SIMPLE SOLUTIONS

FOR

COMPLEX ISSUES

Roy A. Millmore

Self published in cooperation with Createspace, an affiliate of Amazon.

Editing by: Nicole Wilcox
Cover design by: Bernadette Millmore

www.roymillmore.com

ISBN-10:1470038617
ISBN-13:978-1470038618

On the cover is a statement noting my wife Bernadette encouraged this writing. Telling me to quit griping at the news and write about the topics.

So from our davenport to all the American people I dedicate this book. Taken as a sincere statement from my wife; I encourage every American to quit complaining, get up and do something about it. For all those eligible to vote please do! Not just with your wallet per se, but with your conscience. Consider what is best for your Country, not just your personal desires.

Contents

PROLOGUE

I would like to address a perception which will undoubtedly befall those who read what I have written herein. I will address issues which I have experienced, my perceptions of those experiences, and the results of my actions. I will come across as an arrogant individual who thinks he has the answer to all things. Let me state this is not my intention; and I would like to affirm that I have learned through my experiences, the good and the bad.

I do not know everything and I have not experienced everything there is in life. In fact, it is the people with whom I have interacted, collaborated and disagreed; who have taught me valuable lessons that listening with an open mind is the best formula for a content and happy life. I have great respect for the diversity of our intellectual properties and I continue to learn everyday. If my statements offend anyone, it is neither intentional nor mean spirited; it is tough love from a human heart of compassion.

Introduction

In the United States of America, we the people have put great faith in our elected leaders. Unfortunately, it appears they have become so entrenched in their own self serving security of office that they forget for whom they work.

We the people have allowed, by our own inattentiveness, for elected officials to continue in a position of honor and privilege regardless of the obvious fact that with significant arrogance they ignore the people. They have an uncanny gall to believe they have a right versus a privilege to hold their office; and because they win an election, often by small margins, they enter office with an unjustified mandate to do whatever happens to be on their personal or ideological wish list.

It is amazing that every generation of the same surname, with few exceptions, or a close friend of the last senator or congressman continues to fill the halls of public representatives. It is also amazing that so many of these representatives are attorneys.

Why is it that we continue to elect the relatives or close friends of those representatives who did not do such a good job or those whom I refer to as a modern-day attorney? I say this because the past, truly educated, constitutional attorneys are apparently extinct. Could it be the attorneys of our modern America have been successful in convincing us that they are smarter than the common citizen? If this is the case, then I guess the old statement that "the people get what they want" is inevitably the absolute truth and the people truly cannot make the right decisions for themselves. If this is to be accepted, then keep on doing the same old thing; elect the same person with a different face but the same old "doing business without missing a beat", regardless of what you and your neighbors need.

Perhaps we would be better served, if we stopped electing attorneys and relatives or friends of representatives whose performance was inadequate. Instead, we need to look into our immediate communities for interested, selfless, business-minded individuals who still use common sense and judgment which affect society as a whole, versus only trying to please a small segment from a personal wish list. We created this Country to escape the belief that just because someone was born to a royal family they were entitled to a position of status. The hereditary ruling theory is hogwash and the base line for countless revolutions, many of them bloody, throughout history.

The French Revolution, for example, was likely one of the most cruel and bloody ever and certainly without any just cause. Whatever you do, do not relate the French to the American Revolution because they were completely different both in cause and in battle. I do not advocate or believe anyone wants to go there in today's America. Certainly, no one wants or advocates the likes of another civil war, not again.

If we the people continue to ignore or allow our representatives to override every principle and value the Country was built on just to please a small segment from their personal wish list, then the Country will surely succumb to the powers or at best the ideology of those countries we left behind long ago; those who our founding fathers so bravely and selflessly separated.

I will address the attorney issue and many others in the following pages. However, let me state that I am not intending to delve into the depths of our Government and how it works or even what our representatives collectively or individually are doing to destroy our great Nation. Unlike our politicians, I believe most people are far smarter than those who currently walk in the halls of Washington D.C. Therefore, it is not necessary for me to explain the workings of Government.

Many of the attorneys who hold offices are trying hard and diligently to do the right thing. I do not intend to point a finger at anyone specifically. I do, however, point a finger at not one, but each of the primary parties of government; and intend to provide some out of the box ideas and some not so out of the box ideas, by a returned use of age old ideas that stabilize the foundation of our society. I recommend that every American read the best seller *Common Sense* by Glenn Beck. From my point of view, when common sense is extracted out of the equation, we have set aside real or complete justice. This is what I like to call the "Common Sense Doctrine". If you don't recall the history surrounding the French and American Revolutions, then let me recommend a recent book by Ann Coulter, *Demonic-How the Liberal Mob is Endangering America*. Although not mentioned as common sense, I believe that Ms. Coulter's book depicts quite clearly that common sense and facts were completely dropped from the thoughts of the French during their mob-revolution touted by today's liberals.

As we can see and read in the many venues of media in this country, "THIS IS NOT A DEMOCRAT OR REPUBLICAN ISSUE THIS IS AN AMERICAN ISSUE". Therefore, it is time for all good men and women to come to the aid of their party: THE AMERICAN PARTY. I will elaborate in this book on how, unfortunately, our politicians are keeping us down, keeping us from being productive and financing unnecessary project after unnecessary project.

President Ronald Reagan said it best, "I did not leave my party, they left me". This is how the majority of Americans feel today. I will tell why every portion of our society, every project and every issue is a direct result of action or more importantly inaction on the part of those we continue to elect without a thought of how that person affects our daily lives.

It is not my intention to state or reiterate a history lesson that you normally find in books, where opinions come from those who have had high powered positions and ideologies of why things where done; followed by opinions of what should have been done with no real answer on what to do except call your Representative. No, instead I will give you from my perspective and first hand experiences what to do now. Furthermore, if you read this book with a stubborn mindset, i.e., that is not the way things are done or it will never happen, please note it is often that mindset that keeps us from true progress with meaningful results. Read on and maybe you will find an idea or two that you might just find to be a good idea you can support.

Contained herein are simple solutions to build from in order to fix complex issues that plague our society and hold down prosperity and productivity. Additionally, should I recommend a book passage or chapter, please do yourself a favor and read the entire book from which the passage is derived. In fact let me make a suggestion to everyone, take whatever issues you are concerned or passionate about and find two books each of opposing and supporting points of view and read them.

Author's Note

Although this book is not about me, I think it is important to give you some insight into my experiences which have provided the foundation from where the ideas expressed originate. I have held positions of limited authority, such as serving in a dual capacity as an Executive Director for a State of Texas political subdivision and a Chief Law Enforcement Officer with a county position in Houston, Texas. Having earned the coveted title of Certified Fraud Examiner, I collectively supervised and investigated both criminal and civil fraud cases in California and Texas; nearly ten thousand. In total I have nearly forty years of service in law enforcement in one capacity or another. For example, in addition to the above, I was a Criminal Investigator for two District Attorney's Offices in the State of California; a patrol officer and training officer in California municipal agencies; and a patrol officer in a small city in Texas. I was the State Deputy Chief (Manager-Investigator VII) for the Department of Investigations over the Worker's Compensation Commission in Austin, Texas.

At the time of this writing, I hold a Master Peace Officer rating and Training Instructor License with the State of Texas, Texas Commission on Law Enforcement Officer Standards and Training; I maintain the rank of Chief with a local Texas County Sheriff's Office as an Academy Instructor.

I was one of the leading experts in worker's compensation fraud in both California and Texas. I have trained all entities and agencies, both public and private, which deal in this arena on how to prevent, investigate and prosecute fraud cases and have been a keynote speaker for all types of businesses and public agencies in the red flags that lead to exposing fraud.

Further, I assisted in the production of education films by writing the scripts, acting in the films and presenting the education materials on all civil and criminal issues of these fraud cases to audiences from all disciplines. For those of you who think worker's compensation fraud is a hurt knee or a bad back, you really have something to learn by reading this book. I will open your eyes to cases that involve everything from simple civil fraud to organized crime, murder, narcotics, human trafficking and prostitution. The fraud alone exceeds billions of dollars lost every year, not to mention the loss of life and the suffering of innocent people.

I have also owned and operated a successful restaurant and a private investigation firm. These come with their own stories relating to work ethics and loyalty.

I am a Vietnam Veteran with significant first hand combat experience and was one of the youngest locomotive engineers on the Atchison Topeka & Santa Fe Railroad. I will speak to areas that I dealt with regularly in each of these positions and note first hand what I believe is the lesson learned and what solutions should be implemented to fix the severe difficulties and deficiencies.

Because I will speak to a variety of issues including parenting, marriage and relationships, I feel compelled to give you a glimpse of my childhood.

I was born in Queens, New York 1950 and was the fourth in a line of five children. Three sisters and one brother; of whom I do not believe to this date, have even a vague clue as to whom I am as a person. There is no doubt in my mind they all think they do or did (God rest my little sister's soul), but they do not. That said, I admit a great deal of this disconnect is of my choosing.

My mother was mostly a stay at home mom and my father was, I guess, in his early years a good guy with some ambition; but, I never observed that aspect of the man. What I witnessed was a selfish drunk who thought of his family as a burden and, yes, I do believe he was abusive in that regard.

I was never sexually abused by either of my parents and my mother did not physically abuse me; although I can't say as much for my father. He was physically abusive and mentally absent from anything I considered to be a parent.

Our father had absolutely no trust in his five children and I never heard him say anything positive about any one of us. I witnessed him chase my mother around the house yelling a variety of profanities and attempting to beat her, which he did. Frankly, I do not know the "rest of the story", at least not in the early days when I was too young to recall.

Eventually, she found the courage to leave and run away. In those days I did not understand why she left her children in that abusive hell. Her departure was extremely tough for me and I suspect for my brother and sisters; but, only they can speak for what they felt and how it affected them. In later years I came to understand why she had to leave, but that did not change the horrible environment with which we were left to contend. I now know she could do nothing to help us at the time. Her thought, as she told me years later, was that if she got out then one day she would get us all out; and to her credit she did.

Although I believe, we were forced upon her by running to her front door without invitation. Nevertheless, she took four of us in at different times, each with our own set of unsettling troubles. At regular intervals we exposed our individual problems in a dripping mass of uncontrolled anger.

Mother remarried. From one drunk to a second drunk, in comparison the second one was a good man who I believe did care a great deal about us, but he had his own problems and devils with which to contend. Gratefully, he was not physically abusive in anyway. Not to mention this guy put up with some truly disturbed kids, four of us teenagers who came into his life with a hard core attitude about everything and everyone. If he had not already been a drunk that alone may have caused him to become one.

Unfortunately, he was a drunk and I am sure our presence in his life prolonged his struggle; to his credit he went dry years later and I found the only father figure I ever truly knew. He was there on several occasions when no one else would listen or take the time to give some advice. I did not always follow the advice, but I did consider his words carefully and would alter my actions to suit my selfish desires with a twist of wisdom I gained from his insights.

I mentioned that only four of us went off to live with our mother and her second husband. This is because our older sister had long before married her childhood sweetheart even before the real problems began for me. I did witness my father mistreat my sister as well. She, however, hung on to what I can only assume was the father only she knew in her younger years. A man present before the rest of us became such an apparent burden to him.

I believe she tried endlessly to capture the father she once knew and loved in all the years he lived. From my point of view, not that it matters to her, I do not think she found him. Furthermore, I am not sure she ever realized the monster he had become, maybe she did. In my eyes he was not just a monster; he was the devil himself.

I have no illusions that each child in these circumstances will live through the issues and come away with a different perception, which gives rise to different versions of what took place or at the very least what those experiences meant to them individually.

Like I said, four of us went to live with our mother and her second husband. This came about one at a time as our individual troubles arose and became ever increasing between each of us and our father. Our sister, the third oldest, went first; followed by our brother, the second oldest; then myself followed by our youngest sister over a period of a few years.

Imagine our stepfather's thought as each one of us showed up at the door one at a time with hat in hand and terrified that we might be turned away. I am sure he went to the back room and swallowed down another drink to settle his nerves, then invited us in with open arms. He was a great guy who tried very hard to help and sometimes I think in the long run we helped him in some small way. At least, I like to think so.

Before leaving my father's house (I won't dignify it by calling it a home); I thought of running away every day, but I was afraid of my father and the beating he certainly would give me if I did. However, the day finally came for me to go (Thank God). There was not a lot of thought about it that day; it was in the middle of my father slapping me around for not getting a cooking pot clean while washing the dinner dishes. There is a lot more to this story but not for this book. Like I said above - thank God. Had this day not arrived when it did, I had already schemed no less than two plans on how to get rid of him. I do not know if I could have followed through with the plans. I somehow believe, maybe?

I had had enough and to my astonishment I hit him back for the first time ever. I thought he was going to kill me right on the spot or certainly he would beat me unmercifully until I couldn't walk. Instead he stood there and listened to my screaming at him that he would never hit me again or I would somehow even up the odds and beat him back until he would never again be able to strike me. I then told him; if he did not take me to my mother, I would hitchhike the thirty plus miles myself whether he liked it or not. "Just try and stop me, you bastard!"

I will never forget the look on his face! It was a look of amazement and great pain. I think for the first time he actually saw me not as a burden but as his son; he knew what he had done to his children not just me. It was pathetic for a man to travel a path of such ignorance and disgusting actions that his son would have to mirror the hate he created.

Frankly, it would not surprise me to learn that he was awarded a supervisory position in hell.

Therein, lays a brief glimpse into the foundation of my childhood. You might think I would go on to write about how it's everyone else's fault on how I turned out. Truthfully, it is everyone else's fault and a great deal of my own, the military and my wife that I turned out with significant respect for life; realization of what not to do; and how to treat others with dignity and respect. You see, in my adult life anyway, "Everyday is a Holiday".

Now that is not to say that I am a bleeding heart. I am not; in fact, I will kick you in the butt if I think it is warranted. However, I will be one of the first to give you a helping hand, if I see that you want to help yourself and accept some, if not all, of the blame for your being poor or unsuccessful. We all have a different idea about what is successful and what is not. I believe it is part and parcel made up of a wide variety of life's components. They accumulate from both a psychological comfort and a physical comfort; yes, you can gain a little of both from having money, but you can equally have both without money.

You might be interested to know that I have done well for myself. I do not drink alcoholic beverages; I do not smoke; I exercise everyday; and I eat well. I do not attend church, but I have a great deal of deep faith and I am pro life. I have been married for 38 years, at the time of this writing, to a wonderful woman. We have two very productive children: a young woman and a young man. Our daughter is following in her mother's footsteps as a work at home mom; in addition, she edits and writes online articles. Our son is a Deputy Sheriff. We both have an excellent and close relationship with our children and their families.

You do not have to hunt and search for peace of this nature, the one that will give you the outlook, "Everyday is a Holiday". You can find it in your very soul if you simply treat others the way you want to be treated, with respect and dignity. But do not forget there are those that need to be treated in very harsh ways, i.e., tough love. I do not mean by way of physically beating them.

Sometimes that treatment is on the spot. Other times we as a free and giving, honest society have time to provide a fair and impartial insight as to why someone would do harm or be downright evil to others; only then do we take the appropriate actions of holding each individual accountable. Subsequent to holding them accountable, we pray to our Creator and ask that on their judgment day there is compassion and perhaps mercy for the soul.

What does respect and dignity mean? Outside the normal day to day living experiences one might encounter, let me provide an example that exists in the potential experience of a law enforcement officer. They receive a radio call to a robbery in progress at a bank. When they arrive, the bad guy comes running out of the bank and shoots at the officer. The officer returns fire; reacting to his training, he fires three times in succession striking the bad guy twice in the chest and once in the head. This bad guy received his accountability on the spot. The officer treated him with dignity by shooting him only the amount of times necessary, versus twenty times after he was dead. His punishment, in my eyes, came onto him by his own doing and that of divine intervention, saving the life of the officer.

If there had been no shots fired, the bad guy would be arrested and tried in a court of law to determine his guilt and accountability/punishment. In both cases, based on the circumstances given, the bad guy was treated with respect and dignity from one extreme to the other. The officer can find peace with his decisions.

Now for those of you who say "what if this or that", you are an idiot. You are the kind of person that instead of treating people with dignity and respect, you have a long way to go in finding the true meaning of what it is all about. You see, these scenarios are about everyone involved not just the bad guy or one ideology over another.

For my first line of advice on simple solutions to fix complex issues, here it is:

Never change the facts in an actual event to suit your own needs! It is disingenuous and dishonest. If you need to make a point, don't do it on the back of the facts, do it outside the truth and reality of the incident. Use the common way and simply site an analogy that correlates to the incident, but does not change the facts.

Be sure to make it very clear that you are using an analogy or a metaphor or, sure as you live and breathe, some liberal politician or newscaster will distort whatever you said. Actually, liberals can't help themselves, as this is their number one weapon against anyone that does not agree with them. So expect it every time.

CHAPTER ONE
Health Care

Let's get right to one of the issues that is currently plaguing and seemingly crippling our Country: health care. What is the problem here? The problem is that all our politicians want is to control the issues not fix them. Then how do we fix health care? First and foremost, we need to understand the problem is not only health care. The U.S.A. has the best health care over any other country in history. It is health insurance reform that is needed. It is not the insurance companies in totality that are the problem, although they most definitely carry a significant portion of the blame, mostly in special interest groups that find ways to buy off politicians.

Lobbying is another problem, which both politicians and insurance companies promote and use as a legal way to deal from the bottom of the deck. But I really can't hold their feet to the fire for very long because; it is mostly the current laws that allow a private entity like insurance to operate and equally how not to operate. The real answer is capitalism and the free market that should control these issues not the government. Obviously, I do not believe in government control, but I do believe in an established base line which private enterprises must respect.

The first thing we must do is allow insurance companies to do business in all fifty states to create the appropriate competition. I know you have heard this many times. But why do we not currently allow this competition? It is because your politicians – local, state and national- and connected unions mandate ridiculous requirements.

Let me put out a simple solution from where the big boys and girls can start, if they do not read anything else in the following text they like. You take the top ten or fifteen insurance companies in the Country and find the common denominators in coverage, all those procedures that each of them cover. Add a few of the best covered benefits not currently included with all the rest and set the base line for coverage at that point. If any insurance company wants to write insurance in any state, they will all start at the same common covered benefits. After that it is all about competition.

Before I get into other significant areas, I will give you something to think about. There are several specifics in the way our insurance coverage stands in policy that make no sense. I'll give you two examples then you can run away in your mind to other scenarios that make just as little sense.

Here you are a female who has just begun menses. In many cases the primary doctor must, per the insurance policy, see you before you can be seen by a gynecologist. To further insult your intelligence and this referral, you must return to your primary doctor every year for another referral to continue with the same gynecologist or to go to someone with whom you are more comfortable. How much money is wasted on the primary doctor visit and those ridiculous yearly referrals for a very common human necessity that every woman must endure? Millions!

Example number two: you have already been referred to a specialist by the primary doctor for any condition. At some point you run out of a particular topical cream for an itch of some sort, maybe for poison oak or poison ivy. The cream was prescribed by your primary doctor two or three weeks prior, but the rash is still there and the diagnosis is agreed to by the specialist you're now visiting for some unconnected reason.

Interestingly enough, the specialist will not write you another prescription for the same cream. No, instead of calling the primary doctor's office to confirm the cream prescription and write you another, you must go back to see the primary again. This will amount to another insurance bill for an office visit of $300 to $450 dollars. We could save millions of dollars, millions I say!

If anyone is telling you that the specialist will charge the insurance company the higher rates when they write this cream prescription, then everyone involved but you should be criminally punished. The specialist should write the prescription for free, after confirming with the primary doctor. In the report to the primary doctor it should be clearly stated the prescription was written. I am not advocating the specialist go beyond anything reasonable, their fee for being a specialist is already explosive. At the very least the primary doctor should call you in another prescription based on the phone consult with the specialist, without charging you or the insurance.

We all need to understand that insurance is a private business and if left to compete they will out do each other. We only need to establish a base line for coverage which would be fair and equitable for both parties. After all, it is one thing to treat a head injury and quite another to mandate hair replacement for vain or ego purposes. It is important to use medical technology when the individual case provides a necessity but quite another to use the very expensive technology because our physicians are afraid of a potential law suit.

I would bet the numbers of sex change operations that are required to save a person's life are so miniscule they would, in by themselves, make history. To deem these types of surgeries appropriate, insurance coverage is absurd at best. This can be changed with TORT reform and I address that issue later. It is the base line here that will set the standard starting point.

It is worth mentioning there are many types of cases which fall into a general category, yet present with very different manifestations. In these individual cases it is imperative for the physician to utilize our superb technology, as these are the very cases we most assuredly do not want a bureaucrat making the decision on a treatment or a particular test/exam. The reason we must keep these decisions out of government hands is because not all cases fall into general categories.

There are millions of cases daily, while they might all be cancer, come with different twists. How the same disease will affect people differently can be compared with the consumption of alcoholic beverages. Dependent on a person's height, weight, not to mention tolerance, etc, the beverage will act differently in each person, even if they drink the same beverage at the same amount. The same type or different symptoms may present themselves given our independent immune systems. Those medical choices that can mean life or death, especially in major medical cases, need to stay in the examination room with the patient, not in a boardroom in a far away city or state. These are choices to be made by the patient after their doctor advises them of all the options.

A real individual case is needed to make the point and, hopefully, open the eyes of far too many physicians who believe it is they who make the decisions and not the patient. You see doctors, although I have the greatest respect and admiration for you and the tenacity it takes to earn your education, you are there to evaluate the symptoms. Then advise the patient as to what treatments are available (all treatments), and based on your medical knowledge and experience, advise on the pros and cons (all of them) of each treatment. In this way the patient can make their own choice as to what treatment they will endure. The choice of treatment is not the physician's to make! That is not to say the patient will not, as they often do, acquiesce to the physician's best judgment, most will.

I have a very close family member who developed a small lump in an area of the body that was unusual. They went to the doctor and were told to not worry about it. "It is likely a cyst or deep pimple, perhaps a boil that needs to surface." After several weeks the patient returned to the doctor. The lump seemed larger, although there was no discomfort. The doctor elected to prescribe an antibiotic. The patient requested a biopsy, but the doctor and the insurance said it was not necessary at that time. "Let's see what the antibiotics do." After several more weeks the lump, it seemed, was larger again. The doctor drew blood and saw no abnormalities, in fact nothing wrong there at all, everything was normal. As the lump was in the cheek of the face, the doctor said, "This must be a dental infection."

The patient was referred to a dentist, who was not a specialist because the insurance did not approve one. The patient requested a biopsy for the second time; it was again denied. The dentist prescribed yet another antibiotic and again it failed. Several doctor visits passed over many months, each physician taking blood but nothing showed.

Two years after the first sign of this mysterious lump getting larger every week, the patient at my suggestion went to, unbelievably, a plastic surgeon and demanded a biopsy. "If you don't take a biopsy," the patient advised, "I will go home and cut this thing out myself with a knife from the tools in my arts and craft set." The doctor complied and the biopsy came back a week later. Yep, you guessed it...CANCER! It was Non Hodgkin's Lymphoma. After two years of growing, there were stage 3 and stage 4 cells found. "Well, isn't that just great," the patient yelled in a rather emotional tone! "TWO YEARS! What ever happened to early detection, you fools?"

I am not done with this just yet. Following the diagnosis, the patient went to the University of California, Davis Cancer Center in Sacramento, California.

The purpose was to get a second opinion, which was confirmed, and options on treatment. The patient endured endless blood work, bone marrow biopsies, and CAT Scans; it was unusual to note that other than the biopsy from the original lump and other common symptoms of the disease the cancer did not show up. Could this mean it was an odd single tumor? Not according to the eighteen member panel of doctors, all oncologists at U.C. Davis, who completed a second biopsy and recommended immediate chemotherapy. It was comforting to learn these doctors, at least, were not going to waste another minute.

After several conversations with the insurance, a final oncologist was selected outside of U.C. Davis. He ordered even more blood work and then another CAT scan, nothing showed. He ordered a PET scan and there they were: five tumors spread throughout the neck, intestinal and abdomen areas.

It was time to discuss what kinds of treatments were available. Although there were several mentioned, it boiled down to two. Both included chemotherapy: one mild and the other hard core. The doctor recommended hard core. The patient, however, chose the more mild form. The hard core would leave the patient looking like a refugee from one of Hitler's death camps and maybe, in the patient's mind, dead. The patient watched many cancer patients come and go from the infusion/treatment room; it seemed there was no escape from the very harsh effects of the hard core path.

The more mild treatment worked. There was no loss of hair and no pain, although there were some truly uncomfortable days following the medication of oral chemotherapy and prednisone. Subsequent to the eight week treatment, there was still some fairly significant activity of cancer noted in a follow up PET scan, that being the only test that would expose the tumors.

The doctor advised a new treatment: Retuximab, more or less a mild form of chemotherapy. The treatment was explained as going into the body searching out the cancer cells; surrounding each cell; starving out the cancer; and keeping the tumors from growing or spreading. This treatment should have begun two years earlier. If only they would have completed a biopsy at that time.

I am not a doctor and I may be off base in what I am about to tell you, but it is worth some thought. The radio active substance used in PET scans, which is injected intravenously, is full of a glucose (sugar) solution. The solution goes into the body. If there are cancer cells/tumors present, they grab onto the solution. This, in turn, lights up to reflect in the scan, thus exposing the location and size of the tumors. The reason the tumors grab the solution is because the cancerous cells feed on sugar. If this is true, it is another very strong reason to stop eating sugar. If this is true, why do so many oncologist offices serve sugar goodies to their patients, particularly when they are in the infusion rooms?

The Retuximab treatment was and still is so new that there is little known on the long term effects, especially to the immune system. But this worked! All the tumors were either gone or very small. The treatment was one infusion every week for four weeks, followed by one infusion every eight weeks until full remission or unpleasant side effects from the cancer dissipated. The side effects were far less than hard core therapy that is for sure. Several years later the treatments were changed to every twelve weeks. Then, the big one came.

The treating doctor was now different from the first because of insurance and advised the patient, "The Retuximab treatments will be stopped, because we have received information that the immune system in other patients has been significantly compromised."

To give the doctor some credit here, I guess he was attempting to help the patient, but I still do not think that should be the doctor's call. This decision should instead be a collective agreement and the patient should be in charge not the doctor.

"After all, there is no indication in the blood of any active cancer and by all other accounts you are doing well," said the doctor. The patient requested a PET scan, but the doctor felt like that would not be necessary. Now, my family member is back to square one with yet another square headed doctor who believes it is his decision. You might want to know the doctors had already advised the patient, "This disease will result in your death".

Why on Earth, given the history of this case, would a doctor not want to order the PET scan, which is the only test that has ever exposed the cancer in this patient? Because the doctor was told or believes it would cost too much? Or was he truly trying to properly care for the patient? I will give him the benefit of the doubt, but I am not so sure. What is a life worth? What about those medical panels in Washington D.C. or your State Capitol? Do they sound like a good idea to you? Not me! By the way at the time of this writing, the patient now presents with most of the symptoms for Non Hodgkin's Lymphoma and only four months after stopping the treatments. Will the next time I see my family member be in the treatment room for further infusions or in the casket? Great idea to stop the treatment, wouldn't you say? Maybe, but isn't this the choice of the patient and not the insurance or the doctor? It certainly is not the Government's!

Aren't you concerned, as I am, that the U.S. Government will think it is best to cut the cost and let the disease take its course? I think this is dangerous and should never under any circumstances be allowed.

You better stand up and be counted, my fellow Americans! And now that they passed the current health care bill, fight to get it repealed.

Call every elected representative at every level, put the pressure on and VOTE. I do not believe that any elected procedure for vain purposes alone should ever be a requirement mandated for the insurance company to cover. I do believe based on many conversations I have had with insurance executives, that there are some insurance companies that would include some vain cosmetic procedures through competition, if it meant a significant volume of customers. That is what we refer to as the free market. Believe it or not, this policy may show there is a market in San Francisco for sex changes and in New York, hair replacement. Who knows what they will include to gain more market share?

Certainly, we can find common sense and fair base lines in these issues. It is common sense that should dictate what should and should not be covered. Let me give an example of a base line. The patient is walking into a restaurant and slips in a puddle of water. This causes him to fall into a waitress who accidentally spills boiling hot water onto the patient's head, causing third degree burns. The burn requires skin grafts and there is a partial loss of sight. Of course, any surgery should be covered for the grafts. If the patient never wore glasses in the past and contact lenses will restore the sight, the contacts should be covered. Now the insurance will argue that eye glasses will make the patient whole and it should only be required to pay for glasses. This is because the insurance can get the glasses for a cheaper price than the cost of contacts. However, common sense states the patient never wore glasses and is not made whole by repairing sight alone. Not that there is anything wrong with wearing glasses, they actually look good on many individuals and some might prefer them. But many do not like them and that is why contact lenses are so popular. If they don't want glasses and they never wore them, they should not be forced to do so. However, if the patient needed and wore glasses before the accident then replacing the glasses with the necessary prescription should be the coverage.

Do you think this is an open invitation to the attorney's ball, a party in which they get rich and everyone else loses? I say, no. If you are going to apply the **common sense doctrine,** then you must carry it out by way of either limited arbitration or a small percentage – ten or twelve percent - of the total cost to come from the insurance agency directly to the attorney, not out of the patient's settlement if there is one. The settlement in this case should be nothing more than the eye wear plus reasonable attorney fees. I think with this type of settlement there should not be any case brought forward, it would be settled in arbitration. In any case whoever loses pays the entire cost even the attorney fees.

I know the insurance company will fight over which entity is at true fault for the accident, such as the restaurant for not mopping the floor, etcetera. However, this fight is between the different insurance companies and the patient should not have to wait for a final decision. This process is called an investigation to transfer (subrogate) the cost or the blame. Oh, in case you are wondering, the example was a real case that I investigated, including the subrogation. Unfortunately, the common sense doctrine was not in play.

When it is said the insurance companies need to be allowed to do business in all fifty states, we are saying that all politicians need to provide appropriate and fair guidelines to support this competition. Many state lawmakers, the attorney associations, and the strong unions are the ones to blame here. Each of them gets a great deal out of keeping the competition away. The politicians get donations to be reelected, the attorneys get many court cases, and the unions get members to pay union dues and connections with invitations to big names. But what does the union member get? The answer is more union dues to pay, as it is time consuming and expensive to argue for better benefits; and by the way, they receive fewer pay increases because the insurance costs the employer more than forty percent of the member's salary.

If you break the circle with strong competition between the insurance companies, you will no longer need the union. Why? You will get better benefits (let the insurance companies do the haggling to get your business) and you will garner better raises because, your employer will have to pay less for insurance. Not to mention, lower costs means more jobs. I recommend you establish associations versus unions with limited bargaining power; be very sure to include term limits on holding association office; and instill limited dues. In this way workers and management will be able to address issues across the board in a fashion conducive towards an equitable outcome for all parties. This always provides fertile ground that reaps the rewards of better working conditions and better insurance coverage.

Now is the time to allow the establishment of personal "Medical Insurance Saving Accounts." I think there are two ways this can be accomplished. The first is for the employers of like businesses to combine their bargaining power for better interest rates; such as the entire shoe manufacturing industry, all the full department stores, and perhaps all automobile manufacturers (you get the idea). This can be done through credit unions for those agencies/businesses. You would establish a medical account with the credit unions. The funds could only be used for medical payments, medical procedures, and perhaps the co-payments of your insurance coverage.

There should be a cap on the contributions, perhaps the amount of the average yearly income of the state in which the account is established. Furthermore, this account should be as confidential as medical records; wherein, no one would be required to release information as to whether they do or do not have this plan except to the IRS.

This precaution would prevent insurance companies from providing fewer benefits. In this program you have both the insurance coverage and your own medical savings account.

This account will help you save for co-payments and provide you with coverage that the insurance company does not cover, such as cosmetic surgery.

If you have an account, you should be allowed a tax deduction along with your insurance bills. Why did I include cosmetic surgery into your account payments? This is your money and not the government's; is it not? One of the rules might stand that if you use your money for purely elective surgery, then those funds only will be taxed. At least the account allowed for you to save the money for your choice versus having to do other things like pay higher premiums.

The second type is straight forward by allowing you to establish a Medical Account for you and your family without a cap, but to an amount of significant proportions, that would meet a standard of minimum coverage. A base line of coverage is the guide in place of any other insurance coverage. The base line coverage would also be the cut off for a tax deduction on the account. Anything you put into the account over the base line is taxable income, but you can still deduct your co-payments. I would set this minimum account balance at the average earning amount per year of the state in which the account was established.

I also believe, you should be granted a five year grace period to reach the minimum balance of the account without a penalty of taxes on the account. You should be allowed to use the interest on the account to reach the minimum balance. If in the five years you do not reach the minimum balance, then the funds would be subject to income tax without penalty as in a regular savings account. This process will force the account as a mandate, if you want to use this design to pay for insurance. Of course, you will be able to purchase a separate policy without penalty for additional catastrophic illness coverage.

Pre-existing Conditions

Pre-existing conditions are those illnesses and conditions that no one ever wants to see in their own medical charts. Currently, we are yelling about insurance companies not accepting these conditions or dropping the patient who unfortunately develops these conditions. The worst, of course, are life threatening diseases and God forbid it happens to be cancer. Although there are many diseases that are every bit as horrifying, this one is always on our minds.

First of all, I do not blame any private insurance company for not taking or refusing to insure anyone who walks through the door and says they have cancer and they want the company to pay thousands and possibly hundreds of thousands of dollars to treat them. Oh, and by the way, they only want to pay a standard premium. After all, they cannot afford to pay anymore than what the healthy person is paying. That does not make sense. There is no common sense in that statement request/demand at all; once again you toss out fair and equitable justice, if you mandate this coverage. It is simply ridiculous! What is the answer? If we apply the common sense doctrine, the answer is right in front of our face.

When we go to a gambling club we are walking into an insurance house. Like Las Vegas, the house allows you to come in and lay down a bet. The bet is: if you lose, the house wins; if the house loses, you win. There is no difference between this and the insurance game, except the insurance game goes on for life. Pun intended.

If you purchase insurance with insurance company "ABC" and subsequently you acquire cancer, then "ABC" loses and must by law pay for all treatment attached to that cancer for the rest of your life. Even if you no longer work or you move to some other state for whatever reason.

All treatment and bills for that cancer, as long as the treatment is a direct result of the cancer and medically confirmed, are paid for by "ABC". If you want to acquire other health insurance from a second company "XYZ", you should be allowed to do so for all other illnesses and medical necessities; they cannot turn you down because of the cancer. "XYZ" will not be required to pay anything directly related to your cancer.

By approaching this scenario in this manner, let the insurance carriers fight it out on which one of them pays for what procedure. If it's cancer or related to the cancer "ABC" pays; if it's unrelated "XYZ" pays. Let the patient be as healthy and unburdened as possible.

In each case the premium should be appropriately prorated. This means your "ABC" insurance continues at a rate that extracts the premium cost for everything but catastrophic illness, which was separated and clearly documented and stated in the policy at the time of your original purchase, whether the policy came as an independent purchase or through your employer. If your original policy costs $500 dollars per month a portion of that ($100) was for catastrophic illness, then your new premium with "ABC" will be $100 per month to continue the catastrophic portion of the policy. Your policy for the additional insurance with "XYZ", you have chosen or that which comes through a subsequent employer, will be less the cost of catastrophic illness, at least for cancer from that policy.

This is a common sense approach and it is not difficult to implement. In this way you will always have, at the very least, coverage for your catastrophic illness. The costs noted above are examples only and do not reflect the cost of any particular company.

Now, let's take the catastrophic illness of the person who develops cancer when they do not have insurance. This will negate the above scenario for them. Ok, first we hope that person was covered under their parents' insurance so the above would apply. However, if not, then we must find a way to cover them. Here is where we might part ways.

First, insurance companies should be required to set their catastrophic illness premium separate and apart from all other coverage, which is where I get the divide noted above in continued coverage. If a person were in the position that they needed to go on unemployment, those benefits would include payment over the standard payment for which they are entitled. This would include their insurance premium for catastrophic illness only, ensuring they do not lose that portion of coverage, whether they were in a COBRA situation or not.

To make sure this is covered by their own contributions, they would have been paying into the system while working as they do for unemployment and health insurance currently. Of course, there would be a slight increase in that portion of unemployment taken from their paycheck, but it beats having no insurance at all. I do not believe that anyone in this Country should be left to simply die, because they could not afford insurance at the right time in their life. Is this a mandate that so upsets the Country? In some regards the answer is yes, but never for full coverage and not for anything but catastrophic illness.

Perhaps this is a negotiation point to consider. In this case then, in spite of those who say I have ice water for blood, I do think the Government must step in and do the right thing; but only, if it is proven this individual has, by no means of their own doing, placed themselves into such a position. I know this can be tricky and take some resources to accomplish and many will say the bureaucracy of the red tape involved will take too long and be too cumbersome.

That does not have to be the case either. Just build into the law that this issue must be addressed in a reasonable time frame, 60 days, and in the mean time the patient must be allowed to begin the proper treatment.

I guess it must be addressed as to what happens if the inquiries prove the person did place themselves into this awkward position. I can only relate the obvious, which is a bit contradictive I suppose. What if a person elected to live under the bridge believing he would live like a salamander without any responsibility until the unfortunate circumstance raised its ugly head and he acquired cancer? I guess the only thing left to do is up to all of us, let them go or continue the treatment until they can go back under the bridge and never receive further treatment. I must say I am in the camp of completing the first course of treatment, with hopeful success and let them go without any further. Each of us, I believe, has an obligation to be part of our society and contribute, not just take. The line in the sand, as bad as it can be sometimes, must be drawn.

The bottom line here is that the catastrophic illness coverage will be far less than a complete policy. So if we must all pay for others to be insured, let it be there and no further. Treatment will be available for one, two, or three years depending on your condition and we will assist in getting you coverage through employment. I might also add that universities should consider establishing a health care system for students to buy into catastrophic coverage upon enrollment.

If you think the portion about continued catastrophic illness coverage will not work, let me inform you, you are incredibly wrong. How do I know you are wrong? Just look to the worker's compensation plans around the Country.

Worker's Compensation

I am well aware that worker's compensation insurance and benefits are different in many states, so I will speak from what I know was true in California and Texas at the time I was working with those two systems.

If you get injured on the job and it is proven that your injury was work related, then you get lifetime medical for that injury. You can choose to take a lump sum settlement and release the insurance company from any further responsibility, but why? The reason many take a lump sum is because the insurance company will drag out the process for so long you go into further debt, generally because you are not able to work and they know it. This process is promoted by the attorneys and the insurance companies.

(By the way let me enter a side note here, this is exactly what the IRS does; they say you owe x dollars and then threaten you with legal action knowing you cannot afford an attorney. It is cheaper for you to just pay the bullies so they won't break you!)

In the case of insurance companies, it is cheaper for them to get a release from any further responsibility. Which is why this is the real area that needs to be reformed for all insurance matters; i.e., short time lines on the part of the insurance company to make a decision, sixty days would go a long way with a speedy arbitration hearing if necessary, ninety days to settle any differences. If the insurance company misses the time line, then they should be required to pay the bills. I am speaking inside and outside the worker's compensation system.

In defense of the insurance companies, the fraud is rampant, especially in a slow job market or with a poor employee who would have been fired if not for the alleged injury.

This is a complete book in by itself. Perhaps here is the place I can digress a bit with real case history to open your eyes to the types of crime that takes place by utilizing the worker's compensation system.

There was a farmer in California who needed cheap labor. He sent out representatives to the local illegal Mexican population and made a deal. The deal was: "I will give you and some of your friends a job on the farm at a rate more than you might otherwise receive. After a few weeks perhaps a month or two, you will receive an injury to your back and go home to Mexico. We will split the worker's compensation check with you and your family in Mexico. After several months we will bring you back to the States and get you working on another farm under a different name while at the same time we continue to receive and split the worker's compensation check. We have a doctor in Mexico that will provide the required medical reports for you in Mexico City. Although you don't really need to worry about the medical reports because the United States insurance companies cannot mandate those reports from Mexico."

After this scenario runs its course with several workers, even hundreds of laborers, on many different farms, millions of dollars have been fraudulently obtained. This worked well for the farmer and badly for the insurance companies, job market and the general public. Since the scheme works so well hardcore gangsters, who deal in organized crime get involved. They do the same thing with many types of businesses but with a twist. After they hook the laborer into the scheme, they begin to use them for drug trafficking. If they do not cooperate then they murder the family members in Mexico. To step up the price a bit, they take the young and sell them into the human trafficking circuit for prostitution.

It is important for everyone to know that you do not need the farmer in the above real example. This type of criminal activity happen everyday in and amongst the laborers themselves; claiming injury, collecting payment, and simply moving on to the next farm or other work place even the honest businessman's work place. Gangsters of organized crime and our own street gangs run these types of schemes in every business that hires laborers, whether on the farm or in a fast food restaurant and especially illegal alien workers. Given the billions of dollars lost to these scams, it is no wonder our insurance costs are so incredibly high.

There were many cases in Texas where there were legitimate injuries involving illegal immigrants. The agency received a case from a manufacturer outside the City of Dallas, wherein it was reported that illegal workers had received on the job injuries and some of these were very serious. One woman had severed fingers and lost part of the palm on her right hand from poorly designed or reconfigured machinery. She fell to the floor and the supervisor first kicked her, and then made her co-workers wrap her hand to stop the bleeding. She was told to go back to work and only given Tylenol. Professional medical treatment had been refused.

The report was that the supervisor threatened to report her and the family to federal authorities for deportation. This seemed to me as an exaggerated report perhaps from a disgruntled employee. However, I have been in this business far too long and nothing would surprise me. I assigned one of the State Investigators who I knew was honest and impartial at all times.

Bottom line was that her report was heart wrenching. These workers apparently were being mistreated and grossly so. The original report was true according to several witnesses who would only talk outside the community where they were employed. Some of the witnesses were American citizens and all were afraid of losing their jobs and possibly other nefarious retaliation.

I took this matter to my superior and requested we turn the matter over to Immigration and the local District Attorney's Office. Unbelievably, I was told that if I did that, the workers would be deported. I was beside myself and came very close to being terminated. I informed my superiors that getting deported was far better than being maimed or worse and, after all, they would all be back in a week with other jobs anyway. Ultimately, I did the right thing anonymously; but, I do not think it ever saw the light of day because it was, in the eyes of the authorities, a worker's compensation matter.

This is the big tragedy of one agency not working with the other and often times it is a simple matter of ego or misunderstanding. What we hear more than anything else is "our job is more important than other agencies; we just don't have the time". This in by itself is a copout and at the same time true. Each agency has its own responsibility and duty and all of them are understaffed. However, they really do need to establish a liaison officer because many cases cross the boundaries from one agency to the other. Work together at least between liaisons and keep informed on those cases that do cross over, with an understanding of which agency will be the primary lead. But they should never be totally ignored.

Here is a strong note to both the private insurance and the public agencies trying to prove or prosecute worker's compensation fraud and for that matter every other crime: You will very seldom make a strong case by investigating the plaintiffs or defendants via the telephone. Your investigators must get out in the field and do the grunt's work. If all you do is spend money calling people on the phone or go to a neighbor's home and ask a question, you might as well flush the money down the toilet. All this does is provide a weak excuse on paper that you tried to investigate. It is a blatant lie.

This book and chapter, as stated, is not specifically about worker's compensation and the reform which is desperately needed therein; however, please note that we need to address the matter of reform in every state at the state level, before the Federal Government co-opts that right.

Ok, let's get back to the solution for our health care/insurance problems. The transfer of pre-existing conditions (catastrophic illness) will work in our standard system as it is currently set up, if we simply make a few minor adjustments in the rules and not try to change the saddle why we are sitting in it; or worse yet change the horse in the middle of a gallop.

Emergency Room

What do we do about emergency rooms and the costs therein which are driving our health care system and health professionals into the poor house? We all know there are many factors involved, such as the illegal alien population and those who won't work but go to the ER for everyday treatment without paying for services. We also have our own citizens who simply do not want to purchase health insurance knowing that the emergency room will cover them upon walking in off the street.

This area must be addressed if in no other area than services alone. What do I mean by this? If you come into an emergency room with a severed arm and no insurance, then the on call doctor will stop the bleeding to save your life and send you on your way. There should be no reconnecting the arm if it comes in with you and there should be no follow ups, as you would have been given the necessary direction for treatment to keep the wound clean and free from infection.

You might receive a limited supply of medication to assist in treatment and a few days or weeks of pain medication but nothing more. If you come in with a cold, you will be told to go home and get bed rest and drink plenty of fluids. There will be no doctor work releases given and if you lose your job because you have no doctor note, then GET INSURANCE! Of course, the emergency room will treat children, because contrary to what many believe, I do not have ice water for blood.

Let me say the same about vehicle insurance. If you do not have the required vehicle insurance whether you were at fault or not, then your head injury should be treated in the same manner; stop the bleeding only to save your life and that is it. The other guy's insurance should not be required to pay for your reconstruction surgery. Pay for it yourself and learn the lesson on having insurance. If you have the required insurance, you will be fully treated. Afterwards, the battle will be on about who is responsible for what treatment, which is common place today anyway. Let me also state that if you are driving without vehicle insurance, then all the bills are on you. If the vehicle is not yours then the owner who gave you permission to drive will also pay.

Although these remedies are harsh, they are the only way we can continue to meet the need of the Physicians Hippocratic Oath and save money at the same time. Full service at emergency rooms for those who do not have insurance is ridiculous and should be stopped.

Furthermore, if you present in an emergency room with something other than a true emergency, determined by the doctor or other qualified personnel with medical training, you should be turned away. The doctor should not be liable for anything.

Tort Reform

Tort reform is desperately needed to truly cut cost in health care. I mentioned above a few points that would go a long way in this regard, but as with everything there is a lot more that needs to be done. What can be done especially in the case of jury awards? In the case of extremely gross negligence, the evidence should be given to a grand jury to determine if a jury trial is necessary. This would be cases where the physician removed organs as a donor from the wrong patient who was there for an appendectomy; or they did not have the correct information in the chart on a patient; amputating a leg, when the patient was there to remove bunions from their foot.

Unlike many in Washington D.C., I do not believe doctors do these things on purpose to increase the billing or their profits. I do believe, however, they make mistakes and when they are grossly negligent they must pay and there should be no cap on the jury's decision. The judge and jury can and should continue to award in these cases whatever the law will allow.

What about the less serious procedures which are occurring everyday all over the Country? Cases like the doctor did an inferior job on removing the bunion. These cases certainly do not need to go before a jury.

The patient may not like the outcome and they may have some residual negative effects from the botched surgery; but, should the doctor's insurance have to pay out millions of dollars? I do not think so and there are some doctors that I believe, should not have a license. That being said, here is the answer with the incorporation of the common sense doctrine.

The first portion of reform must punish those doctors who continue to make one mistake after another by taking away their license to practice. The seriousness of those mistakes can be taken into account with a three strikes and you're out method. One mistake gets you suspended for a time frame set by the judge and so on until the fourth strike. On the doctor's fourth negligent mistake, which could have easily been avoided, take their license. If only for one, two or five years which ever might be appropriate for the negligence. BUT TAKE IT!

On a case by case basis, the doctor should be first ordered to stand and explain their record and the circumstances of each case in question in front of an administrative judge. By decision of the judge, after weighing the evidence, a panel would convene to hear the case consisting of three to five; an administrative judge; one doctor; and one, two or three people from the jury pool. The cost of legal fees for these hearings should also be set, perhaps at six months worth of earnings that equal the average yearly pay in the state where the suit was filed.

The punishment should follow a sliding scale from which the panel will impose in each of these cases. First and foremost, all future medical bills directly related to the wrong doing (excluding a mental or psychological state) should be covered by the insurance company. There should be no mental or psychological awards in any case, in the new law; except in those cases with gross negligence. A mere inconvenience does not rise to the level of an unnatural mental or psychological state. Get over it; you lost a toe instead of the bunion; you still have your leg.

The scale should be allowed to cover a documented monetary loss as a direct result of the mistake or botched procedure, such as one or two months pay. This should be accomplished without any projections outside the facts of earnings lost.

In other words, there is no element included that states: if this did not happen, I would have been able to be a surgeon or I might have received a promotion, etc. Just the facts in these cases, if you were not earning it at the time of injury, you cannot include the loss into your formula.

A cap, however, should be placed on the monetary award. In my opinion that cap should be no more than five years of salary directly related to the patient's salary. You may possibly include cost of living increases and earning power of the patient had the mistake not taken place. The cost of living is measurable and quantified as part of your earnings, if the injury did not keep you out of this equation. Most cases in this category should certainly be in the lower settlements, such as a month to month and up to the maximum of five years.

The only other cost would be to provide training for transferable skills into a second career, if the patient was unable to return to their customary employment as a direct result of the doctor's mistake or wrong procedure. The new career options, if the skills are transferable or if the patient needs to embark on a new career path, should have a similar pay scale as did the patient's customary employment. Job placement should occur. No one should be forced to lose compensation because of a doctor's mistakes.

On the other hand, we need to protect the earning level of the patient so it will be equal to that of what they were making at the time of injury. They should not have to settle for a position that pays less than what they were earning; but, no one should be become independently wealthy either for these minor or inconvenient mistakes. The judge and panel will not have the power to diminish or increase the medical treatments, so long as the treatments can be verified by a physician as required due to the doctor's mistake or wrong procedure.

These areas should take care of the foundation from which to build a system in the medical field that works and should easily be extrapolated to cross the boundaries of other law suits. One of the very first things that should be implemented across the land - as the law of the land, not just here and there - is if a frivolous law suit is brought before a court, the loser pays all the bills.

Keep in mind the reason these and other ideas have not been brought to the table is very simple. Your local, State and Federal elected officials want control more than they want a fix. Because you see: if you fix it, then their power is diminished. All of us need to be very mindful of the politicians' actions, not just what they say but what they will do. Remember our Constitution gives the people the real power. Be sure to VOTE!

CHAPTER TWO
Politics and Politicians

I have already directed several comments towards politics and the politicians so we need to put this record straight on how to fix the problems. Well, I won't attempt to fix them all, because I can't and I am not sure anyone can with such an expansive mindset of the human race. Unfortunately, I do not think many in Washington D.C. today have any mindset at all except, maybe, how they can spend our money to their advantage vs. ours.

Let us be honest, no one will ever be totally satisfied with any one politician or how the system works or doesn't work. The wonderful part about America is that we have, we are supposed to have, an open and honest system to allow debate and the ability to change the law when it no longer applies or is unjust. Please note, I did not say change our Constitution. We must at all time keep in mind that the Constitution allows for us to be flexible within the boundaries of a free people, as long as we remain a free people with proper rule of law. Our system is built on the law of nature and, if you will, the rules - value, virtue, dignity, integrity and respect- of our Creator.

When you hear that the Constitution is a living document, you must not be fooled to accept this as changing the values and foundation of the rights contained therein for a free people. These inalienable rights which are bestowed onto us within the human spirit, the greatest gift of the universe by way of our Creator, should never be undermined by the legislature. What should be stated clearly is that the Constitution allows a strong flexibility to adapt human needs in concert with the spirit, values and principles of this amazing and I would even say a miracle of divine guidance as it stands.

I beg of you to always keep in mind what I stated earlier: If we extract common sense from the equation, then we have extracted a significant portion of justice. I believe very strongly that our Founding Fathers understood this explicitly. In the construction of the Constitution they were sure to address a balance by establishing three branches of governance to ensure equitable justice, which keeps us out of the extremist margins of being too far left and too far right.

Now what to do – what to do? How about we start a renewed and determined mindset coupled with actions to stand strong and united once again for our founding principles? The first action is to ensure that our children, no matter what their age, are taught those founding principles. We need to be sure they know who the Founding Fathers were; how they came to set the most solid foundation for the prosperity of mankind ever to be known; and how those actions, trials and tribulation allow them to be a free people.

If we do not educate our children about the glory of our Country and how it came about and what we as a nation have endured to become the greatest nation ever, they will certainly fail and fall prey to those who want to destroy the United States and all we have become. The threat is as real as it gets today.

Earmarks

The famous "earmark" issue that every politician is actually sent to Washington D.C. to accomplish. What does that mean? It means we elect our representatives to go to Washington D.C. and bring home as much of the bacon as possible for our community and to make an attempt at voting with a commonsense approach to governing the rest of the Country.

Here is a suggestion: when it comes to earmarks, let us separate them entirely by having just an earmark bill. No earmarks in any bill whatsoever, unless it pertains exactly to what the bill is addressing. **If it does not pertain, it does not remain!** Furthermore, no bill should be any longer than 300 pages and no earmark attached should be any longer than five pages.

Why not pack up a separate bill of nothing but earmarks, which can be argued back and forth and line item cuts can be negotiated in or out by the Congress? If our representatives are worried about someone pointing the finger of shame at them for their proposed earmark, then they should not put it out there or they need to go home and give the job to someone else. Now that is what I call transparency. What does this mean? It means that an earmark bill will be the only bill that the President can have line item veto on and no other. In addition, the Congress can argue all day, every day for a really long time on an earmark bill and the rest of the Nation's business can actually keep moving forward. What a concept!

Education

Here is another place to start; a drive for mass education. I do not mean the Department of Education on the Federal level, that department should immediately be abolished! The Department was created in 1979 and it has failed miserably. Just research the statistics prior and after, you will have no doubts. The education of our youngsters should be left in the hands of the state and local governments with deep and inclusive input by parents and community.

Get this issue on the ballots and get rid of it today! However, if we must have this failing department, then at least take most of its power away by limiting their input to a simple guideline affect and not an enforcement responsibility. At the very least we must cut the Department of Education's budget by fifty percent immediately.

A mass drive for education is a private drive by parents, who should facilitate the reading of *A Miracle that Changed the World - The 5000 Year Leap* by W. Cleon Skousen, which is an easy guide through that history. This book should be read and all of us should demand it be required reading beginning in the eighth grade, continuing each and every year thereafter in all public and private schools. Furthermore, acquire a copy of the U.S. Constitution and the Bill of Rights. Hang these documents in your home and make sure your children know what they say and for what they stand. Talk about it with them as though if you did not, they would run out and have sex.

Wise up! These documents make it possible for our children to live as a free people long after we are gone, to give and receive a positive influence from their fellow man. Hard work and playing within the boundaries of our founding documents, not changing those boundaries, will provide for the hearts and spirits of our children's welfare. At the very least demand that copies of these two imperative documents to the founding of our Country are hung up in every classroom in this country, now!

Boundaries

Term limits for all elected officials, especially at the Federal level, need to be implemented immediately and we need to stop with the special interest groups. Why has this not come about, after all it is always a prominent topic in the conversation on politics and always the first answer for those who are unhappy with their representative? When election time arrives people continue to vote for the same person over and over again. Change who you vote for at least every other time or every third time or stop crying!

Before I go any further, you may have heard the prior Speaker of the House, Nancy Pelosi, reply to a question as to whether or not a recent action taken by Congress was constitutional or not. Her reply was, "ARE YOU SERIOUS?" She said nothing more. Every American, even this arrogant Representative's supporters, should be outraged at her answer. I recommend everyone contact her office (regardless of how much time has passed since she made the statement, don't let this go) and demand she publicly answer the question at length, to include why she believes her response was anything short of arrogant and dismissive of the American people.

What better argument is there for term limits, if not to simply remove anyone who has become so comfortable and so arrogant in what they have come to believe is their right vs. their privilege to represent others? How dare them! I would suggest, onto deaf ears I suppose, to the media that when they gather to listen to the prior Madam Speaker, they ask the same question each and every time they have a chance to ask anything. They should ask nothing else until the bone-head provides an acceptable answer. If she does not, then ask it again and again and again until she does. I would not give her the opportunity to make any statement until she answers the question.

We, as Americans, have every right to know whether our representatives know what it is they are doing and from where they draw the power to do it or not. Here is a clue for each representative in every position: if you serve in those positions, you serve us all not just your own district. Oh, you might have some particular items you want to receive for your district, that's fine because everywhere has different issues with which to contend, but not in secret, not behind closed doors, and not in violation of our Constitution.

If you believe a politician is going to vote in favor of a measure that will put them out of a job like term limits, well then take another dream pill. Let me give you some insight from the fly on the wall. More often than not, if a politician votes to impose term limits on their own position, it is because they already know full well that there are enough no votes to prevent the measure from passing. After the vote they come out strong and say, we tried but the others just wouldn't vote for the measure. Give me a break! Come on, my fellow Americans. Wake up to the shenanigans.

There is one good way to force term limits, but we will have to swallow hard. We do have the final vote and we must make it. If you have someone on the ballot that has been in their position more than 20 years and there is another candidate with the same or close to the same principles with which you can live; do not vote for the incumbent, vote for the other person!

Another way to look at a candidate is their private business experience; if they don't have any, don't vote for them. Now that is not to say they had to own a private business, but they should at least know what it means to have to put in a full day's work for a full day's pay. This business about being born into the position is very old school. I dare say corrupt and certainly leads to corruption, does it not? We ran away from that ridiculous notion over two hundred years ago, didn't we?

How about we define a full day's work for a full day's pay? Everyone needs to look at how many days our politicians actually go to the office and work. If you want just a glance then the next time you're in a bookstore pick up *FLEECED* by Dick Morris and check out chapter 4: THE DO-NOTHING CONGRESS IS STILL DOING NOTHING! This glance will only take a few minutes. Mr. Morris documents the record of Congress with dates and the work preformed, you really do need to take a look.

(I know these books are often timely and our current politicians in Washington D.C. will say that book is now outdated, but don't you believe it. That might be true for the brand new Jane and Joe, to give them some credit, before they get into the way things are done; but, I think at least history shows us they always get back to doing nothing.)

Not only do they spend more time at home or on vacation than at work, when they are at the office, all they do is vote on resolutions to give praise for universities and sports. You will be amazed by the fact they work less than half the time the average working stiff must in order to collect a pay check. But they will stand up and yell what a great job they are doing, if for some political necessity to fool us, they come to the office on a weekend or a holiday. Fact is if the bone-heads came to work everyday like everyone else, they would not have to work on the weekends or holidays. Quit being fooled.

I do not know about you, but I want my elected officials to be doing the people's business every day at a minimum of forty hours per week, not paying attention to the football games around the country. I do not have any idea what a football game can do to win a war or fix the economic problems we are now experiencing. Those dunderhead politicians have their priorities screwed up.

Hey, if they want to praise some athlete that can run fast or pass a ball further than anyone else, do it on their own time not ours. I guess we can allow them to use their - our - letterhead but not our time. I am not dismissive of how much money a ball team can bring to a community, but I think this should be left up to the local community in all regards not Washington D.C.

I really get angry, frankly, when I know that some young page answers the letters of importance to concerned citizens and the football game gets the direct attention of the elected official. Generally, the concerned citizen gets some condescending patronizing remark like, "Thank you for your input, your concerns are very important to me." Then, they forget about it. Later, they ask you to send them money to fight against some law you really want or, worse yet, to fight for a law you really do not want. Either way they don't care what you want or not, they only want to control our money. What a bunch of malarkey! I might have a different point of view; if I ever see someone get real meaningful responses instead of some jock being praised with a hero's welcome for being able to throw a ball.

Hero, that's another term used way too often. Ball players are not heroes just because they have a talent for a specific sport. A hero is someone who puts their life on the line knowing full well that it's in danger in order to save or assist someone else in need, nothing less. Look, I don't mean to belittle someone who can be looked up to and be a role model of what it means to work hard; use the talent they have; stand up with perseverance to better oneself, but they are not heroes.

Here is a short list of those who are not heroes: doctors, ball players, politicians, and anyone else who does a great job, but fails to place their own lives into positions of life or death, dependent on what they do or don't do! Just because a doctor is really good, simply means they are really good.

Yes, they can save a life, but they are not a hero unless they are saving the life on a battlefield with open gunfire and or explosions all around them which might at any minute take their life. That is a hero. Our military personnel, firefighters, and police officers are heroes; so is anyone else who puts themselves in a life threatening position. The rest are mentors, directly or indirectly, or they are simply looked up to and idolized.

Government Housing

One of the things you often hear out of Washington D.C. is that it costs a lot of money to maintain two households: one in Washington D.C. (where it is not cheap) and one in a Representative's home district. Now the newest trend with our young representatives (mostly Tea Party candidates, who by the way I admire), is to make a point by sleeping in their office. That won't last and it should not last for at least two reasons I can think of immediately. First, they should not have to reside in such cramped quarters; second, I am sure it is against the building codes in one fashion or another. I can also see some bone-head page filing a law suit of some sort, such as harassment, because they observed the representative walking around in less than acceptable attire or they had to wake them up because their alarm failed to go off.

What do you say we help them out by eliminating some of their direct expenses by lowering their individual budgets or money out of pocket? How about we build them a housing project? This project should be very nice, but not too opulent, and very comfortable with private gates and the U.S. Capital Police or other Federal Police providing security. You know, like so many of the other Federal buildings.

We should build two complexes one would be called The Congressional Estate Complex and the other one would be The Senatorial Estate Complex. Each state would have a three bedroom house for each of their representatives, paid for by the State not the Federal Government. After all, the Pentagon is safe and our men and women in the military have base housing. Now if they do not want to live in the housing provided, just like our military are not required to, that's ok. BUT THEY PAY FOR OFF BASE HOUSING OUT OF THEIR OWN POCKET! Now that would not only save some real money, but it might actually stop some of the shenanigans. As there, would be CCTV security all around the complexes. So it might be difficult to use our housing for unacceptable social or illicit behavior.

Further, with so much concern about the environment and all those independent vehicles running around Washington D.C., let us run vanpools to and from the complexes everyday three times a day. You know, like the school buses across this nation, these can also be governed by the U.S. Capital Police for proper security. I believe we can create a job or two with these ideas and save-save-save all at the same time.

I do not think the current President or the Vice President arrangement should change and their cabinet members or even the Speaker of the House should not have to take the vanpool. Even in the private sector there are perks for higher position. I do not include advisers to these positions or in these ideas, as I don't believe in staff advisers with responsibilities other than advising, at least not ones who get paid by our tax dollars. Unless, of course, each adviser goes through the vetting process in the same fashion the secretaries or directors of prominent departments must with sworn statements in front of Congress and subject to verification!

There is something significant for all politicians to keep in mind when accepting office, whether elected or appointed. I am talking about a duty to prioritize the people's money as they are charged with spending it from a budget collected from the people and of the people. This charge is not simply the task of developing programs and securing bids to eventually spend the money on anything, just so they can say they did in an attempt to accomplish a meaningful task. It is to prioritize all expenditures arising out of their prospective budgets. I mean this sincerely and I think most people agree with me. How many times have we heard of the ridiculous expense of furniture in the remodeling of some public office? This exact scenario occurred in my own office and brought me to odds with my Board of Directors.

I was the Executive Director for a public office and taxing entity of a State of Texas Political Management District. One of my first tasks was to locate and secure ample office space, followed up by having the office furnished. This included remodeling any space, should it be in need, by way of designing walls, doorways, bathrooms, kitchen and break area, and the conference room. Given the numerous conferences necessary almost daily in order to accomplish the mission and vision of the District, each of these issues were of great concern, as there would be hundreds of visitors representing every stakeholder in the community. I won't bore you with the countless meetings and arrangements, then changing each of these as required to fulfill the mission but the following makes my point very well.

The Board of Directors had many loyal friends who supported the legislation and promoted the State Legislators of the 77th session into enacting the District, many of whom provided assistance in the development of the vision. (You might refer to this group as special interest.) The directors were insistent on favoring many of these loyal partners.

I, on the other hand, believed that loyal or not the people's money was far more important as a fiduciary duty, and the best price for tangible resources that met the needs should prevail. I also believed we should make every attempt to spend those funds within the District and, in fact, that is part of the design: collect the money in District, spend the money in District, in order to benefit as many of the stakeholders as possible. I did not, however, think that the doubling of prices, whether in or out of District, was a proper expenditure.

One director found a new conference table; it was an eight foot oval with laminate covering and plastic edges and cost $3800.00 dollars. A great price, he said, and it was from a loyal supporter in the District. I went to untold numbers of used and reconditioned furniture outlets. I found a fourteen foot oval, solid wood, beautifully refinished table in rich dark mahogany at a cost of $800.00; I bought it immediately. I was steadfast when told to reconsider buying the new table from the local supporter not the cheaper one and nearly lost the battle. I was able to win this one and bought the reconditioned table with significant negative comment towards my team building ability in question; and I lost the next order of business.

The next related to the office desks. From yet another refinishing and reconditioning outlet, I found solid wood desks in a mahogany finish for each office at a cost of $1500 to $1700 delivered and set up. The Board of Directors found beautiful solid wood also in mahogany at a cost of $2800 to $3200 each with an additional charge of set up. Of course, their choice was from a loyal supporter. They won this one, go figure? I might also add, in order to prevent another foolish expenditure; I donated a desk for one of the back offices. The Deputy Constables put it to good use. I was told but never confirmed there were some who were very angry over this, as it broke the cycle of purchasing any further furniture from the special interest groups.

There were several instances like these; most I did win because I learned from one of the two people I look up to with great respect: President Ronald Reagan. Taking his lead, I spoke openly about most of my proposals with the stakeholders before I made them officially to the board. I kind of went over the heads of my directors and I did hear about it often. Regardless, we managed to be a quasi team and did good things for the District. I would not have been able to accomplish much without their support in the long run and, of course, the support from the stakeholders. I left on very good terms and decided to retire before those terms turned negative. It became apparent to me that any negative infighting would translate into the lack of positive growth for the District. Neither the board nor I would change and the community was the priority.

Political Correctness

An area that I think is very dangerous and, frankly, will continue to degrade our best efforts is POLITICAL CORRECTNESS. This is a virus, a cancer, which takes apart equality and justice throughout our American way. For some weird reason we, as a society, always overreact to everything. We must stop and reinsert common sense into our attempt at repairing damage or assuaging someone's hurt feelings.

First and foremost, we cannot forget the basic principles our Country was founded, which beyond any doubt were Judeo Christian Beliefs. Therein, we need to understand this business of separation of Church and State.

This does not mean you or the Government cannot worship or recognize the Country's founding principles. It means that the Government cannot mandate a religion for you to participate in or worship.

It also does not mean that religions of other nations MUST be allowed in the public square, especially if they stand on a principle which seeks to destroy our Country. After all, it is a matter of National Security and always has been.

Nevertheless as a layman in these matters, I must confess there lingers the question and imperative concern of national security within our current struggles. These perils are, as I have alluded to, in the extremists of any proclaimed religion who use their cause to bring about the evils of destruction. Perhaps these should be treated in a manner of criminality vs. religion, if we can see our way past their camouflage. I know this is a tough issue and I do not proclaim to make any real religion illegal. But we need to look very close at those who are intent on destroying this Country when they use the camouflage of a religion.

You can, as an individual, worship whatever religion you like in America; but, you should never be allowed to insist on any religion of any other country to be publicly recognized by the USA. This country's founding religious principles should always be recognized by the United States Government. In other words, we won't prevent you from practicing your religion, in fact we encourage it, but we do not and should not have to recognize your religion in the public square of this country and we should not allow you to prevent ours from the public square. Even if you have no religion at all, Mr. & Mrs. Atheist!!

When Thomas Jefferson wrote the words - a wall - separating Church and State, he was referring to the individual states and not the Federal Government. The Constitution had already been written and clearly separated the powers of the Federal Government in these matters. The Constitution further gave or left these matters up to the individual states. It appears clear to me that Jefferson made this point without the need of further interdiction by the Federal Government, both as a legislator for Virginia and as the President of the United States.

Therefore, the Supreme Court of this land has indeed overstepped the boundaries of our Nation's Constitution. It is my opinion then; should a matter of regulation in question of religious worship be brought before the high court of this land, it must be rejected and returned to the high court of the state, without comment or ruling.

Lately, there is a run on preventing Christmas Trees and Nativity scenes to be displayed in and around the public square. Therefore, we need to find a way around these absurd and disrespectful antics against the founding principles of our great Country. Here is one way to fight for our right. Get together with your group, the Church if you belong to one or the immediate community members, and each accept a role to play in the Nativity. Everyone dresses up, being sure to represent each of the figures. I am quite confident that there is a newborn in the community and the mother to gladly play those roles.

Then, you need to visit all the public buildings in your community and take up a position. You do not need to request a permit and you do not want to put on a play. I would recommend that you all walk together at least a block or two to get to your destination. Do not interfere with any traffic, vehicular or pedestrian, and do not carry any signs.

Remember you do not want this to be a parade, so do not advertise it, just go visiting and the news will certainly find you. To be sure the message is sent to our supposed leaders, try and have several groups out visiting various public buildings at the same time and or traverse the community over the twelve days preceding Christmas. If you make this into a parade, then the community leaders will state that your group will need a permit, which they may very likely deny. You just need to stand around celebrating the birth of the Child, or just visit with one another.

Be sure not to forget the local library, as I am quite sure the employees there will be glad to help you locate the religious section and check out the appropriate books.

Discuss the content amongst yourselves, softly but aloud. Do not preach to anyone outside the group and only answer questions of why you're dressed the old fashion way as: you like the clothing style. Be sure to keep anything and everything you or your group undertakes peaceful. **Do not carry signs**.

Be sure to stop and have discussion near all the capitol buildings and if you can take a tour, do so, especially the White House. If you know where your representatives reside, walk slowly past their homes to and from a neighborhood store or coffee shop. I am sure you may want to hesitate (very briefly) near or in front of their homes.

Do not carry signs and do not block any traffic vehicular or pedestrian. You do not need to say anything to anyone except amongst yourselves. Those in opposition will be hard pressed to stop you, as it is still legal to dress the way you want as long as it is socially acceptable. I am pretty sure the way folks wrapped themselves up 2000 years ago is okay today. Oh, and don not carry signs.

When it comes to the African-American title and all the other titles which I believe are negatively attached to American, I am as baffled as the majority of other races and many of my own friends who are Black, Hispanic, Asian, Indian, and many other Americans. All of us, or at least most, consider ourselves to be only Americans. Why, then, do we and more importantly our politicians continue to use these titles that segregate us from one another?

Come on; after all we have recognized, have we not, that all men are created equal and interracial marriage and interracial unions are okay. The same drinking fountain is okay. All other rights and privileges are okay for each of us, which is exactly the way it should be!

If each of us is to live and experience this great Country and all it offers as Americans, then why not drop the statements that are intended to separate and segregate.

In this particular category we often hear about the hatred and the slavery of long ago. For today's society to continue trying to pay the debt of our grandfathers and grandmothers for their horribly wrong actions is like punishing me for my father's abusive onslaught. How do you think that would work out? It keeps you angry and makes you even more resistant to authority and society.

Many will speak to the fact there is still racism alive and well in this country; it is in every part of the world not just in America. The reason for this and many issues is because it is impossible to people proof anything. Individuals who can't get by these issues are idiots. Those who continue this ridiculous race garbage must stop or it will never become a level playing field. No matter whom you are or which position you hold, you must stop. The insistent badgering of the race issue, especially as written in our laws and work policies, is forever keeping people angry, promoting racism towards each other. STOP IT!

The ridiculous statement that is often made to end or discourage someone who wants things to change is: can't we all just get along. No, we will never all get along well enough to educate those idiots who just can't see past their own self interest. We must stop insisting on title markers which do nothing more than keep people angry.

I am all for keeping laws making it illegal to discriminate, for any reason, and we need not change those laws. However, all the hate crimes are foolish and only provide a furnace for more hatred. There is no reason to say because you hate that someone is gay, you murdered them. Therefore, instead of life in prison or the death penalty, you should receive for your punishment "LIFE IN PRISON OR THE DEATH PENALTY".

Or maybe you should get two life sentences and two death penalties, which would be okay if you murdered two people? But come on is that stupid or what? Murder is murder!

Why should a person who punches some passerby in the nose get anything less or more than if they punch the passerby because that person is gay, black, short, tall, belongs to a union or does not? Maybe, they punched them because they did not like the look received. That is not a reason to punch someone for sure. But hey, just punish the offender with stiff penalties perhaps with both monetary and public service and/or imprisonment according to the level of violence and let it go. Just make the violator do all the time to which they are sentenced, instead of letting them slide on some stupid technicality.

Technicalities, now that is truly an overused excuse presented to a jury; that is for sure. If the wrong was illegal - not in line with the Constitution rule of law, etc. - okay, I get it. But, this baloney of someone forgetting to check a box on the booking form; put some minor information in the documents that was obviously nothing more than an oversight or misunderstanding - which can and should be merely ordered fixed by the judge - must stop. Fix the document and hold people accountable.

The only reason these law enhancements exist is because of our politicians who want to say, "I feel your pain." This way the groups who fall into these categories will vote for the politicians and keep them in powerful positions. The reason a politician votes in favor of these laws, which will not necessarily gain a vote per se, is because they need the other politician to support their own legislation or they know full well the other side of the aisle will demonize them for being a racist, a homophobe, soft on crime, etcetera.

It is nothing more than spineless politics, my friends. Unfortunately, the action or non action by our politicians has dire consequences for the American citizens. It keeps us at the very least angry and sometimes brutally violent towards each other.

The politicians use these issues, especially race, as an excuse to fund projects that are often times extremely controversial and do little to fix anything. Instead, these issues and programs ignite the flames in that old time race feud and keep us all segregated. When the politicians keep handing out the fish and fail to teach those in need how to fish, they will forever be dependent and the politicians know it. Those who become dependent will never fish for themselves and the politicians know that all too well. Why then do the politicians keep doing the same thing? Because they have control and lots of tax payer money to spend where they know it will keep them in power.

What is the answer to this perpetual cycle of keeping the minority down by degrading them and keeping them dependent? Stop shoving these excuses down the throats of all Americans and just maybe they won't be so angry all the time. Maybe they will stand up and learn how to fish along with helping others. These will then teach even more to fish, finding themselves to be truly a free people like all Americans should be regardless of their race; creed; gender; religion; or any other display of; I am different than you so give me, give me, give me.

I often hear that we have come a long way and there is still a long way to go. That is true; unfortunately, they go on to try and justify their statement with nonsense like, just because we have come a long way doesn't right the wrongs of the past. Again I agree but they should follow this with another statement to give the first statement new life i.e.: it has been put aside and now we are moving forward.

The historical wrongs should never be forgotten, but they don't need new and distorted versions extrapolated into our more understanding and accepting society either. History should be studied and taught as it occurred in order to learn from our wrongs, but never used as a weapon to do more or rather constant damage to the human psyche.

The best analogy I can use here - which I believe everyone will at least have observed play out in movies, if not in their own life - is the one of a marriage gone wrong. If by the grace of God a spouse can forgive the other for having cheated with another, they must truly have forgiven. If they have not truly forgiven, then by way of continuing to bring this tragedy forward they will always be on the losing end of their relationship or the lack thereof!

Before leaving this subsection there is one other item to be addressed I do not believe there is a mandate to print federal, state, or local government documents in any language but that of English. There is one exception to this and that would be instructions on how to become a citizen of this Country, to include the need to learn the language before citizenship is granted. Again with the exception of printing instructions on how to become a citizen, these issues can lie in the lap of state business and not at the federal level, in regards to printing material.

If a state votes through their legislative process to print the material in more than one language, it is their budget. We will save millions of dollars, if we enact this common sense policy. By the way, if someone needs an interpreter; then they can pay for it; unless they can't afford one in a criminal trial. Civil trials and common communication are another situation. If they brought the civil action and win, then the ruling can be all court cost including the interpreter. If you believe I am a racist because of these measures, I can only say you are very wrong.

Political Dependency or Illness?

It is time to speak - not to the exceptions because even I know there are exceptions in all matters - to all those who believe they need to be paid in order to stop eating, stop smoking, stop peeking into the internet porn sights, etcetera, etcetera, etcetera. These issues are not anything more than a lack of will power in the hands of weak-minded individuals. They use the excuses politicians hand out like candy, so they can keep doing what it is they are doing, believing it to be a real addiction or disease. But it is not! These problems are the result of their own weak mind and their lack of will power. Many just really like what they do and they can blame it on someone else, not to mention getting paid for doing it.

If what I say isn't true, then the placebo effect would never work. I don't care if it's in your genes or not; just because you inherit a weak brain does not mean you don't have the power to overcome it, if for no other reason than simply out of necessity or be miserable. In this case few will like you, but many will unfortunately coddle you and put up with your poor-little-oh-me-syndrome. The key is in having the tenacity to keep after the demon and stay the fight. All you need, more often than not, is your brain and a bit more good sense than God gave a green grape. Come on, people; the side of the package states very clearly, YOU WILL GET CANCER IF YOU SMOKE THIS CRAP, or words to that effect.

Here is something for the exception category. If someone is going through the trouble of cooking all day and putting their talents on display for a family tradition or holiday festivity, then enjoy the food! Help yourself to their gracious offering and eat as much as you are able without getting sick. Go back on your diet tomorrow.

Quit insulting your host with your guru diet out of some book or from television paid programming; if you really don't like the food, don't force yourself.

Of course, if you are truly allergic, don't eat it. But if you like it, eat it and say thank you! As I have said, I am not a medical doctor and I am well aware that there are very real diseases, such as Celiac Disease. For you people and others with diseases that the pharmaceutical companies don't pay much attention, you need to be your own advocate. Do your research. There are many books out there to be read and questioned, such as New York best seller *The G Free Diet: A Gluten-Free Survival Guide* by Elisabeth Hasselbeck.

Back to those so called diseases and illnesses of which the politicians and self-help, self-appointed gurus' have convinced you that you are a victim, so they can do nothing more than make money or keep power. Sorry people, you simply lack will power. Reach down and find it in yourself or there will be those who say you are nothing less then weak-minded. (Like I did) If you are fat, stop eating so much and exercise at least three times a week for ten or twenty minutes.

If you really do or suspect you might have a true disorder or disease, then as noted previously do your research. Stop depending on nothing but doctors who often do not listen to what you think because they believe they know better, true or not. Especially do not depend on politicians who think they know better than you. They very seldom do. They must be questioned.

Then there are the medicines that have significant side effects, often one of which is a symptom of your own complaints. Research; question; and, then, do something about solving your problem, not just masking the symptoms with some drug that has a list of side effects as long as your leg.

By the way, let me make a strong suggestion to you. Nicely, of course, ask your doctors how much training they received in medical school regarding nutrition, supplements and the subsequent effects on the human body?

Did they learn how nutrients are best absorbed and what type of nutrient they would recommend for your particular deficiency, disorder, disease, or whatever has brought you to the medical expert's office? Ask the politician what school of medicine they attended and what did they learn about nutrition.

Oh, have you ever gone to a really nice doctor for weight control or worse heart disease and found them to be extremely obese? My mother did. I was with her and I for one was absolutely appalled. It was kind of like going to a proctologist named DR. Butt; it is just hard to believe and you keep retelling the story. The physician above used the entire political garb to justify his lazy fat self and scolded my mother on proper diet. I came close to slapping this guy upside the head.

If you smoke, stop it. You do not need, in my opinion, any medication of any type to stop smoking just will power. If you like pornography, stop it or own up to the fact that you like it; become a part of it and go to hell or shut up and stay in the closet with your unwelcome antics. If your wife or partner catches you scanning the porn, please read the above sentence again. Follow the advice and your loved one might forgive you or you may have to hit the road and pay up for the violation of your vows and promises. When you stand before your Creator, well, you took the chance. Didn't you?

For those fat people- oh, I am sorry was that politically incorrect? For you fat people, I will give you a break here because the overweight do not always get good advice and for some reason they are too lazy to do any research on their own on what to eat and what not to eat. Fact is: if you just stop taking in so much food you will lose some of the fat. I don't buy into the excuses that you try really hard and you just can't lose weight.

Hum-bug! You don't stick to it or you don't truly try. I am not saying you must boycott the chain restaurants. To the contrary, I think it is a good idea for you to go down every now and then to grab a McDonald's Big Mac or whatever your preference might be. Everyone needs to cheat on their diet once in a while, just be careful and be wise. Why? Because, it shows or holds up the fact that you and you alone are in charge of yourself and everything you do!

Here is a good place for you to start. This is just an opinion, I am not a doctor of any kind and I strongly recommend you speak to your doctor before changing your diet. **(Because, I have to say that.)** You should go to the internet and look up the "cut diet", which promotes a life style diet; show it to your doctor and have a discussion. If your doctor is unwilling to discuss this with you, get another doctor; your current doctor is on an ego trip. There are all kinds of great tasting foods in the diet from all the groups that you need and none of what you don't. There are variations in the diet, if you don't like something recommended. You just need to stick to it!

If you must change over slowly go ahead take your time but get there. Stick to it!! I read in material, which the International Sports Science Association put out, that seventy-five to ninety percent of all dieters who lose weight can expect to regain all of the weight they lost within one to three years of completing the diet. Come on; we can do better than that can't we? From my perspective this information means there is an answer; stay on a diet that is healthy for you. But, I am not a doctor! Do your research. The most foolish thing you can do is depend on a politician to advise you or your child.

I personally hate most food good for you; but, I have done this diet for well over three years. I will confess though, I did not need to lose weight. I know there are those out there saying that I don't have to worry about a weight problem. This is wrong, especially if you look at the rest of my family who struggle with weight.

I get fat just like other people and quickly, if I do not work at staying healthy. There is no luck at all; it is just awareness and doing something about it. I am just trying hard to be as healthy as I can, in order to live a full and complete life. I am never hungry. Guess what? You get to eat five to eight times a day. My weight stays within three pounds, either up or down. Oh, here is one of the best features. I do not take any prescription drugs.

I do take vitamin supplements; but, that is a choice I made long ago. **Of course, I would strongly recommend you speak to your medical doctor and a nutritionist before changing your diet or even sticking to the standard of life you have chosen for yourself. I said, "The life you have chosen for yourself." I also said, "There are always exceptions."**

I understand that drugs and alcohol are addicting and I will address this issue. However, for now let me say this: it will take friends and family to take the hard line in these cases. Never indulge these addicts and always do whatever you must to keep them from those substances, which includes having them locked up for their actions either in a public jail or a private hospital. Never stand for any violence brought upon you or another person by these addicts; by allowing them to be violent, you will be enabling their addictions.

The sooner you get them away and off the drugs, the sooner they will return to a normal and productive life. Always keep in mind, these people must hit bottom to get them clean and sober. If necessary help knock them down, figuratively, whenever you have the opportunity, and one day you will be in a great position to help them back up.

You may recall, I made mention of placebos earlier. Sometimes they can work in a way you might not think. Let me relate a story about my mother and step-father. They both had difficulties with alcohol, but his was far worse.

My mother emptied all the bottles of booze in the house and replaced it with colored water and just a hint of alcohol - not in the bottle but around the top of the outside to keep the odor or the aroma present. My step-father drank them all and without leaving the house (which was the intent to keep him home and out of trouble) it worked and he appeared to become, at least, slightly intoxicated. Placebo, go figure!

If you think some substitution drug will help them because a politician told you it was better for them than the drugs, wrong. Many addicts I have spoken to and arrested say that when they can't get drugs on the street without committing a crime (most do until they get caught), they purposely get arrested; they can then go to jail and get a fix. They get it from the institution or another inmate. I will address this drug issue later and how to stop it in our prisons.

These issues are in this chapter, because it is the politicians and us who are allowing the politicians to keep most individuals on an addiction which could be overcome with some self control. We need to give true assistance instead of entitlement programs. If we will just go back to teaching those in need how to fish or swim, they won't starve or drown – or die from an overdose!

There is one disease that I truly do believe is completely and forever imbedded into a person's mind and actions, for which there is absolutely no cure or fix of any kind other than death itself. Therefore, death it is for any pedophile. They do not change, which has been proven by their own repetitive actions throughout history.

If you find and prosecute one of these devils and there is no doubt to their guilt, demand that they are executed as soon as possible. Life in prison is not worth the chance of parole or escape under any circumstances. If we do not get rid of them and we let them onto the streets for any reason at all, they will eventually kill someone's child, maybe yours.

Frankly, I don't care why they are sick. In this regard there is no cure. Execute those we know of now while the research goes on, to one day find a cure. I am not willing to sacrifice anyone's child until that dream cure is discovered, but you can continue to research. By all means after we execute them, take and dissect their brain.

While we are at it, let's give them all the experimental drugs possible until the day of execution. Perhaps that will lead to some other cure. There are individuals, even experts, who will tell you that pedophiles don't do harm, like cutting their victim's throats. The pedophiles themselves don't believe they are doing any harm to their victim at all. I respectfully or not so respectfully disagree, because even if they don't cut the throat they have still harmed that child both physically and physiologically. How can they not?

Yes, I know I said that I am pro-life and there are those idiots that try to play this ridiculous game of equating the death penalty to the right to life at birth; but they are simply foolish people. I believe these people have an agenda and it is one of two things: politics or ignorance with a dash of ideology. One issue does not cross over into the other, especially not where pedophilia is concerned.

Previously in this segment, I spoke a great deal about health, habits, real or not so real diseases, medications, and solutions that many would say should be in the chapter under health care. I put them here because I disagree. I think that which I spoke to in this chapter is so closely related to politics and politicians that it is actually changing our society. Please think hard about these issues for yourself and those who you love not to mention our freedoms, values and standards in this Country.

THE VOTE AND THE DRAFT

I think it is important to address these two issues because here too we have lost our way. I know there are many who simply do not agree with me, even those who stand shoulder to shoulder with me on several other issues. However, please let me make my case.

To give the vote to a kid, who is an eighteen year old child – ok, ok, a young adult - without any exposure to the world, is equivalent to a baby bird that just left the nest and swoops down onto a rattlesnake for dinner versus a worm. The snake is beautiful and gets your attention; but, there is no doubt if you don't know what you're getting into, the bite is deadly.

I recall the fight over this issue when I personally would have been directly affected. I did not agree then and I do not agree now! The rationale then was exactly what I hear today for lowering the voting and drinking age to eighteen, which is also foolish. The most common was if they are old enough to be drafted or enlist and go to war, they should be old enough to vote and drink alcohol. Oh, hogwash.

I said then and I say now: if we draft them and put them into our military, then give those individuals the right to vote. Those who don't serve don't get the privilege until they grow up. What is the grown up age for voting? How about at least twenty-one, as this seemed pretty adequate in times past?

Although I believe, twenty-five years old would be far more suitable. After all if we continue to raise the life expectancy, why not raise the voting age. They will have plenty of time to get the desperately needed exposure to cast a valid vote while having some understanding of what the measurable impact might be.

It doesn't matter if they are married and have children or not. Getting married is only one of many steps it takes to have real meaningful exposure. Give the marriage a couple of years to see if they were even mature enough for that step, before putting the Country's future at stake. Oh, did I hurt someone's feelings? What is the matter youngster, can't you handle the truth?

I realize that most will not agree with me over the grown up age, but I stand by it. I have been in law enforcement and public service long enough to have witnessed that these kids, by a wide margin, do not have the maturity to handle the vote and they especially can't handle their alcohol. I know there are those exceptions. Yes, I thought I was one of them; but, I was not, at least not until I came home from the battlefield. I did grow up by the time I returned. Real life and death issues can have an extreme affect on all people, both positive as well as negative.

When I married, my wife was too young to vote and too young to drink. The age then was twenty-one. I was twenty-three, she was eighteen. I was too young as a soldier to cast my vote, but the military allowed us to drink on base, which was and still should be the policy. Each soldier will turn twenty-one during their time in the service or shortly after they are discharged.

Paying attention to the draft, I think we should. We need to ensure that our troop levels can be built up quickly in time of need. Not to mention that we currently burn our troops out. How many times have we recycled each of these soldiers into battle: two, three or more times? I personally know several active military personnel who have deployed four, five and even six times. If we initiated the draft, we would not have to do that. That does not mean those drafted must stay in the military for two years like days past. Unless they decide it might be an opportunity, after they have had a taste of being part of a team and learned some discipline.

This will allow them to break the apron strings and perhaps find a trade in which they can prosper. Really, was the past all that bad; I don't think so? This will give them time to learn who they are, not what some movie star eats for dinner or who they dated the night before. No, this gives them up front, personal, and in-your-face experience. This is exposure to real life, not reality television from the living room.

I would suggest they enter boot camp right out of high school, male and female; learn the basics and stand by for a four or five year period in the ready reserve. If the Country must, upon a declaration of war **only by the Congress,** activate them. This would allow a jump on the training and they could have a very brief refresher's course and advanced training, should they be called up.

Obviously, they can go about their life during the standby period. I would also like to see a two year enlistment versus the draft which would void the standby time, if they choose. As far as that voting and drinking measure, if they are active duty after boot camp, then go on give them the vote. If they are inactive after boot camp, no vote and no drinking until they become of age.

Let me be very clear, before I leave this section. I am very proud of all those who volunteer for our armed forces in any capacity and back them one hundred percent. I also would stand with them today in any theater of combat.

However, I am adamantly against our government going out and offering citizenship to anyone who is willing to enlist in our forces. If this is not a back door for our enemies to enter, I do not know what is. This type of recruitment must stop. Become a naturalized citizen in the normal and legal process or be born here, then enlist or be drafted.

UNIONS

For some reason we have allowed the Government to transfer a perceived power of regulating into actual governing of the private market place and we have allowed them to use the unions to do so. This action is in direct conflict with a free market. It is often necessary for government to step in for the sole purpose of ensuring the individual is not unfairly taken advantage of or harmed - in a way that prevents **citizens'** constitutional rights from being hindered or prevented from being exercised.

Although there are many examples of this unfortunate action, it is most prevalent in the establishment and strongholds of unions in the free market. Keep in mind that unions try to turn a privilege into a right and they are incorrect. We should never allow a union to deem a privilege to be a right and we should never allow the Government to force a privilege. Being free and equal as all men is a God given right, not a government privilege to rule upon. It is the job of our government to protect our being a free person, which once again is a God given right not a government given right.

I have mentioned my extensive work history in fraud and worker's compensation cases in two states. I have been in the work place and investigated just about every type of business both public and private that exists; I do mean just about all, both legal and illegal. Within these dealings I have had hundreds of conversations and intense investigative insights with every level of every social economical position of the corporate world, private and public, rich and poor.

I can tell you unequivocally that those businesses which are not unionized have far less complaints overall than those that do have a union, particularly a strong union.

Furthermore, the nonunion shop has far less injuries, far less complaints about management, and especially far less fraud. The less the employer is pushed and demanded to do things, the simpler it becomes to acquire the best work environments. Yeah, yeah, you can beat me over the head with the exceptions, but that will not change the facts I know to be true.

My statements and firsthand experiences come from my direct investigations, conversations, and eye witness accounts. I am not speaking from some distorted analysis, manipulated statistics, numbers chart, or financial budget. Most of these types of reports are subject to subjective measures and protocol that inevitably lack necessary criteria to be anywhere close to being accurate.

If the employer won't budge at all, slow down the work place or strike if you must. Tell the customers why and let the free market take its course. By the way if your job is public safety DO NOT STRIKE, as you must fulfill your obligation as a public servant or quit. I have no problem with you taking your time on service calls that won't increase the danger or jeopardize the safety of the public. Explain to them why it took so long, but never sacrifice anyone's safety: not the public, not yours, and not your fellow officers or supervisors, never! If you lose your job over the fight, the job may not have been worth the trouble. You should always keep your eye out for a better job, even if you're happy in the one you have; you never know what opportunity may come your way.

My uncle used to tell me, "If you always walk around never looking down, you will never find a dollar in your path." After that, you would be surprised at just how much money I found in the gutter and on the sidewalks. Get the point? Oh, the advice did come with a stern insight: it is just as important to look up every few feet to stay on the right path and to ensure you don't trip or bump your head - or get pooped on by a fly-by-night politician, I mean, bird.

Here is a very important distinction. A nonunion shop is not always a shop without representation. There are many employers who have associations instead of unions. In a union shop many employees do not want to join but are either forced because there is no job if they don't or they are harassed to the point of no return. Further, they **must** pay the dues and those dues are taken from their paycheck automatically, like it or not. That is not free choice and it is a mandate without representation.

I have investigated cases where I found that middle management were voting members of the association. When I was working with the Amador County District Attorney's Office in California, the investigators were a part of the Deputy Sheriff's Association. Investigators were fine, but the lieutenants in the Sheriff's office were also voting members. Here was the problem in this case; the Sheriff was not well liked by the investigators and many, if not the majority, of the deputies. The lieutenants were middle management and reported every detail of the closed meetings to the sheriff, a form of intimidation.

Why was that a problem? The investigators and the deputies were unable to complain openly - getting it off their chest - to the Association for equitable remedy. Instead, their complaints were taken to the Sheriff and used against the individual deputies. Do not allow middle management into the same group of voting members, the association loses any value of keeping the "union" out and the possibility of equitable solutions.

Why does this force the issue of having a union? Employees become extremely frustrated in the above scenarios and vote a union into affect. The employer who allows this frustration cuts their own throat; eventually, the union will violate every opportunity for an equitable work place. The frustration simply builds and the equity of the job decreases.

Associations, when organized properly, allow the employee to join if they like and choose to pay the dues or not. If they do not join, then there are privileges they might not receive, which are up to the association rules. I admit that there are some who will still feel that obligation to join, but in the associations it has proven to be far less pressure on the employee and the dues are almost always far less than unions. Not to mention that, more often than not, the employee still has a job. Additionally, it is rare for any employee not to join and the team type relationship becomes prevalent without even trying. Of course, there is give and take.

I can say, unequivocally, that the union shop over and above the nonunion shop has significantly higher stress; extreme low level morale; and a strangle hold on the hiring and termination process which, contrary to propaganda, stifles growth and increase in both monetary and benefit compensation. I have investigated many cases where an employee should have been terminated; but, because the union was so strong it was nearly impossible to drop a nonproductive employee. (Just look closely at the U. S. Post Office) When the chance came, it was extremely expensive and it was often a fraudulent worker's compensation case. Fraudulent by the employer because it was the only way to get rid of the trouble maker; and on the part of the employee because they did not have or receive the injury of their claim as a matter of work.

The unions are more to blame for this flagrant blockage of termination than anyone. Without doubt the union is also responsible, at least indirectly, for the fraud and the rising cost of worker's compensation insurance.

This might be one of the most important statements I write. **If you do not see the connection between unions and the ever-growing, all-powerful special interest groups in America that wine and dine and flat out buy our career politicians, then you might just be fooled forever.**

You may also be the victim of unions, forever bound by the unequal and inequitable rules mandated by the union bosses and your politicians. Why would anyone want to start or own a business under the rules that prevent them from good and prosperous management?

Just think of the jobs lost in this process! If you don't think I have it straight, then please look to the government offices we always gripe about: the U. S. Post Office, the Department of Motor Vehicles, etc. Who do you think keeps that wonderful, service oriented worker behind the counter, where they can screw everything up and blame the problem on you? Here is a clue; it is the union! I know there are those who will say the union is not in the Federal Government. Do you want to bet? Better think about special interest groups, my friend. There is a very deep connection to be found between federal policy and the procedures in every federal agency.

In connection and hiding in the shadows with the special interest and the unions are the trial attorneys. If we keep electing attorneys, it is the same as having the fox guarding the chicken coop. I have stated time and again there are exceptions to everything, including attorneys. If I must pick a type or personality of an attorney to elect, then give me the likes of Congresswoman Michele Bachmann from Minnesota. At least she says what she means and means what she says.

Mostly, however, I prefer attorneys in the court rooms, on advisory boards, or in an advisory capacity (on retainer) to keep us out of hot water or get us out when we do not belong in the boiling pot. I do not want them to have a deciding vote in matters they argue for or against, except in the case of a judge who understands the totality of the argument based in law and gives the final vote to the people.

This is similar to a jury or the general public (through the elected or appointed officials) in matters of legislation and the enforcement of law. Judges should not legislate from the bench; instead, they need to be judging the accused and the case by the law already present on the books.

One of the best actions you can take in addressing politics and politicians, in addition to placing telephone calls and writing letters to their office, is to pressure and push the political party in which you belong and believe to find new candidates every eight to twelve years for the U.S. Senate and the U.S. Congress. Do the same at your local level with mayors, council members and sheriffs to keep the ball rolling forward. Do not let them come to believe that the job is an entitlement of their own; it is not for just the rich, not for an individual, and not for a family dynasty. If we continue on the current path, it will lead to tyranny and there will be - I believe and God forbid - another bloody revolution.

If I have not said this and I may say it again in some other context, it is important we all know who is running the Country and what is their value, principle and vision for the Country. If you will take the time to read *The Rules for Radicals* and learn about Saul Alinsky's plan for bringing down America, you may agree that those running this country today - those who currently have the power: George Soros, Andy Stern and, yes, the entire Obama Administration, particularly the President's advisers "Czars" – are doing just that. If you can't see the plot, then say goodbye to our freedom.

I don't really believe this is a plot by design from our President's part (is it?); but instead, I believe it is his very left wing ideology that the foundation of the plot takes advantage. By the way, why do our presidents need advisers who do not go through the standard system of confirmation? The answer is simple: if they went before confirmation, they would not be confirmed and the President would not be able to hide their true identity.

No president should be allowed to hire, on our dollar, any advisers other than those who go through a complete confirmation hearing. Aren't these jobs already in place in the form of secretary department heads? For what is a cabinet secretary position, if not to advise on their responsibilities directly to the President?

I continuously hear the television news, opinion shows, and read articles in the print media, wherein it is said this current administration seems to simply be out of touch with the American people. They know exactly what the American people want at least in the true American spirit, but if they comply with those terms, values and principles there will not be a crisis and it will not comply with the "rules for radicals". Will it?

I think our current President, Barack Obama, said it best, yet too many grasped at a preconceived meaning, in their own mind instead of what this President actually meant. What did he say? "We are only five days away from fundamentally changing the way America does business." Then after being elected, he went about apologizing throughout the world for America and all for which we stand, calling each of us arrogant. How dare you, Mr. President! I think you have confused arrogance with pride. Or did you mean what you said? Of course you did and I believe you have shown yourself for whom you really are; dead smack in the middle of the George Soros, Cloward-Pivin doctrine, The Rules for Radicals.

Frankly Mr. President, even I had high hopes that I might have been wrong, but I was not. You are who you are and this Country desperately needs to get you and your cronies out of office. I want a good solid conservative in that office no doubt; but, even if another Democrat is elected, I can only pray that he or she truly believes in the American people and the American way of freedom, liberty and prosperity.

CHAPTER THREE
Economics and Business Management
Jobs + Jobs + Jobs

This chapter will incorporate issues of job creation, taxes, social security, medical accounts and, of course, management; what I like to call the "Millmorian Management Style", derived from my last name. This style of management is nothing more or less than good common sense, a give and take of respect, and hard work. I will incorporate each in this chapter because it is here that I believe these issues can be solved. Like everything else, these issues intricately intertwine with the rest of this book.

Every business owner and, for that matter, every supervisor and every employee at any level must understand the necessity of earning respect not demanding it and demanding accountability not fudging or overlooking it. Starting with job creation is like addressing all the above because each issue must be taken, not so much as individual components, but as a whole.

But let's try to break it down. You and your employees should look, act, and speak professionally, no matter what your industry or business. Professional does not mean just an educated staff; it can mean being polite and respectful to others both in-house and outside the business. I hear everyone at one time or another address the use of profanity. If you or staff uses foul language, your work place is unprofessional, period. Is anyone listening in Washington D.C.? Mr. Vice President, you also lose respect, a ton of it.

Furthermore, if anyone allows bad language (if there is such a thing anymore) you are setting you and your business up for the inevitable frivolous, or not so frivolous, law suit and it can be extremely expensive and a job killer.

You must do everything possible to keep a safe and clean working environment. Always address any safety issue immediately; even if you do not think it is a safety issue, you must do something to prove you addressed the matter. One way to prove you addressed the issue is to have documentation and have someone other than the owner or supervisor sign the document.

Alternately, have them and a second signature to witness the action taken to address and or fix the safety issue. In some cases you may want to spend a bit of money and call in a third party to address the matter, dependent on the expense and whether there might truly be an issue at all. In this way there is always proof that the issues were addressed. Of course, not every complaint will warrant outside policing.

Look closely at your pay scale and how it is an employee receives or earns a raise. I would suggest building in a merit increase to enhance the common seniority steps. This will invoke initiative and make sure there are particular criteria to earn the merit enhancement. This does not have to be much, but it should be enticing. Make sure you have a documented policy and procedure manual; be careful not to allow policy by practice to supersede the written policy. Hold everyone accountable to the rules and follow them as a matter of example.

I believe in participative management, to the degree that you need to listen and include good ideas. Don't summarily dismiss an idea because that isn't the way things are generally accomplished. Study the idea for what it is and what benefits it may have on the industry. Specifically, look to the cost and what it might save.

Is the expense worth the productivity and/or safety, not to mention the morale factors? You must also exclude bad ideas for the same reasons, but in either case you must communicate your final decision. It is not always necessary to justify your decision; however, productive communication is rarely harmful.

There are always times when it may be necessary to improvise. In these situations do your level best to have on hand the proper and necessary tools of the trade, both for your employees and your customers. All equipment should be kept in a safe and good working order.

It is imperative to negotiate salaries and benefits with your employees, but you should establish the starting point before the meet and confer. It is not necessary to always justify a compensation package but it can often help. I have also learned without communication the unions seem to find their way in under the door, like a rodent searching for food. Happy or content employees do not need unions, due to the lack of founded complaints or abuses. Most reasonable people understand the employer is the one taking most, if not all, the risk. If you're fair and honest, they will understand you will make more money for those risks than they will.

Customer Service

There is no other place more important than meeting excellent customer service than the public entities. It is, after all, the public who pay for these services in their taxes. Take note of the public's concerns or complaints and do something legitimate about those concerns. Don't just appease the public issues with public relation statements and happy-go-lucky BS. If you do this, the public will very soon see through your words and distrust you and your profession. Make sure there is feedback to the people regarding your action. They do not have to like the outcome, but they deserve the feed back.

In the private sector there is nothing that will drive your customers away faster than a filthy establishment. It really doesn't matter whether your business is a hotel, a garage to repair vehicles, a car dealership or an office place providing some type of document or research or legal service.

Restaurants are a given in these cases. However, if you operate a service station or conveyance market or any business that provides restrooms, check the restrooms continuously throughout the day. I don't know how many times, but it has to be hundreds, where citizen complaints came to me as a Chief Law Enforcement Officer regarding filthy restrooms. The inevitable follow up was a query into which law I could enforce to make the store owner clean them.

Time and again, they reported rude reactions by the store managers or their request to clean the restrooms would simply be ignored. For those who care, here is the most popular complaint: "There is a trash can in the stalls to be used for disposing of used tissue." They would rather you place them in the trash instead of flushing these unhealthy and possibly hazardous materials down the toilets. Not only do they stink but often times the used paper only makes it to the floor and not the receptacle.

These trash cans do exist in thousands of establishments all across this nation. The complaints come from customers, both local and the traveling public, who stop at restaurants and convenience stores that serve food. I have been told more times than I like to remember, from the owners of these establishments, that there are many people from other countries that don't flush the paper where they come from and the trash can is a better alternative than the floor. That is, if the paper gets into the can.

There are several other measures that should be taken by management to remedy this health hazard. If they choose to not do so, the establishment should be severely fined for this public health hazard. I would go so far in this matter to have the local police become involved, if there are not enough state inspectors to issue citations that impose significant mandatory fines. I do not care if the owner and the majority of customers are those from the other countries; it is still a health hazard.

First, how about the owner installs a lid on the can and some sort of disinfectant system to kill the germs; similar to the containers where female sanitary napkins are put, but larger and more advanced with disinfectant chemical sprays. Second, try posting signs in several different languages on the inside of the stalls. Who cares if someone gets upset at the sign? It's a severe health hazard.

That is the nice way I suppose to advise the general public; however, as this is the United States of America not a third world country, do what it takes. If the business does not have a sewer system, then make sure the paper is bio-degradable for the septic system. For goodness sakes, next to the employees, the customers should be the highest priority of doing business. It should not matter if they are regulars or not.

Taxes

The best way to create jobs is to lower the tax rate across the board; especially the corporate tax. Frankly, I would be remiss if I did not promote the obvious. No matter who you are, there is no way you can PROVE that a fair tax or consumption tax would not work. I know there are those who will argue against the fair tax, but they cannot prove their case. At least not without changing the facts or assumptions within the correct data that proves it can and will work.

That being said, I am also well aware of the problems and disruptions a fair tax would cause, like all those IRS workers who will truly have to learn what it means to be a kinder and gentler person. Hey, under my social security plan they can still do audits while harassing individuals, employers, banks and very likely accountants.

Isn't hope and change what we are all looking for today.   There were some who thought they might have received this in the last presidential election; ha, ha fooled again. Friends, listen to everything they say, not just portions of what you want to hear. Remember, an election is like reading just the headlines of a newspaper article. If you don't read the entire article, you will never know what the story was even about, let alone what was really stated or intended.

The fair tax is a solution that I believe will never be accomplished on the part of any politician in office today; yet, another reason to vote them out and new blood in. If you want a good understanding of the fair tax you should read Mike Huckabee's *Do the Right Thing*, you will find it in Chapter 10 (The Fairness and Force of the Fair Tax). Let me paraphrase, in part, what Governor Huckabee states in this chapter.

"Flat", a flat tax on consumption of purchased items new at the retail level. This will not punish anyone regardless to their economic level.   Taxes should not arbitrarily create winners and losers, by a process or any other means. Those who earn more money will spend more money and thus will pay, "their fair share" as the saying goes.

"Fair", it should be obvious to any demographic; those with a liberal mindset speak to the creation of a fair tax and do so on behalf of the poor. But this always turns out to be disingenuous. Fair is not raising taxes on the wealthy in excess of forty five to sixty percent of what they make in order to give it to those who don't work. What the liberals really mean is if you make more we will tax you more and more and more, without end.

Therefore the poorest will never rise up to a fair share. So where is the fair share in a world where those making the rules decide who is wealthy and who is poor. Well that is easy; the standard is what ever they say it is. The earning numbers are manipulated and the formula works out to meet the criteria. Those are arbitrary numbers. Without the clear and appropriate criteria as to variables for individuals, the only thing left is an imaginary line of wealth. This is irrational and lacks common sense.

"Finite", it is transparent and fixed with no hidden cost. Because there is a limit to the tax burden even our youngest business minded people; like running a lemonade stand, can understand it. The most important factor in starting a business is having a solid idea of what all your liabilities will be from start to at least five years out. This is one reason numerous entrepreneurs recommend a five year business plan. As Governor Huckabee said *"The Fair Tax is the same for everyone, regardless of what a person does or where or why or how. Best of all, it is fixed – it doesn't vary from person to person or over time."*

Look simple is fair and flat is simple no matter what your status or arrangement.

Our government should allow any business who is keeping and investing their money elsewhere in the world to repatriate this money. The conditions to repatriate funds without the burden of extraordinary taxes should be to invest in creating jobs in the United States. After all they took their money offshore because the government taxes here are far too burdensome now. Additionally, the business tax rate must be dropped, somewhere in the vicinity of twenty-two to twenty-eight per cent, but the experts in this field will be able to put a better handle on this rate than I. Regardless, our current rate is higher than almost anywhere else in the world.

The U.S. Government continues to speak about creating jobs as if those in power have the only answers. Although I am not in favor of big government, I do believe there are departments of the Government that must be staffed appropriately to comply with our Constitution. Let me help them out with a good idea or two. Please don't forget the comments on our military; we do not have enough personnel serving given the instability in the world today. I implore everyone to reconsider the draft.

We should allow Federal Law Enforcement officers to be hired after the age of thirty-seven years old. The reason given for age discrimination in this arena is that these officers must be able to complete twenty years of service to gain the benefits of retirement. What a bogus excuse! What should be policy is that anyone regardless of their age - particularly those with prior experience who can physically and psychologically pass the requirements of the position - should be hired. The retirements can easily accommodate these employees with a five or ten year retirement benefit, similar to the many city and county police and fire retirements across the nation.

While I am on retirements, the same should pertain to those elected officials who serve; wherein, their retirements should be adjusted to fit the time in service vs. the position. You are aware, aren't you, that if elected to the U.S. Congress you only have to serve one term for a lifetime retirement? Hey, there is a great selling point for the friend you think might make a good representative in Washington D.C.; use it and convince them to run for office.

I will exempt the President of the United States, because no President should ever be allowed to fall into dire straits. The rest of them can take the time served - as they say in the court system -towards their retirement. Pro rated ladies and gentlemen! This idea may very likely open a few seats (jobs) in Washington D.C. all by itself.

History has proven to be the best teacher time and again. Why not roll back the taxes to accommodate the cost of living from when those taxes in place worked? If we took the tax base both for business and individuals in place during those years of President Ronald Reagan, add the cost of living, then we will have a tax rate that will create jobs immediately.

For those of you in current elected positions with only the brains God gave a green grape (there is a long list to choose from), let me enlighten you. The U.S. Government will receive by way of volume and less fraud more money to control. I put the money part in there to get the Pin Heads' (to quote Bill O'Reilly) attention, because I am sure most people with the ability to reason or read will know this instinctively.

Now, if Washington D.C. truly wants to cut the budget so they can then create jobs, why not start with a program of cutting foreign aid? I know we need to assist many places in the world. It is a given that there are countries that only use the money we send to pay corrupt government officials, not help the people. Luckily, many areas are certainly helped by our generosity, particularly when no one else will help.

But, give me a break; does it really make any sense at all to give over $300 billion dollars in aid to China, when we are borrowing far more then that from none other than China? That is correct, I said China. We could save at the very least the $300 billion we give to China by just borrowing that much less. I realize it would be difficult for Washington not to spend a windfall like this, so why not spend it where it might be needed such as on police or fireman? Or I don't know, put it towards the deficit?

Energy

I guess I should state the obvious here with "Drill Baby Drill"; do it and do it now! If the current world situations don't look freighting to you, I just don't know what to say other than it is time to become energy independent! Don't you think? Open our drilling for petroleum, natural gas and coal. Build refinery plants and create real jobs for Americans now. Look, I am all for researching new energy solutions like wind, solar, etc.; but, our technology is not yet proficient enough to get us what we need now, right now.

Keep up with small short term projects and one might work down the road - which would be great; but for now, use what we have right here in our own soil. Between drilling the pipeline, new transport vehicles, roadways, building structures and refinery plants we will create hundreds of thousands of jobs. I am in favor of building new nuclear plants as well. Now that we know strong earthquakes are inevitable, let's build them with proper failsafe systems in the event of nine point five or ten on the Richter scale. Just think of the jobs all this will create!

If anyone out there has the power, do me a favor will you? Put the price of gas in real terms at a per gallon rate; drop the ridiculous nine-tenths of a penny. What a fraud! Think about it. They charge you, say $3.39.9 per gal; but you can't buy one gallon; because they can't give you change. They force you to buy more than they advertise. I mean come on! If you want it to be $3.40 per gallon then say so, quit with the stupid stuff.

All we need to do for this and the rest of these suggestions to at least be discussed, refined and tested in pilot programs is to ELECT SOMEONE DIFFERENT THAN THOSE WHO HAVE BEEN THERE MORE THAN THE AVERAGE CAREER. Keep the positions moving forward with new blood and we will see real change, not purchased wishes for special interest groups.

For the independent states look to Texas or Arkansas for some answers, they got it right and are doing pretty well. The right-to-work states have a pretty good system, although I find some difficulties. I do not think most police officers in Texas and other places are paid what they should receive for the job they do. Here is a recommendation to lower the cost of pensions for public service and increase take home pay. It is time to negotiate a new contract with the employees. Oh by the way, listen up employees; if you want better deals, get rid of the union.

I believe where these matters are concerned, especially for those contracts and programs entrenched in our minds as absolute rights vs. privileges, the best and perhaps fair way is to grandfather them out. How about we renegotiate any new employee contracts for the future and let the old ones die out? (Pun intended)

Drop the retirement amount to a point viable, for explanation I will use fictitious numbers. If the current police officer or any public servant receives eighty percent of their full pay at retirement, cut that to fifty-five or sixty percent. Increase the employees take home pay by ten per cent. Then use whatever is left from the total amount cut to pay down the debt. The leadership certainly should be capable of finding the right formula.

In case I don't say this enough, here is a note to the new employee: get rid of the union, negotiate from an association and you will take home more money. I would also drop any maximum amount a retired person can earn.

If they worked for a retirement, they should get to keep all of it and earn however much they want or are able to in some other field without any penalty to the retirement. For goodness sake let people earn as much money as they can and they might just spend a bit more at the store and they might not need a government entitlement plan.

Social Security (Here is the current formula – Ponzi + Madoff = Social Security)

This is the biggest fraud scandal of all time and each of us knows it to be true. It sounds great and for those who collect the money they put into the program, it has been a life saver which cannot be disputed. There are millions who have depended on their monthly checks just to get through everyday and it is the safety net to be sure for them.

However, by allowing this system to become not just a safety net but a dependent system to sustain us or die has been a mistake driven by the politicians. But it is now time for the "Bernie Madoffs" of the U.S. Government to stand up and admit to this scam once and for all. Do not let this continue; it will be the death of millions who believe the money will be there in twenty, thirty, forty or fifty years to collect. It will not be there. If it is, so to speak, it will not be the money put into the system; it is the money of their grandchildren.

Today the money you put in is hidden or camouflaged in such malarkey as being in a "lock box". What that really means is the money is used and even spent long before it is collected. The politicians use and spend it on every type of program under the sun.

Most of these programs are nothing more than entitlements and welfare handouts to keep people feeling good; so they will vote for those who implement and support the program from which they collect and depend. Of course, these programs will keep those who depend on them depressed without any initiative to get off the public dollar.

Our grandchildren will not be able to afford and should not have to shoulder the burden. There is no "lock box". There is no box at all and there is no savings account. There is nothing but IOUs in the fictitious lock box.

From my stand point this is the same as saying, "Well, maybe if we can, we will pay you back on your investment, but maybe not." We all know how it works or supposed to work, so I will not get into the matrix of this fraudulent system.

Let's just discuss the way it was designed and you figure it out. In the beginning, you paid into the system until you turned sixty-four years old; then, you could collect a minimal amount the government thought was enough for you. That is, if you lived to the ripe old age of sixty-four, as the life expectancy was only sixty-two years. People bought into this. Well, if they bought that, then there is a real good chance they might buy into something that actually makes sense today. We need to find a better way. By using the same money from your working pocket to your retirement pocket; instead of from your pocket to the U. S. Government, who will then give it to others they feel are more deserving of your money than you.

One of the real problems with the current system is they give it out to people who never paid a dime into the system. Take my friend's nephew for example. He was a good kid who took his chances with a life style that was very risky and he knew all the risks. He became sick, - go figure - and for years before his death, he received social security. He never had a job other than working under the table for this and that, a dollar here a dollar there.

He never paid a dime into the social security system. Every government worker who helped him get the money was well aware of his circumstances, all of them. He did not lie to them and he did not commit fraud. In my opinion, the system and those working in the system committed fraud.

I say, mandate by federal law your employer take out the same amount of your pay as they do for Social Security right now. But instead of sending your money to the Government, send it to a "Security Retirement Account" of your choice (electronically of course).

Then, report to the Government that this mandate was complied with, just like they do now with Social Security. Some say this will cause havoc because of the different accounts and I say that is bunk! Almost everyone today has electronic direct deposit for their pay checks. The social security portion simply goes into a separate retirement account noted on the pay check for confirmation of compliance in government audits.

For those without automatic accounts, then the bank where you cash the paycheck will be required to deduct the red line amount on the check and put that amount directly into your retirement account. This goes for any business that cashes a paycheck and they all must have an auditing account for inspection to insure the direct deposit, with a mandated receipt. For those who are self employed, the same rules apply. They pay into their retirement account; report the amount along with the financial institution where the account is managed and the account number for audit, if necessary, to the Internal Revenue Service at tax time.

Here is the added benefit. This plan will pretty much eliminate the fraud, as you cannot collect from the system because the government has no oversight on who gets paid out of your account. The payee is you and only you, as long as you're alive.

When you die, your social security account should be allowed to be divided as you see fit in your last will and testament. If you do not have a will and/or your death was by any means other than natural causes, your money will be divided among your heirs equally.

The program would be mandatory for every working citizen to participate and carry all the same requirements as social security for the purpose of collecting at the appropriate time (age) and under the exception circumstances (your disability) in the current law.

Now, how in the world would we undergo such a change in order to get it right, fair and equitable? The best way to abolish any government program, particularly those that have been depended on for years, is simply to grandfather them out. This means we come up with a formula which allows the entitlements to dissolve over time. The idea is to have replaced the program with equitable measures that have far more positive effects than negative.

How do we accomplish this daunting task wherein there is so much dependence on social security? Well! How about we start at the beginning and work forward?

Number 1

Those who have not been born and those who have not had a job and those who have not earned enough money to count or tax, leave them out of the current system altogether. Instead, put them into the new program outlined above when they begin to make money. What will your retirement account number be? How about the same as your current social security number along with a personal pin number and name?

Although our social security numbers are pretty vulnerable now, we do currently depend on those. However, I would rather come up with new account numbers, perhaps the account number of your retirement account with your bank and pin number.

The pin number is not for withdrawal; it is for checking on the status, so you will be sure your employer, banker, etc, is doing what they are required to do. When it comes time for the monthly payout, the financial institution that has the account will distribute the funds. This will be reported to the Government, as they do now on other payout programs. As stated, the employer will continue to deduct the same amount of social security funds they would normally deduct.

The deduction portion of the payroll check would be electronically deposited into the employee's account now known as the "Security Retirement Account". This is an account of the employees' choice, not the Government's. These accounts would be subject to Internal Revenue audits and subject to all the same rules the current social security system regulates for the purposes of collection and dispersing of funds. The accounts would be secured by the FDIC up to the amount of the same FDIC protection for current savings accounts; or greater if the economists believe that to be necessary, as long as that FDIC program amount is reasonable. The interest rates should be set at no less than the standard prime but without a cap for earning power.

This system will in fact be the new security net our politicians pretend they care about and there would be no question at all that those funds will be available for and at the time of your retirement. I guarantee each person in this system will be far better off at retirement than at any other time in history. You will have made far more interest; and if you did not, you will at the very least have what you contributed, all of it.

Number 2

We need to address the middle working populous. I believe we need to set these individuals apart by earnings. Give them the choice to get into the new system and out of the old.

Arbitrarily for our purpose here, let us start at the national earning average, and the poverty line. Meaning if they are below the poverty line, the Government buys them out of the current system. The Government returns to them, in the way of a refund allocated over a number of years, the money they have already put into social security and it must be placed into a "Security Retirement Account." The refund will be sent directly to the account versus to the employee.

For those who are above the poverty line and above the national average, they have a choice to get out or stay in the social security system with all those currently retired. The choice being that they can take three quarters of what they paid into the current system over five years and convert those funds into the Security Retirement Account. Same process as before; if they take the buyout, it goes as a direct deposit into the retirement account not to the individual.

Second choice: they can leave the money in the current system for ten more years and then take the three quarters amount noted above in the same fashion over five years. They will receive only the amount of prime rate at the time they accept the buyout by the Government; that decision will be final. Everyone will be given the opportunity (choice) to buyout or stay in conditionally in the same year or at the time the new system takes effect. In this way the buyout will be at the same prime rate and the Government can project and adjust the national budget accordingly.

Number 3

Those who are rich or earning (net) above a million dollars per year - I do not believe you are rich in this country until you have netted at least a million dollars or more - will also have a choice in how they get out of the current, in my opinion very flawed, social security system.

They can leave their money with the Government without further deduction and accept it at retirement in the current system or they may will it to the Government for the good of the Country. This will be their choice not the Government's. I suspect there might not be that many who choose to give it away. Or they can will the funds to their family members who may or may not fit into the first category; wherein, those funds go automatically to the Security Retirement Account upon inheritance.

Future funds collected subsequent to the enactment of the new system will be deducted and forwarded to the Security Retirement Account. Obviously, all those who currently receive social security will continue to do so until they are no longer eligible. When they are deceased, everyone else will be subject to the new and improved rules for the establishment of a "Security Retirement Account" and once and for all we can get rid of this inept government Ponzi scheme. For those individuals who only watch television, that is the equivalent to Bernie Madoff, only in social security the entire American population is the victim. Oh, by the way; it was not Bernie Madoff who put it to us; it was our politicians.

THE MILLMORIAN MANAGEMENT STYLE

In the beginning of this chapter I referred to my style of management as "The Millmorian Management Style". I cannot take credit for this title and some believe it is derogatory with negative implications. Well, that is true based on its origin. Years ago I found it necessary to fire an employee. I do not believe any descent boss wants to fire anyone, particularly a person they have come to like.

In this case I did not like this person's past behavior which I learned from a background investigation, because he took questionable advantage of his position as a law enforcement officer that led to his termination with the force.

He did have pertinent experience for our needs and we discussed his past; he gave a good story. He did not do anything criminal; he did have some justification, although in my opinion it was unethical. I decided to give him a chance and we had a common background in law enforcement which made conversation easy.

After approximately a year of his turning in mediocre investigative reports, I began to see a significant drop in the work product. His work lacked a great deal of pertinent information and way out of bounds superfluous information. Generally, that means the author of an investigation is banking on prior experience rather than the facts in a case. I began to work with him closely, in order to assist in better work products.

This led nowhere. He simply reverted to the same antics as soon as I left him to his own doing. This, of course, was troubling to me. Those reports are often the end result of evidence leading to prosecution, whether in criminal or civil court, and could have resulted in justice being thrown out the window. His reports were riddled with inconsistencies and mistruths.

I had to recall every one of his reports and have them reinvestigated by another investigator or myself. Luckily, there had been no legal decisions of any kind in these cases because the wheels of justice turn very slowly in both criminal and civil matters. I was able to correct any wrong and save the cases before they went into the system for disposition.

Even the amount of time he reported to obtain the information was altered by many hours, as was the mileage driven in most cases presented. This was extremely important as he would be paid for time and mileage.

When I began to suspect there was wrong doing, I followed up on the case and followed the employee several times, before I took action. I learned that many of the so called interviews never took place, certainly not the follow up interviews I asked him to complete. Although many were declared as in person, he actually did them by phone or not at all. Before I did any of my own investigation and tailing of the employee, I made it a point to ask him several times if everything was okay and if he needed further assistance with his cases.

I entered into conversations of general subjects in an attempt to gain insights that he might not want to disclose for personal reasons. I was not trying to pry into his personal life; I was trying to find good reason for his decline so I would be able to take positive action vs. negative action.

I was not successful and his lack of cooperation; mistruths; out-and-out lying, coupled with injustice, led to my having to terminate him. Three months after he was terminated, he responded with a rebuttal letter. It stated in part, "I do not know how anyone could work under your Millmorian Style of Management." No doubt, he meant that negatively. I learned later that he chose to write the letter after consulting with attorneys who apparently advised there was no case to sue me for wrongful termination.

Let's take the time to analyze the particulars of my management style, which I strongly recommend to everyone who owns a private business, the CEO of a private or public business or entity and all the supervisors at every level in the private or public sectors.

First set the example! Understand the business or public policy and procedures, rules and regulations and the laws that govern your particular responsibilities. Be sure you follow all the above and always give more time and effort without asking for additional compensation.

Be available as a mentor in the business and not a conflict between management and line workers. If there is a difficult employee who stirs it up negatively in the workplace, try and have them become, at least in part, the solution to those issues that they yell loudest about. If there are no true problems and even if there are, be sure to hold everyone, supervisors and employees, accountable to their responsibilities. When you have held true to your responsibilities, then you will earn respect.

There are always documents of all types to be filled out timely and there must be a constant standard for carrying out the process in order to accomplish the task. One of the most egregious mistakes all employers do, public and private, is not follow the written policy and procedure manual in all cases.

When you do not follow the written procedure for one employee but you follow it for others, you have just superseded the written policy. You will lose, more often than not, a court case for these reasons. On the off chance you do win a wrongful termination case or discrimination case when you have violated your own policy, it will have cost you far more money, perhaps in the thousands, and often times hundreds of thousands, and more than it ever should have.

A quick example; one of your employees cannot produce an acceptable work product and there have been numerous attempts to mentor them, give them further instruction, and even extend their probation period. Subsequently, the employee becomes indifferent and even insubordinate to supervisors. It comes time to terminate and the firm gives notice and lets the employee go.

The now-fired employee comes back with suit in hand for unlawful termination and/or discrimination. The investigation provides the employee had very good evaluations, made a point to sign in and out of all instruction classes and was well liked by co-workers. In fact, it was the supervisors who had been known to skip out early from work and seldom stayed in the training classes to the end.

Further, the supervisors handed out good evaluations when they should have been poor on the productivity issues and other reasons for termination. This becomes a he-said-she-said situation except for the documentation noted above and you lose more times than you win. Why? Your written policy has become superseded in a way known as "Policy by Practice"; you did not do your job.

The supervisors did not do the proper documentation. In the interest of time or trying to be politically correct or simply being too lazy to be a proper supervisor vs. being a friend, like a bad parent, your supervisor or you have just superseded the written policy by practice.

Why is it that we do not hold all levels of the work place accountable to follow procedure? Why are we so compelled to be lax when we like someone and so hard when we do not? All employers and their supervisors need to reinforce the policy and procedure by simply following it.

There is legitimate concern over policy and procedures being too strict or too lax. In these cases and in all cases, look closely at those procedures and be open to participative management. You will often find when employees have questions or concerns, like all myths many times there is some truth. Listen to them and address the issues. If you do or do not find a problem, explain the findings and settle the matter as soon as possible. Be sure you have documentation to prove the issues were addressed. All policy and procedure must be flexible within reason, but they must also have boundaries for which they cannot cross and this must be very clear at all times.

I feel compelled to address the issue of nepotism, the employment or supervision of your relative. I do not see anything wrong with having your relative working for you, as long as they are treated **exactly** like everyone else. This means you do not have to make an example of them when they violate the rules just to prove you are fair and you do not let them off the hook either. Treat them exactly like you would everyone and follow the rules, policy and procedure. It can be problematic and a cancer in by itself when you allow your relative to fall in a category by themselves. If you make an example of them with harsher punishment, you will lose respect of not only the relative but all the other employees and possibly the family ties. If you allow them to get away with violations, you lose respect from everyone even the relative, which will raise its ugly head in time. But far more devastating, especially if you run a public entity, is the loss of morale and command, trust, respect, and dignity. Each of these will be carried into the public eye every time and will forever become a measure of your own leadership or lack thereof and a poison that will fester into the distrust of all your counterparts within your profession. It is extremely dangerous in the Law Enforcement community and is one reason that many agencies have difficulty in recruitment. I will expand with examples in the chapter on Law Enforcement.

So to close this chapter, I expect every employee - especially government employees who are spending the people's hard earned money - to come to work on time, early if possible, and stay at work for the minimum of hours they are paid to be there. Also, they need to accomplish, maybe not finish, something every day. Each employee should make a good faith effort to meet any and all deadlines. If they do not, then they should be able to articulate why not. Hopefully, employees who are doing their job will be aware of the deadline approaching and be able to articulate, if need be, a proper request to extend the necessary time.

Furthermore, do not expect excuses. I want reasons and legitimate ones so there is never a need for negative managerial reaction. I do not believe anyone should be given a raise in compensation for mere seniority, with the exception of steps in grade for performing adequately up to a limited point. Performance is a measure across the board in all issues for employment not just meeting a deadline of a work product. This means a work ethic, a positive attitude, and treating everyone else with respect and dignity in a professional manner. Furthermore, if you have an opportunity to mentor a coworker so they improve, do so versus ignoring them.

So, if this is "The Millmorian Management Style", I welcome the compliment.

CHAPTER FOUR
Law Enforcement and Firefighters

I want to start this chapter with a clarification of my position particularly to my fellow peace officers, firefighters, veterans and those who actively serve in our military. There is no one on this Earth who has more respect and appreciation for each and every one of our peace officers, firefighters and military personnel, than I; although there are no doubt many who share my position.

I will not start the next sentence with a "but" or a "however" because, as I learned from Dr. Laura Schlessinger, that negates my noted clarification, instead let me state there are issues I think must be addressed. I will begin with a memo to all in uniform.

MEMO:
With nearly forty years serving collectively in law enforcement and the military in one capacity or another, one common denominator amongst the bad guys stands out. It does not matter if they are a common thief, fraudster, burglar, bank robber, rapist, murderer, pedophile, or any other type of criminal, they all have a garbage mouth using foul and disgusting language regardless of who might be in earshot.
---------------THE CHIEF.

Then why is it that I can sit in the lobby or restaurant of the Embassy Suites hotel next to the Dallas Airport and watch the disgusted look on the faces of parents with their children as the peace officers sitting at the tables next to them vomit such terrible language? Why does any citizen, no matter gender or age or position in life, have to stand in a line or near their vehicle under any circumstances and listen to a peace officer or a firefighter or our military personnel spew out vulgarity? How many times have we heard a police officer talk about someone's attitude and/or behavior? As officers or professionals we expect everyone else to respect us, then how about we show some dignity and professionalism and respect them.

The above situation did take place, but it was not the Dallas Police Department to which I was referring. In that incident they were Federal Officers and not just one or two, there were ten to fifteen of them sitting at several tables. I have had this same experience hundreds of times all over the Country with all levels of police, fire, and yes, even military personnel. I have heard the same vulgar language from all rank and file personnel and in some of the most advertised family-friendly establishments.

Recently, I was at a birthday party for a six year old and his classmates. I was having conversation with a Lt. Colonel in the U.S. Army, who also happens to be a doctor. He did not hesitate to use the "F" word several times, even though his daughter was standing nearby. What really amazes me is that they don't care and they even get angry at one of their victims should someone request they stop it, just like the bad guy does.

Additionally, I was recently sitting in the office of a local police chief. We were discussing new programs that might better serve the community, when he saw a fellow chief from a neighboring city outside on Main Street. The chief - in full uniform - stood up and opened the Venetian blinds to insure his friend would hear and see him.

He then knocked loudly on the window and when his friend, the other chief who was walking with his wife, looked up the local chief flipped him off by placing his unmistaken hand gesture onto the window. Some say, what is the harm? I say it is harmful because there were several citizens walking on the sidewalk. In addition, there were two local kids who looked towards the knocking on the window and saw the Chief of Police give the hand gesture. They also observed the other Chief of Police return the gesture. How professional, wouldn't you agree?

I have no problem with gestures between friends and joking about with antics in private but not in the public eye. However, I say each and every one of you should be absolutely ashamed of yourself, if you participate in these types of public displays! What will they do if someone takes it upon themselves to stand up to a police officer and adamantly tell them they need better manners or, worse yet, a punch in the mouth? I can tell you; they will arrest them and charge them with assaulting a police officer. This kind of setting the example for our children is simply not acceptable. Is it no wonder our kids are so rude and without respect in today's society?

This is a good time to advise our elected officials and their appointees of the same concern. I can tell you if I was a congressman or visitor to the White House and the President's previous Chief of Staff (Rahm Emanuel, who now serves as the Mayor of Chicago) or anyone else directed the type of foul language that has been reported in the news towards me, which he apparently uses during his angry tyrants, then he would find himself with a fat lip and lying on the floor - behind closed doors of course. There is no doubt it would be worth my being arrested and the subsequent court trial. This guy is an international embarrassment and a hard-nosed punk who needs to learn some manners.

On the other hand, when they act accordingly with respect and manners, then there is no problem. At least not with their language, I cannot say the same for their politics. I have no difficulty with anyone who simply disagrees with me. For those of you who are saying, "Oh, tell me you have not used this language towards the bad guys." I will admit in some very few cases I did, but very few. I found ways to communicate in ways even the stupid could understand without dropping to their level. It is called COMMAND PRESENCE and in all my dealings I have treated everyone, even the worst of human rot, with dignity and respect because my actions are a reflection of my profession and our society.

I read Governor Sarah Palin's book *Going Rogue* and recommend it to anyone who wants a good look at the idiocies within a campaign. I have high regard and respect for the Governor and truly hope she keeps involved and focused on the White House. But let me say, even in her campaign and around her children, those who do not have enough respect to keep from such foul language need to be in their place. Get some manners, you jerks! I know the Governor does not need me to stick up for her and that is not what I am doing here. I am reiterating the need for all of us to return to respect and, especially, public manners!

Taking into account the issue of respect, there seems to be a significant lack of it - which maybe I adequately expressed above - or there is a misunderstanding of what respect is and what it means. The first two formal definitions from the dictionary state:

1. Respect: To take notice of, to regard with special attention; to regard as worthy of special consideration, hence, to care for, to heed.

2. To consider worthy of esteem; to regard with honor.

When I read these two definitions, I think of the protocols which use to garner and generate respect in all things public and private. You did not use foul language in public; certainly not around women and children; in church or any other place which gave access to the general public. You wore appropriate clothing so as not to offend the general sense of common decency. Out of formal respect you wore your best attire to display the depth of your human nature, the spirit of pride and soul unique to mankind and endowed by our Creator.

Why then, when the entire world witnessed the formalities of a funeral service for soldiers killed by an extremist lunatic on the United States Army Base Fort Hood, in Killeen, Texas, did I immediately take notice of the Commanding General of the U.S. Army and the rest of his soldiers wearing their work fatigues? Oh sure, there were a few in the green Class A uniforms, but no one was wearing the honored and formal respectful Dress Blue uniform. Now the first thing that my opposition will say, "Those soldiers were working, in fact they were coming from and returning to their assigned jobs on the base. Do we really want them to stop and have to take the time to change their uniforms?" My answer is a resounding: YES!!!

However, I do understand the delay this might take in meeting the dead line of certain assignments with many but not with every soldier. Certainly the commanders, all of them, should have been in their Dress Blue Uniform without exception. What in God's name has happened to formality, decorum and respect in the United States? We should demand that appropriate respect, decorum, and formality are put back into practice immediately in our military and police forces now and to heck with the liberal ideology.

While I am speaking about proper attire, especially in the work place, let me say I believe this business of dress down Fridays in the work place is bunk. Dress for business everyday and stop allowing people to show up in their lounging clothes. I have investigated many work sites where this idiotic policy gave rise to discrimination and sexual harassment cases that cost thousands of dollars to defend and, figuratively speaking, raped employee morale as a direct result.

Okay, I have captioned and highlighted a few things generally. Now I would like to speak on some specifics regarding police work, then I will move on to firefighters and the military. I have a lot to say and a few programs to outline, so hold on and enjoy the ride.

Before I go too far, I want to set the record straight. In no way do I advocate a "Police State" I am well aware that we cannot have a police officer on every corner and it is not just about law enforcement in my opinion like many have accused of me. Additionally, I do not believe in big government. However, the government in one capacity or another is where law enforcement officers derive. Therefore, there must be a minimal number of officers in relation to population in order to have effective policing.

Some say they are a necessary evil. I say they are an absolute requirement to ensure a free people and do the work of GOD. (Romans 13: 1-7). But make no mistake about it, without a strong visible reactive and proactive law enforcement policy every community subjects itself to higher crime rates, less productivity and a poor economy.

Each community without lawful and effective policing will experience less jobs, more pathetic affordable housing projects turned bad and full of the down trodden, more homeless, more beggars on the corners taking advantage of good hearted people, and above all higher and higher taxes to sustain ineffective services.

Here is a response to those who will call me shameful or worse regarding my comment about the "beggars". In a large city I was involved in a surveillance filming the bad guys, when I observed a young man in his twenties ride up on a motorcycle to a coffee and donut shop. There was a beggar standing in front of the door. He was dirty and disheveled and stated he was hungry, would the youngster give him money for food and a cup of hot coffee because he was cold. The young man said, "Wait a minute, I will be right out." When he came out he had a cup of coffee in hand and a bag of donuts, which also contained a chicken sandwich from the store. I was able to overhear this conversation clearly, as I was not more than ten feet away.

The beggar slapped the bag and coffee from the young man's hand and yelled at him, "I want money." The young man stood still with a frightened look on his face. I became furious. Although I said nothing, I believe my anger was obvious and I began to walk towards the beggar. He immediately ran around the corner, jumped into a new Toyota pick-up truck, and drove away. I did not get the plate, lucky for him. I witnessed more than one of these occasions in several different cities. This is why I have separated the homeless from the beggars; I do not believe most of them.

Let me come to the defense of our sheriffs, chiefs of police and directors of law enforcement agencies across our country. All of them must by law respond to the emergency (911) call before any other request for assistance. Secondly, they are reactive to all other immediate service requests and make every attempt to prioritize those calls in the most effective way possible. What do I mean by an immediate service request versus 911? An immediate service request is "someone broke into my vehicle/ house and stole/damaged my property". Citizens want an officer now and the crime scene may still be fresh, but it is not an emergency. You get the idea.

I am sure most officers will agree with the above. Now we get into the holy grail of policing which is on the wish list of every police administrator to whom I have ever spoken: proactive policing. Where is the budget? There is rarely a budget for this, the most productive policing of all. What is proactive policing anyway? There have been numerous books and opinions written on the subject, so may that they would fill many libraries across the nation. Several do their best to convince the general public of what must be done and yet there is still no or very little budget to accomplish this necessity.

Now more than ever, we need proactive policing (not just at the federal level). Administrators have a great deal of difficulty in small town America and in our large cities because, to put it plainly, we are no longer trying to deter the local bad guy. These are the criminals who traffic in narcotics and prostitution; the loan sharks and bullies; the burglars and would be bank robbers. Many of these continue to do business in plain view, because the entitlement programs are soaking up all the money in the city budgets.

We also need to deal with TERRORISTS WHO WANT TO KILL ANY AND ALL AMERICANS JUST BECAUSE WE ARE AMERICAN. REGARDLESS OF WHAT ANY ONE INDIVIDUAL'S IDEOLOGIES MIGHT OR MIGHT NOT BE.

We cannot and should not wait around in our smaller communities and big cities hoping the Department of Homeland Security or the FBI has it all under control. They do not. They do not have the budget, or the time for that matter, to wait around and receive the 911 call that a terrorist blew up the downtown building. Through community proactive policing we (police officers) can spot many criminals and terrorists in plain view, casing the town if you will, while they go about what looks to be a normal day. To others they may look harmless, but not to a trained peace officer.

We train our officers in community policing methods and then we send them racing from one call to the other without any time to take notes on what they are passing. Meaningful Community Policing is out the window as we currently operate. Further, do not let anyone fool you by taking a stand on "we are very progressive". That is nothing less than bunk as none of them mean progressive per se. They mean liberal thinking and programs that do little to nothing, except spend a great deal of money to appease you.

Here is a notice to everyone - especially to the county supervisors, commissioners, mayors, city managers, councilmen or aldermen, however your local leader is addressed - the time to allow and to insist your law enforcement CEO has an adequate budget for proactive policing is now! You must give up some of those self serving public relation programs that garner nothing more than a vote and begin looking to saving lives and property in your community. You will be a better leader for it and I would guess reelected overwhelmingly. Just ask or look at the record of Sheriff Joe Arpaio in Arizona. Why do I say this? Proactive policing will and has worked where allowed to be implemented and set into regular active policy.

However, if I cannot convince you and you can't get by the extremely foolish attitude and mindset of "THAT WILL NEVER OR COULD NOT HAPPEN HERE", I urge you to read the book titled *Terror at Beslan* by John Giduck. Read it now. If you do not like to read, you should do two things; first, read the first forty three pages of that book; secondly, resign immediately, if you are an elected or appointed public official.

Foreign and local terrorists are a prominent concern for all communities. Unfortunately, many local leaders still have that blind and idiotic attitude I described above. This does not alter the fact that we still have our home grown typical bad guys who need to be dealt with through reactive and proactive policing. We do and always will.

Every chief law enforcement officer must deal with being accused of "profiling" and more often than not "racial profiling". In my design of community policing, I requested my Senior Sergeant, Richard Smith (one of the best peace officers with whom I have ever worked), to have the deputies stop and talk in kind conversation for no reason at all with everyone on the street as time allowed.

Please take note, I did not say stop everyone or make a traffic stop on people to talk to them. I said the deputies should stop and have common and friendly conversation with every elderly lady or man, every young kid and every suspected gang member. Further, they should go into every business possible and do the same with employees, managers and owners but not in a disruptive fashion. I do not believe this is profiling. I believe this is good police work when it can be done.

We did it every day and every chance we were able. We gathered significant intelligence on the bad guys without doing anything but having normal incidental conversations. We assisted numerous citizens and created a partnership with the community and youngsters. In addition, we improved the law enforcement image, even if just a little bit, for the entire profession.

However, I also had a citizen accuse me to my face and in my own office of racial profiling, simply because I asked him if I could be of help. I won't forget the look on my office assistant's face - who has many times requested that I do not identify her by name, but I must say she is and always will be a trusted friend who did a spectacular job.

I was standing in the reception room of the District office talking to my office assistant when I noticed this gentleman enter the building lobby. He was looking about as though he was lost or looking for someone as opposed to looking for an office; he was not reading the directory, which was in front of him and it could not be missed. He looked in my direction, as we had glass doors and were in plain sight.

It did appear that he might be in need of some help; so I stepped outside the office and asked him, "Are you looking for someone or an office and can I help you?" He said he was looking for a particular office and fumbled around in his pockets and came up with a business card. The address on the card was not in the building and it was not on the same street. The address was maybe a few miles away and I directed him to the approximate area. He said thank you and off he went. No problem and I went back into the office. I saw him drive out of the parking lot in a silver sedan.

Approximately three minutes later, I saw him from my office window as I sat behind my desk, drive back in. He stopped his car and I noticed when he got out he slammed the driver's door. He had an angry look on his face. He came in the lobby with a truly cocky gate and before I could get up he entered the office. I heard him demand of my assistant as she sat behind her desk, "Where is that guy with the tie on?" I stepped around the corner and went up to him blocking his ability to harm my assistant. In a boisterous voice he said, "Do you have a problem with me because I am black? Do you think because I am black I was doing something wrong?"

I knew from years of experience two things: this guy was not under the influence of alcohol or drugs and he was looking for a reason to either fight, sue or both. I calmly advised him that I had no problem with him at all. I told him I had tried to help him. He raised his voice, I think because he believed I was intimidated. This was far from the truth and I snapped back. I told him with significant command presence that it was he who had a problem with being black and he should be ashamed of himself. When the look on his face went flush, I thought the incident might become truly problematic. It was time to introduce him to whom he was speaking, in an effort to calm him down. I showed him my badge and identification.

He immediately backed off with an apology. I reiterated my statement, "You should be ashamed of your actions and it is time for you to leave, so as not to get in so deep you cannot get out". He left, I took a deep breath of relief, but I was sure this young man would file a grievance or law suit with the county or my Board of Directors. He did not and I never saw him again. My assistant said, "Wow was that guy crazy; he scared me!" She was visibly shaking. You never know from where or in what situation these accusations might come, but you must never back down because of political correctness. Stand your ground and do your job.

Sharing information and working together:

It has been extremely obvious, from the time of our founding fathers, that one police agency to the next believe they are the best. This is true in every industry both public and private, no matter what anyone tells you. In law enforcement this often times arrogant attitude of superiority can give rise to very dangerous outcomes. It also exists, in part, between our military.

With the military the soldier is embroiled with what it takes to win a war and unity, above all else, will always come out on top. This is because the war in by itself is the mission. Like President Ronald Reagan stated, "We win they lose."

Although there is significant camaraderie in law enforcement, the mission, or more appropriately the way they go about the mission, changes from one jurisdiction to another. I don't just mean physical boundaries; I also mean the scope of responsibility in policy for a particular agency. This is why you find one agency making statements regarding another like "they don't have a clue" and, as such, they are reluctant to exchange information.

If this message is widely used by the commanders of any agency, then this will be the prevailing thoughts of their subordinates and the effort to work together and exchange information will be damaged, slowed or even thwarted altogether. This is very dangerous in today's world and it must stop. There must be leadership among all the department heads to emphasize it does not matter what your badge or uniform or credentials read, it only matters that our mission is one in the same, public safety.

When I speak of this to other department heads the standard answer is, we all get along well on the street even though "they don't have a clue". In one of my many conversations with a prominent chief of police surrounded by his command staff, I was requesting for a combined effort of departments and was asked by the chief, "Why not just use this department?" I advised the larger agency was simply too expensive and the time allotted for the program to truly have a positive effect on the community would be cut in half, thereby, lacking in efficiency. The chief replied, "But you would have quality officers."

I admit I was taken aback, given this chief's experience. I tried to reconcile the statement in my own mind with the chief trying to make points with his own staff and or simply trying to promote his agency into a more prosperous position. But I also believed, then and now, that the message was reverberating in the ears of his command staff and would filter out into the community through his own officers in the field.

I was compelled to point out that every officer in the State received the same training in the academy; thereafter, the State requires continued education for which they were very strict and held each department accountable. Although I conceded that some departments, his included, went above what the State requires.

While this was commendable, the fact remains the other agency were peace officers like any other and they were not going away. Furthermore, if they were inferior then why not work with them in a way they may learn to be better officers, by way of example at the very least. I went on to say; after all we all work the same streets. Are we going to ignore them as a resource in an emergency or tell them to go away when we or more importantly when the community need their service? I made my point and from then on this chief worked with me in a friendly, professional and cooperative form, as though I was one of his own.

This is the time to return to the nepotism I referred to earlier. Here is the expansion of how it hurts a law enforcement agency. In one large agency where I worked, the department head hired his son. This deputy (the son) was assigned to an important position but certainly not a crucial assignment per se. It was his regular position and he was a deputy without any rank above having a few years on the job. Because the son knew his father would protect him, he carried arrogance with an attitude and behavior reflecting the beliefs "I will do and say what I want to anyone at anytime like it or not"; and he did. I can assure you; I was not influenced at all and stated as much.

One day I walked into a public forum and there were numerous citizens and uniformed officers from many agencies all within hearing distance of a loud, filthy, outrageous conversation between the department head son, two Sergeants, and a Captain of the department. The son was stating, "I told that f-ing Lieutenant and the Chief Deputy, they better do exactly as I said with their units. If they don't, they will have to answer to me." Not one of his superiors called him on it. The other personnel from outside agencies laughed and stated, "Well, that's who they are."

The general public stood with mouths dropped and obvious shame at what was being stated. I said, "In my opinion, you should be fired now!" I was later told this was a common place occurrence and nothing was going to be done; now, I was ashamed and amazed. So much for proper accountability and leadership, and no wonder the other agencies found it difficult to work with "them".

I am well aware of the liability factors involved when an officer rides in another agency's patrol vehicle. At least this is the excuse many departments and elected officials use as their crutch, to keep the uniformed patrol force from intermingling. Yet, they have no problem accepting funding for undercover operations or working in a task force for such things as narcotics and organized crime penetration. Please do not get me wrong; I am a strong supporter of the task forces and undercover officers.

The problem I have is we forget the necessity of our patrol officers patrolling together, not just in adjacent communities. What I think is a good idea is rotation spots in uniformed patrol at least one or two, several if the agency is large enough within every agency and/or divisions of each agency. So departments can integrate themselves with each other on a standard basis, not just when they need help or in cost hindering and proportionate partial training exercises that are far and few between. It seems to me this would be cost effective and the officers would know exactly what to expect from their counterpart when that emergency does happen; and it will.

I know we have established the training Critical Incident Response programs - in fact, they are mandatory - but we need to do more than develop a program in the classroom and periodically practice the plan in the field.

These steps are imperative and should continue, but they are expensive. If we cross-patrol together, there will be no more expense; the officers from different agencies will get to know each other like a partner, not just the camaraderie of another cop. The sharing of information will take place in a patrol car between officers with great detail and spread faster then waiting for it to arrive in a briefing room, so why not do both.

I am told, "We need to use the task force in order to gather intelligence information, so we know which bad guy to focus our attention." I agree that is great for getting to the top of who is the supplier. This should always continue, but again have we just set aside the uniformed officer to run from one call to the next? Is it just too expensive to go out and do up close and personal police work? For those who think it is all about leaving this segment of good police work up to the detective or the investigator or special agent, if those titles make you feel better, you are very wrong. These positions are necessary and have expertise. However, I think this is used in the general public's mind and budget departments' minds as an excuse to hide from or not pay for proactive policing.

In the past when I was on patrol, you could stand at the water cooler, so to speak, in any police station and collect intelligence information from every officer there. Each had the names of several bad guys, the places, what they were up to, or crime they were suspected of committing. Amazingly, in numerous agencies today this does not occur. What happened to the officer's note pad? Where are the first line supervisors who are supposed to carry that information up the chain of command and into the heart of the task force, so they can focus on what we do know or already suspect?

By the way if you poison the bad guys' water hole (market place) with uniformed cops just stopping to have friendly conversation as often as possible, you will force the horse rider (Mule, get it?) to go elsewhere, which will monetarily cripple the bad guy loading up the saddle bags.

I know the Federal agencies, like the Federal Bureau of Investigation (FBI) and the Drug Enforcement Administration (DEA), get all bent out of shape when local agencies disrupt their undercover operations and justifiably. But excuse me! Are we not talking about sharing information? Of course, I am aware of occasionally keeping the loop as tight as possible. This sometimes means keeping information within their own agency, especially for the federal agencies in a variety of cases. Mostly though, these are the exceptions and that is perfectly understandable.

However, someone in the agency should be assigned to be liaison in every operation to determine when notification must be made to the local police or vise versa. This person must have the freedom and authority to make the notification at their discretion and without punitive damages. The Feds say they do this and they do more now then in the past; but, they need to do it better. I think my points here are elaborated in the recent "Fast & Furious" gun scandal.

During the recent Congressional hearings on this scandalous "Fast & Furious", our top two law enforcement directors - the Attorney General of the United States, Eric Holder and Secretary of Home Land Security, Janet Napolitano - either lied or exposed their arrogance, egos, or just plain old incompetence! What did they say? Eric Holder stated, he did not even know about the program or wasn't briefed on the program until "maybe two weeks prior to being asked".

Janet Napolitano said she had not even had a conversation with Eric Holder about the matter at all! Can anybody tell me why the top two department heads of our federal law enforcement agencies did not find it important enough to have a conversation over this matter? A matter with TWO DEAD FEDERAL AGENTS AND HUNDREDS OF CIVILIANS IN MEXICO NOW DEAD, BECAUSE OF THE IDIOTIC PROGRAM FAST & FURIOUS!

What is (hopefully, was) this program? In short, the Feds arranged to sell thousands of weapons, many of them automatic rifles such as the famous AK-47 and the rest semi automatic weapons like hand guns your standard police officer carries, to the bad guys - the really bad guys, you know those notorious drug cartels. The ones known to murder everyone and anyone who get in their way: cops in any country, federal or local; military soldiers; even civilians in any country without any regard for human life.

The idea was to track the guns that (maybe) had locators built in them. The whole thing stinks and I, frankly, don't believe either of these two department heads. I mean, you do watch the news right? How many massive grave sites have been found in Mexico with numerous bodies of men, women and children? How many were shot to death by our federal program of "Fast & Furious", just how many? How do Napolitano and Holder sleep at night?

There is one other egotistical attitude getting in our way. When the Feds get involved, they take all the credit no matter who is leading the charge. As common citizens we say, "What should it matter who gets credit as long as the job gets done?" I agree as long as we are speaking about an individual per se, but we are not here. We are speaking about an entire agency. Every agency should be recognized for their efforts, it is only human nature to want this acknowledgement and it fosters better morale among everyone.

There are still department heads that will not share information or work cooperatively with each other because this attitude stands in their way. They cannot stand to give any other agency credit where credit is due; they want it all and will cover up anything that bends the credit or shares it with other agencies. You say, "Then fire them or demote that person and replace the position immediately." If you can expose the right person, I agree. Identifying the right person, however, is tough and the wrong individuals may get hammered.

One way to alleviate the problem is with a liaison officer who has the authority in every individual program or case. The liaison officer should not have to contact a supervisor and then wait for that supervisor to go up the chain of command repeatedly to get answers days or weeks later; by then it is often too late.

I will come back later to different agencies working together from a completely new angle because the idea includes a system never applied previously. I think the system will work and I strongly believe the Country needs a system of this nature, now more than ever. However, before I do this I want to provide some basic steps I think will assist local governments in recruiting and retaining officers from the top down, especially small police agencies in the poor community.

Recruitment is highly competitive between all agencies; however, the small one man departments to sixty personnel are especially affected, due to the lack of tax base and other funding resources, wherein they must compete with much larger agencies. The majority of these recommendations are not new by any means. We can historically find the following measures in just about every new community developed in the building of our great Nation since the time of its inception. This concept has either been forgotten or we grew so far away it became politically questioned as a conflict of interest.

I don't think there is any conflict of interest when the interest of the community is obviously first and foremost. Every agency, both small and large, should include as a matter of a compensation package to their Chief Law Enforcement Officer, ROOM AND BOARD. The appointing authority would provide housing for the chief and their family.

The housing payment and utility bills would be paid by automatic payment by the appointing authority every month. Certainly, some sort of configuration as to the amounts and depth of the ROOM AND BOARD policy can be worked out by the appointing authority. I do not like an allowance for this purpose, which is currently done for transportation today, but it is one way to accomplish the task. The allowance becomes more cumbersome at tax time.

There are a couple of ways to accomplish this. First, rent the appropriate home in a nice area of the community to accommodate the chief's family. Use the same home as the last chief, if possible, and only sign a leasing agreement with the landlords that match the chief's contract. Be sure to stay away from conflicts here; the city manager should not be the landlord.

Second, if necessary establish an account for proper accommodations in a nice local hotel, which may be attractive given the cleaning perks. There are many hotel suites with plenty of room and very nice accommodations, such as the Embassy Suites. Security measures can be established between the chief and the hotel staff.

Additionally, in many of the hotel suites breakfast is included, so the appointing authority would be able to drop the lunch idea. If the appointing authority does not want to accommodate ROOM AND BOARD in compensation, then this should at least be considered in the short term say three to six months.

However, only the chief would have his lunch reimbursed daily not the entire family. I would be in favor of the cap idea on lunch because the chief may want to eat and probably should eat in different restaurants around the community. The solution is simple, a credit card from the appointing authority for food only with a yearly cap, a certain amount per month multiplied by twelve. When the cap is reached, the chief pays out of pocket.

Of course, if the chief eats at home, he pays the grocery store out of pocket. This food cap can also be used in the per diem portion of necessary travel, which offsets the additional travel cost.

For line officers there are communities that provide room (housing) for the officers and their family, generally in public housing projects. This is believed to be a good idea for those areas in rundown neighborhoods, because cops in the project may help curb the violence. This does not, however, sit very well with the officers and certainly not with their family; they seldom take advantage of this concept. The idea is good; if the housing is in a good or not so bad area. But I question the motives of the authority and would rather see a better effort to address morale and safety of the officers.

Addressing all positions in recruitment, if the appointing authority would assist the spouse of new officers in the form of headhunting through the networking of the appointing authority, this would go a long way in capturing new recruits at all levels. I do not mean the authority should hire the spouse. I mean; if the spouse is a nurse or a legal secretary or whatever their career happens to be, help them find work.

This does not mean to only provide them a list of who is hiring or links to job sites. Although that is a good idea, there should be more. Help them network; try to assist in promoting them and set up interviews for them. This should not be all that difficult as all appointing authorities have a network system and there are a multitude of work places that would sign up in droves to assist; all you have to do is ask.

If nothing else when you are the authority and you do not have a friendly network, then you should establish one for community relations or quit; get out of the business, you do not belong in public service. Also, the place of employment for the spouse must release, unconditionally, any and all liability on the part of the officers' hiring authority.

Obviously compensation is extremely important to hiring good people. Younger people do not necessarily look at the benefits as much as they should, but they do pay close attention to the actual money in take home pay. Advertise your benefit packages with as much strength as you can. Entice the recruit and take advantage of the current and long term projected economy to enhance the benefits even more than the take home.

Provide a step pay scale with merit pay on top of seniority steps, if possible. Merit pay is a morale builder; giving raises just because you hang around doing only what you must to keep your job is a morale killer. It is brought up every time there is a promotion and handed out to those with seniority only and no track record of being on the team for the team. Think about these issues, especially compensation in the merit category and remember that it does not have to be much. It is a simple recognition of excellent work product and productivity.

For law enforcement officers there is far too little attention provided to physical fitness. Well that is just not true, say my colleagues! We have strict hiring standards and physical agility testing. Is that RIGHT, I ask? You may have strict hiring standards, but you drop those standards after your recruit is on the job. Anyone who does not believe me can take note of all the fat cops, those who can hardly get in or out of their patrol vehicle. By the way this is also true of our military, but not quite as extreme.

They might have standards, but they are not complied with or there is no accountability to keep them in shape. Mostly because we have all bought into what I have coined as the "Huggie-Bear-Smackie-Poo" syndrome. Everyone has a real excuse vs. reason for their being out of shape, when what they really have is a significant case of being too lazy and no leadership.

I am aware that the officers are often not willing to take care of themselves and may even threaten to bring suit against their agency, if they are made to exercise without extra pay. To the officers, you should be ashamed of yourself, because this tells me it's all about you and not the community you serve. My friend, this is the wrong reason to serve in any public place of honor and privilege. If police work is nothing more than just a job, get out, please!

You see, fat cops, you not only put yourself in harm's way, you also put the citizens you are sworn to protect and serve in harm's way. Don't mention the liability you place on the shoulders of your hiring authority should something happen due to your poor health. If you are a chief of police or a sheriff, then get out from behind your desk and get down to the gym. Set the example!

I will give you two stories that are true and pitiful from my point of view. First, my wife and I were in a large shopping mall in the Hill Country of Texas. We stopped to have lunch. When we exited our vehicle and crossed the parking lot, I could not believe my eyes. In a full size pickup truck was a deputy sheriff in full uniform sitting behind the wheel, waiting politely for us to cross.

I should say, he was sitting AROUND the steering wheel, the dash board and the passenger side of the truck. He had to be five hundred pounds, if he was an ounce. I am not exaggerating here, believe me! In fact, I might be underestimating his weight. I truly could not help myself from staring!

This man, I am still sure, must have been shoved into that truck every Monday morning and popped out on Fridays, because there is no way he could get in/out by himself. He must, I thought, drive up to the take out window of fast food restaurants every hour or so and shove the food down his gullet.

My friends, I am not kidding this man was so large his driver's seat was all the way back and his abdomen was overflowing across the top of the steering wheel, which was in its highest position. He asked me, "Can I help you?" It took me a moment and I said, "Are you a mall security guard?" I was hoping desperately that he would say yes! He said, "No, I work for the Sheriff's Office. Do you need a security guard?"

As I looked to read his shoulder patch and then his badge he said, "You don't believe me?" And I said, "Yes, I believe you. I just don't want to believe you." He looked at me like I was crazy and I was sure if he could have pried himself out of the truck, he may have done so to find out more about me and my strange statements. But, frankly, I don't think he could. I went into the restaurant shaking my head in amazement. He drove away.

Let me relate a second story about a friend of mine, who will remain anonymous. He was a Chief of Police and a great person. He is an intelligent man who understands the complexity of law enforcement as well as anyone in the business. The problem is he is one of those really obese cops that have significant trouble getting into the patrol vehicle.

He said to me as we got in the police vehicle, "It's a good thing the department has an SUV, because I can't get in and out of those patrol cars." We would go to a restaurant and he would order a lot of food, all of it loaded with fat. He hardly fit into the booth and had to ask for the condiments to be passed, not out of politeness (although he was polite) but because he was too fat to reach them.

He related the following story to me in response of my asking why he left his chief's position in another city. He said, "When I was the Chief, the City Manager came to me and told me he wanted me to establish a physical fitness test and follow up program for all the officers. I told him I would; but I, as the Chief, would not participate in the test. I am too fat for that kind of physical agility."

He lost respect from his men and from his City Manager. Inevitably, morale in the department went down. Furthermore, he gave rise to dissention among the officers towards the test and getting fit. As the department head you need to earn respect not demand it. The best way to earn it is to first be one of your own and second abide by your own policy and that of the appointing authority. This does not mean follow blindly. Instead, lead by example! Believe me, there are many who have died when they did not have to because of the officer's poor health: the officer, the citizen and the bad guy.

How do we get around this dilemma? I say the first thing a hiring authority should do is create a "Memorandum of Understanding" ("MOU") with the officers' association. The "MOU" should include that all sworn officers, regardless of their rank, will participate in a physical agility test every six months or, if necessary, once a year to accommodate negotiations.

Note I did not say union, as I do not believe first responders should have unions, only associations. I also do not believe any first responder should ever go on a complete strike, but a blue strike may be in order if the employer stops playing equitably. This means answer all emergency calls and stop the bleeding. But never call in sick just to make a point! I hope school teachers are reading this as well. Take your time getting to the secondary calls.

These can be answered by the command staff or perhaps the Mayor, they will certainly have to answer to the community when officers don't arrive on a secondary call for a very-very long time. Further, I did not say the "Blue Flu" when officers do not show up for work. Come to work as you should, never leave the community to the fate of an emergency. By the way, I did not say cry to the public; just tell them the city has not approved a strong budget for services and leave it at that.

The departments need to affix a sliding scale to accommodate age but not to accommodate girth. The authority needs to provide a complete physical for each officer once a year. If there are under lying problems medically confirmed, the authority needs to have a training program and/or physical therapy program designed appropriately. It might go a long way to have officers on each shift who are trained in physical fitness and proper nutrition programs.

It would be a small token to morale and a small sum of compensation to have a Certified Physical Fitness Trainer (Officer) trained through a course from the International Sports Sciences Association. This would go a long way towards effective budgeting and the training is minimal. Look into the weight lifting magazines for where to go and get officers to volunteer for the training. Just because the weight lifting magazine is a ready reference does not mean you are turning all your officers into bodybuilders. Read the advertisements and know there are several choices.

If the officer does not pass the agility test, they are given a second chance to get in shape for the next test. If they do not pass the second chance, then they must go into the training program and get fit. If they cannot or do not make it the third time out and there is no medical reason for the failure, they need to be put on one year probation to get fit.

If they cannot pass after a year and a half, then terminate on the grounds of being unfit for duty. Only change their assignment when absolutely necessary, not to save their job but to have time to get in shape.

Okay, if the officers will not cooperate unless they are compensated for the time to exercise, then arrange a shift plan such as a "four-ten" (where the shifts are four days of ten hours each) or a "three-twelve" (where the shifts are three days of twelve hours each). There are several formulas to negotiate. But it is imperative that three hours a week are assigned to the gym for exercise and to work with the training program.

The officer only needs ten to fifteen minutes usually for strength and fifteen to twenty minutes for aerobic exercise and the rest can be for personal goals and hygiene. If you can't do anything else, use an extra day or two off as floating holidays during the six month period to make up eight hours of exercise. Do not allow overtime for exercise, unless there is no other way. When I worked in agencies that implemented these plans, morale was always higher than the department down the street and the injuries to officers were always fewer and less severe. Our pay was not always the best but our physical fitness program was a great recruitment tool.

Above I mentioned the gym. I believe every law enforcement and fire department should have a gym. I also think that safety is of the utmost concern and there are two ways to fulfill this requirement. First, the department should invest in as many Bow Flex machines as possible. (I don't mean this in the way of recommending the company Nautilus or their line "Bow Flex", although I do like "Bow Flex" and own one.)

An individual can work on these machines by themselves with little risk of injury. Keep in mind that if the motor vehicle industry can give public safety a break in the price of purchasing our vehicles, we hopefully should be able to negotiate with Bow Flex.

If the department cannot afford to buy equipment go ask the private gyms in the area to make a deal for the officers or have them donate their older equipment when they purchase new. It is best to have a private gym for the police and fire personnel. Find a way to get the officers in the best physical shape possible. We owe it to them, the budgets and the community they serve.

There are numerous departments who mandate officers purchase their own weapons and other necessary equipment. They buy their own uniforms from top to bottom. This is unfair, even if the appointing authority is poor.

I understand the cost up front is tough, but maybe we should think about reimbursement to the officers over a year or two on the job for that expense. If the officer chooses to be reimbursed, then the equipment becomes the property of the department; if not they keep it, but the offer of reimbursement should be available.

This brings us to the entry pay. I understand there are small cities who want to have their own police officers. However, to offer a person as little as $20,000 per year or less is ridiculous for putting themselves in harm's way every day. If in fact this is the case in any department, then a life insurance policy for at least $50,000 or more should be offered.

The premium should be paid by the hiring authority, in addition to all burial expenses. I have said for years, without much argument from anyone, that police and fire personnel are extremely under paid; and if a city cannot pay a minimum of $35,000 per year, then they should use the Sheriff's Office.

If the Sheriff cannot afford this amount, then raise the taxes to do so; just make sure the citizens are onboard. When tax dollars in other areas are not working, you can bet there are these cases, then drop that program and use the dollars for first responders.

The police and fire departments will get you better results in the way of serving the community. You might be surprised and find you have actually cut the budget, which will make you more effective. There are always programs currently in place that do not provide positive dividends to the community and are only in place as pet projects, wasting tax dollars. Find them, get rid of them, and use the funds more wisely.

While I have addressed the Sheriff, let me point out a significant disconnect from that honored and elected office to the people and the voters. I have been told numerous times.

"The Sheriff doesn't really want to write traffic citations or ordinance violation citations and in many cases does not want to have their deputies make any arrest during policing initiatives!" In many areas of the Country, the Sheriff's Office writes very few traffic citations in comparison to other agencies, wherein the head of the department is not elected.

I get it. The Sheriff has specific duties different than other agencies, but the duty to be diligent in the full scope of their office includes making arrests and writing traffic citations, when the deputies observe the law being broken. It is a complete dereliction of duty, when they look the other way. The only reason the Sheriffs (with exception) enter the community policing initiatives is to soak up as much public relations as possible. They don't want the finger pointed at them for having arrested or issued too many traffic citations. They have stated it plainly, "I can't get their vote, if they are mad at me."

If I were Sheriff, I would think good people who vote count more than those who want favoritism. I would want those citizens to view me as impartial and serving justice equally. Tell the Sheriffs to do their job and hold them accountable at the voting booth.

Perhaps this is the real reason small city leaders don't want to contract with the Sheriff's Office. The Sheriff directs the deputies to patrol with a caveat of don't make an arrest or issue a citation unless you have no choice. Given this to be true, the people are not served. Are they?

Let me clue you in on the same shifty politics in many small city, towns, and village police departments. I was offered a position as chief of police for a small city and I discussed the very low salary and the two-position opening with the acting city manager. This particular acting city manager made it very clear he was not interested in this position, as he was a full time city manager in a neighboring community with much higher compensation.

I said, "Well, I am certainly qualified for both positions, so why don't I take on both positions until a full time city manager can be put into place." It had been made clear by the mayor that the city was limited on funds and they were purposely stalling to fill the position of city manager. However, the temporary fellow was being paid a significant sum to do the job. I would be willing to do both jobs at the minimum step of the chief's salary and half of what the temporary fellow was taking.

You may not agree with the premise of one person having both of these positions and consider it to be a conflict, but it is done in many places. Furthermore, in this case both of these positions answer to the city Mayor and council. You just bypass one step, that of the chief answering to the city manager. Nevertheless, that is not my point in this scenario. The point is this. I was told by the temporary city manager, "If you want more money, then you just need to go up on the state highway and write as many traffic citations as possible. By doing that you can raise your income significantly; however, do not write citations to citizens of this city." That is in my mind unethical, criminal and a long way from justice. What a rotten shame! I turned the job down, regardless to what the final offer would have been, and left.

Going back to recruitment, send out a representative from your agency to every job fair you can; in addition, have the department head or representatives speak at functions such as career day. Do not wait for the function. Create the function and take all the agencies in your area with you. Get with all the agencies in your area to set up recruitment offices, if at all possible, like the military does. Each department can tell everyone their agency is the best and it is fun, not to mention each agency will share the cost. The recruitment office can be mobile and or space sharing from one department to the next.

Don't compete so much with one another; instead, help each other and you will find a deeper and wider pool of applicants. Pool the department resources as often as possible in all things. The public deserves nothing less. One test plus several departments equals money saved!

.

IMMIGRATION

This issue has become so poisoned by politics that the entire policy, from either side of the aisle, must be trashed with a complete and new back-to-the-Constitution approach

Let us first understand and agree that this is an issue addressed and put to rest by the U.S. Constitution. The Constitution does so by allowing immigration to be left directly to the States and not the Federal Government. It is an interpretation, not a fact and not the law, through which the Federal Government maintains this power.

It is a fact and Constitutional that the States retained this power noted without exception, in Article 1 Section 8. "To establish a uniform Rule of Naturalization" - These are the seven words that pertain to immigration or naturalization and have been construed in case law to mean and extend into federal law. But it is not factual and one can research these issues with only one conclusion; one which Thomas Jefferson stated directly:

"[A]lien friends are under the jurisdiction and protection of the laws of the state wherein they are; that no power over them has been delegated to the United States, nor prohibited to the individual states, distinct from their power over citizens; and it being true, as a general principle, and one of the amendments to the Constitution having also declared, that "the powers not delegated to the United States by the Constitution, nor prohibited to the states, are reserved, to the states, respectively, or to the people," the act of the Congress of the United States, passed the 22d day of June, 1798, entitled "An Act concerning Aliens," which assumes power over alien friends not delegated by the Constitution, is not law, but is altogether void and of no force."

If you don't like what Thomas Jefferson said, then look to James Madison who stated:

"The powers delegated by the proposed Constitution to the Federal Government are few and defined. Those which are to remain in the state governments are numerous and indefinite. The former will be exercised principally on external objects, as war, peace, negotiation, and foreign commerce with which lasts the power of taxation will, for the most part, be connected. The powers reserved to the several states will extend to all the objects which, in the ordinary course of affairs, concern the lives, liberties, and properties of the people, and the internal order, improvement, and prosperity of the State"

If that is not enough, then listen if you will to Chief Justice of the United States, John Marshall, who wrote the following when delivering the unanimous opinion of his brethren of the court in McCulloch v. Maryland (decided in 1819):

"No political dreamer was ever wild enough to think of breaking down the lines which separate the States, and of compounding the American people into one common mass. Of consequence, when they act, they act in their States. ... In America, the powers of sovereignty are divided between the government of the Union, and those of the States. They are each sovereign, with respect to the objects committed to it, and neither sovereign with respect to the objects committed to the other."

Ok, if you want to bring it up a notch, then let us quote Amendment 9 and 10 of the Constitution:

Amendment 9 (Ratified 12/15/1791) – *"The enumeration in the Constitution, of certain rights, shall not be construed to deny or disparage others retained by the people."*

Amendment 10 (Ratified 12/15/1791)--- *"The powers not delegated to the United States by the Constitution, nor prohibited by it to the States, are reserved to the States respectively, or the people."*

That is what this is all about, my friends; the rights given to the Federal Government and/or retained by the States and the people. We are the people and without question we, as the United States' and individual State's citizens, have retained the right to protect our borders. Given that the above has been poisoned by the politicians, let us come up with solutions that may well work within their distorted brains, so they can maintain some power. Let us tap the foreign aid funds we provide to Mexico. Why should we use the foreign aid funding route? They will never pay a bill per se and it is a reduction in the total budget. Here is how it might be spelled out in formulating a base policy.

1. We demand our law enforcement agents would be allowed to be armed appropriately when in Mexico, for self-defense. If this issue cannot be agreed to by both sides, then no funds in any form under any circumstances.
2. For every illegal immigrant we arrest, detain, and process we subtract the cost of those processes from the aid package.

3. We send a United States' appointed budget specialist/accountant with any aid package to administer and oversee the proper allocation of funds as designated by the Mexican officials. What do I mean by "designated by the Mexican officials"? They request the aid and establish the parameters of what and why they want to spend the aid and we ensure that is exactly what takes place. In doing so, we can limit or arrest the corruption, for which Mexico is famous.

4. We can place onto any aid package the necessity for the Mexico side of the border to be reinforced, secured, and properly patrolled.

5. If it is possible, the aid package should also include our support and their reimbursement of at least fifty percent within a reasonable time frame to send our law enforcement and/or U.S. troops to train their enforcement agencies properly. The fifty percent can easily be set out in a long term loan amortized as appropriate.

We must stop giving money away without some sort of payback. I know our politicians and others might say the payback is in the safe border or simply the international order of business and relationships with allies. But we can't afford this kind of give our all and get little back any longer. Because this is literally our backyard, someone needs to show us something, anything that it will work. So far the current policy has not.

Later I will; I present a plan to establish the Federal Rangers and this is a great area for their supplemental efforts to be placed into effect, in conjunction with state authorities and under the supervision of U.S. and local authorities. By the way I would highly recommend, wherever possible we should utilize a mounted patrol in the remote areas. That's right; the good old fashion way - on horseback. They are fast, quiet, and efficiently cost effective.

In other portions of this book, I also point out the use of our U.S. troops to be utilized in and for the explicit purpose of training on and around the very diverse topography area of our borders. I would suggest we first use the two thousand miles along the Mexico border for a pilot program; and if need be, then also use the four thousand miles of the Canadian border. These training operations can be sporadic and limited but in the way of illegal immigration and drug traffickers.

Somehow, I think that it might be difficult for the drug traffickers or illegal trespassers to pass through a battalion of soldiers on training exercises. Oh, they may go around them, but if the troops are efficient in their training and continuously on the move, well it might not be so easy. When all is said and done, this will be a policy for training U. S. troops not border patrol. Get it?

Look, if all else fails - so far this seems to be the case - then we need to come up with a solid program addressing each component of immigration. Recently listening to the Republican Presidential debate, for the first time one of the candidates (Newt Gingrich) came up with a brief outline that made some sense. Let's look closely at his entire program and at least put into practice those portions we can impart on a trial basis now. I do not believe in amnesty, but Newt did not say amnesty.

He said those who are here illegally for twenty-five years or more whose children are US. Citizens and who have been paying taxes should be given a visa to put them on the path to citizenship.

I say follow that up with a time frame which is reasonable, three years maybe, to force those who get the visa to become citizens or risk the possibility of being denied a second or extension on their visa. I might also put in a caveat to look close at those families who have not bothered learning how to speak the English language, which in any case must be a requirement in the path to citizenship under every circumstance. We can get this done one way or another!

Maybe our Government should borrow some cojones from the Australian Prime Minister. She is not afraid to speak the truth and apparently does not hide behind political Huggie-Bear-Smackie-Poo rhetoric in regards to immigrants.

When you read the following, replace Australians with Americans. It is very apt. In case you missed it when it went viral; here it is.

Quote: Prime Minister Julia Gillard - Australia

'IMMIGRANTS, NOT AUSTRALIANS, MUST ADAPT... Take It Or Leave It. I am tired of this nation worrying about whether we are offending some individual or their culture. Since the terrorist attacks on Bali , we have experienced a surge in patriotism by the majority of Australians.'
'This culture has been developed over two centuries of struggles, trials and victories by millions of men and women who have sought freedom.'
'We speak mainly ENGLISH, not Spanish, Lebanese, Arabic, Chinese, Japanese, Russian, or any other language. Therefore, if you wish to become part of our society, learn the language!'
'Most Australians believe in God. This is not some Christian, right wing, political push, but a fact, because Christian men and women, on Christian principles, founded this nation, and this is clearly documented. It is certainly appropriate to display it on the walls of our schools. If God offends you, then I suggest you consider another part of the world as your new home, because God is part of our culture.'
'We will accept your beliefs, and will not question why. All we ask is that you accept ours, and live in harmony and peaceful enjoyment with us.'

'This is OUR COUNTRY, OUR LAND, and OUR LIFESTYLE, and we will allow you every opportunity to enjoy all this. But once you are done complaining, whining, and griping about Our Flag, Our Pledge, Our Christian beliefs, or Our Way of Life, I highly encourage you take advantage of one other great Australian freedom, 'THE RIGHT TO LEAVE'.'

'If you aren't happy here then LEAVE. We didn't force you to come here. You asked to be here. So accept the country YOU accepted.'

Love it or leave, in my opinion, is not what is being said by the Prime Minister. It is all about assimilating into the country of choice. You can be proud of your heritage and bring some of your customs with you. But in order to be a positive and productive citizen vs. destructive of where you choose to live; you need to assimilate.

If you find something you think will improve your new environment, make soft recommendations vs. demanding them. This will lead to conversation and thoughtful, respectful insight, which may in turn implement change. If you demand and attempt to force that which is not acceptable to your choice of citizenship, you will not be accepted anywhere.

The Department of Corrections

I have been inside the workings of hundreds of detention centers, local jails and prisons over the years. These range from minimum to maximum security penitentiaries. I have investigated thousands of fraud cases and assisted in hundreds of internal affairs cases which originated within the walls of these facilities. I can speak directly to California, but not to every state and federal facility other than affirming the thousands of investigative leads and conversations that took me outside California and Texas. However, I do not think there is anyone inside or outside that will argue against the fact there is extensive drug use and drug trafficking inside those walls of confinement. You may recall, I said that alcohol and drug abuse is a debilitating disease that grabs you and won't let you go.

In our society is there anywhere to find a more captive customer base than inside a prison? No, there is not. I know some might talk about the poverty stricken streets and neighborhoods and they are indeed troubling. But they are not captive, per se. I have listened to politicians and law enforcement professionals for forty years in my career. Before even getting my first job they said and continue to say; "It would be nice to fix it, but it is what it is." Then they seem to forget about really trying. What they do is implement some absurd program originating out of some idiotic ideological mindset that gives rise to sympathy. Nowhere is there any real substance to what takes place in the true setting of addiction, other than the fact that people need help.

Oh I know, let's listen to the drug addict that will do or say anything to get drugs or the psychologist who can state one theory after another, again without having a clue to the real world or has been proven wrong time and time again throughout history.

The old adage in these cases is: It is worth it, if only one is helped. That is nothing less than Huggie-Bear-Smackie-Poo BS. I am back to they do not want to "just fix it", as the former Presidential candidate Ross Perot would state. How do I know there is a way to stop drugs in its tracks within all these facilities? I have been asked what my solution is while sitting around the table with high ranking officials who keep coming up with "great ideas" that often sound good but do nothing. Many are implemented and again do nothing but cost money, a lot of it, just to say "I feel your pain", a statement made famous by President William Jefferson Clinton.

Once again that is because of politics and unions. When asked, those who know me would smile and say here it comes. Others would say, "Oh, no they ask Millmore?" Why did they have this reaction? I have the answer that no one wants to hear or even try. They certainly do not want this answer to get out to the general public, because they have done such a great job in scamming the average Joe and that would put a real crimp in the power and money which funds the rest of the story. Read the first line in this paragraph (in bold) again and again and you will get the idea.

These higher-ups, as they like to be referred, are more interested in the HUGGIE-BEAR-SMACKIEE-POO state of mind, than they are about actually doing something worthwhile. Alright here is the answer: K9 units (drug sniffing dogs) period. How would that work? Easy, each facility will assign a K-9 unit to every entrance and every exit. It should not matter if you are an inmate; an employee; a visiting dignitary of any status; or a vender who delivers the food, mail, or medicine.

Everyone and I mean everyone, whether you wear a uniform or suit or you are just visiting and every vehicle and every letter and every package should be required to pass a dog.

If that dog hits on you, you are searched. If you are found to have contraband, appropriate charges will be filed; subsequently, due process should be followed and the system is at work.

So what is the problem? Why are the politicians against this great idea? They do not know how to sell the idea to the public and God forbid they lose a vote over a situation that is in such desperate need of fixing. How should they sell it? With the truth, first of all, and with the rewards this type of action will produce, especially for those individuals who are hooked on the dope.

Not to mention, those we will take off the street and out of their jobs they do not deserve for trafficking in this menacing crime that cost lives and billions of dollars. You know the war on drugs. Wouldn't it be great to try a real solution versus a bunch of money-sucking, do-nothing programs, just one time?

Why are the unions against this great idea? They say it will take away jobs, their budgets will be cut, and there are not enough officers now. If you are not getting the job done now, it is not because there are not enough positions within the corrections system. It is because, as all union shops and government run entities, they do not use the funds or the programs in place efficiently.

Now look, I truly like the officers and the command staff who work in atrocious circumstances and I would not wish to be employed in their shoes. But there is far too much evidence to prove the lack of efficiencies. As you read on you will see that the plan will not cost jobs, but instead, rearrange jobs and most likely put a different face on what type of jobs might be needed or added.

The special interest groups say this would be a violation of the Fourth Amendment of the Constitution - Search and Seizure. I say that too is bunk, because at every single facility I have visited there are Federal, State and local laws with plainly stated signage to advise everyone that they are subject to search just by entering the property.

So get over it or don't go to the facility! Yes, this would subject even attorneys to be searched! Look, just because an envelope is smelled by a drug sniffing dog with training - court after court has upheld this practice in search and seizure issues - does not mean a prisoner's rights have been violated. It does not even mean the letter is opened or read. It means there is no dope inside the package and if it is 'hit on" by the dog, then there is probable cause to believe that a crime is being committed and therefore legal reason to be searched.

But wait, K-9 units are expensive! Do they cost as much as the ridiculous programs now inside allowing a prisoner a substance that will keep them high and hooked for life? I can guarantee that these highly trained dogs are far cheaper then the ridiculous medicines given to the prisoners in place of heroin or other illegal drugs, the staff required for administering and monitoring, not to mention the number of medical doctors on staff.

I know we need the doctors, but not as many. Certainly, we do not need them to administer drugs that keep the population of rotating prisoners hooked for life. These addicts do not come out "clean". Instead of using heroin, they use "just methadone" or some other substitute. Then they go right back to using heroin or their drug of choice. Don't they? So very few stop using drugs; it seems to be hopeless. Ok, then lets do it another way or at least try another way in a prison near you?

Here is a method I believe will work and I believe we will have a real chance of getting these prisoners off drugs, at the very least. If we stop the drugs - and we can, then we can truly focus on building a skill set for the prisoner. But before I go there, let's talk a bit about prison time to be served.

Say the prisoner receives a five year sentence in a state prison for robbery or aggravated assault with the use of a weapon.

Ok, we can parcel out which type of crimes fit what type of "rehabilitation", which mostly doesn't work. However, they must truly be clean and then it is worth a try. But they truly must be clean or forget it; we will forever be in perpetual rotation from the streets to prison and back again.

The first three years of the five should be hard time, getting clean and working hard within the prison. Few privileges should be given during this first step. No conjugal visits for the first two or three years. No dessert with meals, no meals except the very basics to keep them healthy. In fact, follow the local school menus without any of the frills attached. No coffee, no tea and no soda; they can have hot or cold water, it's good for them and it's good for their bowel movements. The only exercise allowed will be mandatory, but they can only use their bodies no equipment. You know PT, like in the military.

After a successful two or three years without any further privileges (i.e., no trusty perks for good behavior) keep them in line and EARNING the next two years of their sentence. By then they will have learned the meaning of getting along, following the rules, and knowing they will not be mistreated. Instead, they will be given a chance at never returning. Now clean from drugs (because none entered the prison) and healthy from no sugar, no spices and a diet consisting of the nutritious food groups, we and they are ready to move forward. Don't tell me it can't be done. It can, we can.

Any lawsuits that arise out of following these rules should be dropped and thrown out by the courts, period. If there are abuses outside of following the rules, then by all means let the suit go forward.

The third or fourth year provides a real dividend return for the prisoners' effort at doing what they must: serve society by serving time and getting right in the head and the body.

Now, they can EARN the trust and the right to be free, instead of captured by the ills of society with the politicians keeping them suppressed and in the gutters. We begin to focus on education, in order to establish a skill set. They should not be permitted to acquire a law degree or some other education on the public dollar that costs the common citizen a fortune and deep debt to get ahead in life.

A skill set would be fine, like mechanics or operating heavy equipment, construction or building furniture, maybe working in an office or in sales and other such careers. They should be given certificates (Not degrees, unless the college/learning institution or family is willing to pick up the tab, not the public dollar in any form) from outside learning institutions that offer these trades, such as junior colleges. The certificates will be earned from inside the prison (no passes to outside classes) under appropriate proctors, but the prison will not be mentioned on the certificate.

They may start to choose a cup of hot or cold coffee or tea for doing well in their classes and continuing to work hard at the assigned job inside. Without incurring penalties and behaving themselves by obeying all the rules, they will begin to have dessert with meals. Towards the end of the fourth year and with one last year to serve, they might be allowed conjugal visits.

I have known soldiers who have gone one or two years in the jungles and other war zones without meeting these needs and they did not violate everything or anything sacred to our society. Frankly, I do not believe in conjugal visits at all, but even I am willing to budge in order to make a deal that has a foundation with sustenance from which to build.

Six or eight months before release, the prisoner begins to work with a human resource officer who will network the outside and assist in a first job. The network will have long before been established with companies willing to help and give them a chance.

There are many employers that step up and there would be several more, if we demand a system that will truly make the effort to get these prisoners straight.

If while serving time a prisoner cannot straighten up and get their head right, if they break the rules and the agreement of incarceration, then they receive an extended sentence. The extension can be set into law for the crime committed or at their sentencing hearing. If they return to prison, it gets harder and they will not be eligible to participate in a step program, just serve hard time, forced to get clean and no privileges from beginning to end. Now look, if incarceration is hard, most clean and sane people will not stay on the perpetual turn table and our recidivism will lower significantly.

If anyone out there thinks for one minute that many of our correction officers do not participate in drug trafficking, then man are you naive. I cannot tell the number of officers I have filmed in my surveillance cases and how many statements I have gained in interviews and through interrogations that prove it. I could cite hundreds, if not thousands; but let me give you only one case, as brief as I can, to drive this point home.

This investigation involved a medical prison, included eight officers, ten inmates and several outside drug dealers. All of this was known and little was done to prevent the continuance of shenanigans because of political correctness and union rules. The officers, self-proclaimed lesbians, lived with one another off and on. I have no problem with their being lesbian, that's up to our Creator to make a final judgment; but, it is a fact in this case and I believe a significant portion of reason to the rest of the story.

Two officers had been caught engaged in sexual activity with prisoners in the cells and in the yards. All were caught in sexual acts with other officers and all were on duty. All eight had been disciplined but not terminated, with the exception of one who was actually permitted to resign.

That officer relocated to another part of the State and moved in with a paroled prisoner. The prisoner was a career criminal known for trafficking in drugs and sometimes weapons. The other seven officers realized they might be terminated in time, so they filed numerous grievances with the union. Then three of those officers filed worker's compensation claims in addition to their union grievances stating stress and poor working environments. That's where I came in.

Not only did each of these officers have a stress claim, but intertwined were several physical injuries like knees, backs, hips, etc. These worker's compensation claims are common place in thousands of employee disciplinary actions of all types. The officer files them with mostly bogus injuries to ensure they will not get terminated. The union tells them in one way or another, if they file the claim, they can always turn around and accuse the Department of Corrections fired them because of the claim.

This protects them from termination as a result of the other wrong doing that began an investigation into their participation. The claim protects them, because it is illegal to terminate for filing an injury claim and the employer stands back. Additionally, the employer sees a way to get rid of the criminal officer through the worker's compensation laws via retirement versus termination.

As a result the seven officers still on the books were put onto worker's compensation leave, where they each collected full salaries tax free. That is the way it worked then and I do not believe it has changed much since I left that portion of my career. Now is it any wonder why our insurance rates are through the roof?

During my investigation I learned and proved they were all deeply involved in drug use, trafficking, and although many other suspicions of criminal activity arose, I only proved the drugs, per se.

Proof as it relates to other criminal activity in this case was circumstantial, but certainly not out of the question. Unfortunately, my investigation was satisfied, and the rest would be up to other agencies, mostly Department of Corrections, to follow through. They seldom ever did. Furthermore, if these cases and suspected violations were handed over to any other law enforcement agency, they would simply kick it back to Corrections and so the circle goes.

Each of these officers told me they were in love with the other and each stated they were angry at each other. Yet, they continued to run around and share each other with one another. When I asked what they meant by "share", I was told "drugs and sex mostly". It was common place, according to them, for all to be involved with one another during sex and the use of drugs. At some point, for reasons only their twisted minds could invoke, jealously would take over leading to physical altercation and psychological games.

By now you are saying, "Hey, I thought this account would be brief." It is, I am only giving you a very small part of this very involved and deeply troubling case (one of many). You will not like this part at all, I hope! A regular portion of my investigations was to complete a brief background on the subjects involved.

I will cite one, as they all in this case had unbelievable life styles and criminal behavior in their backgrounds long before they became employees of the Department of Corrections. "Wait a minute," say you. "Aren't correctional officers required to undergo a complete background before they are hired?" The answer is, absolutely. The real question is, do they? The Department will insist they do or did and no one is hired with a criminal background, at least not one that is too severe. Or are they?

Here is part of the brief inquiry I made on just one of these eight officers. She stated on audio tape: (Paraphrasing) when I applied to the Department I was working in San Francisco as a lighting technician in a private club. I have used many different drugs as a recreational source, including heroin, LSD, and of course, marijuana. I use LSD and marijuana regularly even now. I was arrested in San Francisco on prostitution charges, because I worked for an escort service and the same private club where I was a lighting technician. There were many other times I came in contact with the police on various other issues, but after being hired for the Department I only prostituted myself with other officers and the occasionally parolee. They don't get much sex inside, so I give it to them when they get out or whenever I can. On the other hand, if they are inside for life sentences or really long periods, I/we try to give them blow jobs as often as we can. Sometimes we can satisfy three or four at one time, if the other officers who are afraid of getting caught are out of the way. Many will make that effort, when we tell them what days and times we plan the "cell search" or "prisoner assist". In fact, if we plan things just right, we can all be on the same shift and not worry so much about getting caught.

I had asked these questions, because I was able to find the drug and prostitution charges in the system. She did not hesitate to confirm them. I was surprised at what I had discovered and her confession. Out of the abusive cases I investigated within our system, this one was rising to the top of discouragement and abysmal. Unfortunately, it would not be the last.

As it turned out, all eight officers had been in trouble with the law at one time or another. Furthermore, they had all been disciplined by their superiors for various issues at work. A lot of what was known about these officers was regularly circulated in and about the work place. Gossip at its best but with strong witnesses and tons of evidence if only properly investigated. (Thank-you unions!)

Furthermore, there were video tapes of parties; there were up to thirty different tapes at separate parties having taken place at the officers' home, wherein numerous officers were participants. Drug use and sex were prevalent and there were known drug traffickers in attendance. All of this was confirmed.

I went to Internal Affairs and requested assistance from the special agents I knew to be honest hard working officers. They confirmed that "a mailing background" had been completed on each of these and many other officers. They explained that a mailing background was just that, completed by mail only. Although it was to include a records check, there was no guarantee this occurred, at least not with any check and balance.

I, of course, stared at them in disbelief and they explained further, "A few years ago there were several institutions extremely understaffed. The union made it clear that the Department must hire the necessary staff and do it at any cost, and be sure there was a significant percentage of minorities." I am not saying that all the officers in these cases were minorities, they were not. I am simply repeating what I was told.

The problem in the background checks was there were not enough background investigators/officers to complete a thorough investigation - i.e., mailing out paper inquiries to references and no field work - resulting in hundreds being hired who should never have made it in to the Department. While I am at it, let me say that the unions keeps the number of Internal Affairs special agents to a minimum and you can't believe how overworked and under staffed those agents are! Can anyone guess why the union does not want an efficient number of special agents on the job?

Just let your mind dance around with that issue. The references were mailed to those who knew and were friends of the applicant.

What do you think was returned? Do you think there were any phone calls to confirm the returned documents or the lies simply stood as "a good reference"? What about the drug screens? No one could explain it. How was it they passed? Did they even take one? Maybe they were clean enough at the time to pass and simply returned to their lifestyle after being exposed daily to their fellow criminals. Or maybe, just maybe, there are others in the background checks or backrooms that simply took the chemical tests for them or doctored the results, if there were any real results to doctor.

You know the applicant here described her lighting technician job to me as, "Standing on a table over the top of the "John" and dancing while placing hands over different color lights, then I would provide sexual acts for bonus pay." The term lighting technician was good enough to pass the background without explanation. "Sales" may have been good enough for the escort business and the drug use, who knows? Perhaps "recreational use only" was the passing grade?

You might also be interested and I hope relieved to know that none of these eight work for the Department any longer. That is not to say they were terminated; they did indeed collect worker's compensation benefits and moved away, thanks to the fouled laws and the union backing them up at every turn.

The one officer, who moved to a different part of the State with a parolee, was visited by two of the others. These two were fighting (according to them) over who was going to "marry" the third. (They made marriage certificates up between themselves.) But when they arrived at the third officer's house she wanted no part of either. She was now in love with the parolee who gave her everything she wanted, according to the two visitors.

They told me the parolee was "pimping her out for drugs." Traveling with the two visitors was a known drug trafficker (one of the same who had attended those parties mentioned earlier) and the three of them apparently gave drugs to the third officer before leaving. When they returned home, the two got into a physical fight; one put a .357 magnum into the mouth of the other stating next time she would kill her, if she got in her way of having whomever she desired.

Traveling to the third officer's new home for a statement, I learned from local authorities her body had been dumped on the step outside a hospital. She was dead from apparent heart failure after ingesting "Bad Dope", cocaine. The parolee had been arrested and charged for the possible murder. Is there more to this story? You bet there is a great deal, but not for this particular book. I will leave you with an image of the last time I saw and spoke to one of these two, who is now retired with life time worker's compensation benefits, a monthly check, rehabilitation rights, and whatever else it takes.

She lived in Northern California in an old ranch type house with one of the other eight. As I was taking a follow up statement requested by an attorney representing the State, a cow walked into her kitchen, defecated in the middle of the floor, then turned and made its way past the urine soaked mattresses laying on the back bedroom floor to another open door. They were selling eggs for extra cash to the general community. I advised the city. Who knows if they listened to me about a possible health hazard?

The point here is, do you think we need K-9 units (drug sniffing dogs) at the entrances to our prisons and other lock up facilities? I do. As I said, they may be expensive but think of the money we will save in programs like worker's compensation claims, drug addiction and so on.

Just think about the possible lives we will save by getting the drugs out and maybe, just maybe, clean these prisoners' bodies and souls, so they have a real chance to become productive citizens. I do not know about you, but I can't help thinking we might also get rid of bad officers with a program like this one. I believe this is worth a try, at least as a pilot program somewhere. Don't you?

Firefighters:

I won't spend much time on this topic, only because my experience in the fire department is limited. However, while serving two years as an officer and then Administrative Sergeant, I supervised a full complement fire department. I was employed by a Police & Fire Department under contract with the U. S. Department of Defense, 1000 acre "Hughes" aircraft plant for construction, research & development of helicopters; both private and military.

I had worked along side these brave men and women for years as a police officer within the municipalities and county. But this experience gave me deeper insight to their profession. There was no doubt in my mind, they would put their own life in jeopardy on a moment's notice to save another person, regardless of who they were or what the circumstances. Act now to save a life, ask questions later. This was the same work ethic and professional pride exhibited everyday by my fellow police officers, although the firefighters were just a bit different. Meaning the firemen/women are generally called upon to save someone's life during a fire or immediately following a tragedy. Unfortunately, police officers respond during the commission of a crime which often turns tragic. Here the police officer is both taking and attempting to save lives, perhaps giving CPR to someone they just shot.

Both professions have a distinctive inner drive towards their fellow man, much like mothers protecting their children. It does not matter what they did wrong - fires or criminal activity - they must be saved now; then, we will look at the circumstances leading up to the rescue or protection of their life. The firefighters and the police will handle the emergency/service call and the investigation to sort it all out, but discipline and punishment is someone else's job.

The firefighter was ninety-nine percent of the time in excellent physical shape and in the early days most police officers were too. Somewhere along the way that rate dropped significantly for police officers. I think we began to run short on military veterans; the police started growing large bellies and weak arms. I also took notice that the police officers stopped shining their shoes and the police units they worked in everyday always seemed dirty. On the other hand, the firefighters were well built and they were forever washing or waxing some equipment, between fires of course. Now this is a trait motorcycle officers have in common with firefighters.

I must say that my own experience in the fire department was mostly training on controlled fires and milk runs. I did respond to a few fires that were not controlled and did some of the heavy lifting as directed by real firemen.

Although we were like the majority of city fire departments, it was slightly different as we had an airstrip to accommodate large fixed wing aircraft and helicopters. This meant training on the runway and tarmac for the possibility of emergency landings. Turning out the foam was a great deal of fun like most of the training, as we all made it a training game with a serious necessity to learn and perfect.

The Howard Hughes plant is an interesting place with underground hallways and rooms like a large underground military bunker or vacant missile silo.

We trained in these block long underground hallways all over the one thousand acres by fighting fires within confined places and I, as one of the supervisors (with a top secret clearance), explored many of the dark undisturbed places often. On one of these training days, I was convinced the officers were trying to kill me. (Just kidding guys)

The training was to set up a burn in one of the tunnels just below one opening and we would then enter from both the top and a secondary opening. They were not supposed to set the fire until I arrived and knew I would come through the tunnels to get there. I would be with other supervisors and we were on our way inside a connecting tunnel.

We entered the controlled tunnel and half way down (walking) which was maybe five hundred feet from the burn, they set it on fire. They had poured fuel onto the rubble to set the fire. We did not know they were using fuel and that was not part of the plan, nor was it part of the training. To this day no one has copped out to whose idea that was.

I recall thinking at least they maintain their "I'll cover your back" attitude. Regardless, the fumes from the fuel had rolled down through the tunnel. As they set the fire, it came at us fast and furious. For the first time I knew exactly what they meant by fire is its own kind of living breathing animal, a true monster with really hot teeth. I will never forget the growls and moans as we ran like hell!!! We could feel the heat on our backs and exited the tunnel in record speed, slamming the hatch behind us.

As I stood one day in deep discussion with my brother, a retired Chief of Police from Southern California, he stated, "You know they should take all the fire trucks and paint them blue, because the police are always on the scene first." Certainly, he had a point. Indeed, the call comes out and the police are already on patrol with units rolling towards the scene.

The firefighters are getting ready in record speed, but they still have to get ready and get in their apparatuses and drive. It is also true that in most agencies the police are not firefighter trained and their primary duty is to direct traffic, insuring the firefighters can quickly and safely get in position to fight the fire.

However, this brings me to the recommendation under firefighters. Although this will cross over to police, the need is there for smaller agencies versus large agencies. You can see where I am going here as, yes, I believe it would be cost effective to cross-train. There are several agencies that do this and save money, not to mention they attract a different type of recruit and a wider pool of applicants.

For the small agency it will pay to cross-train, if for no other reason the officers can help when necessary should one or the other lack manpower at a particular scene. I would also recommend that one of the fire crew, regardless of cross-training, should at least be a trained Fire Marshal, as they fall under the category of Peace Officer in many jurisdictions. In this way the fire investigation can begin immediately; if there is a suspect on scene, the police do not have to intervene and make the arrest. Perhaps, a good idea would be to rotate a Fire Marshal with the crews on a regular basis, particularly in the larger cities.

I do not mean the police officer should dress out in their fire gear, although that is the case in some cross-trained agencies. I mean, they need to learn how to operate the fire apparatuses, so the firefighter can enter the fire and assist inside, if need be. Additionally, the firefighter can assist the police with traffic control and talking down a suspect should they need the help. I know they assist each other now under several circumstances, but cross-training is extremely important to accomplish any task correctly and professionally, not to mention save on the liability issues.

Unfortunately, there are many individuals who fall into the type of personality I am about to expose. All receive some sort of sexual gratification from fire. I am told you can find one in just about every jurisdiction, referring to small agencies here versus large ones. In *The Anatomy of Motive* by John Douglas and Mark Olshaker who are two of the leading experts in FBI profiling, when speaking to officers of the New York Police Department they were told at most fires there are numerous persons standing around masturbating. (This book is a great read, a necessity for law enforcement personnel.)

Let me share a story of an arsonist. Unfortunately, there are many individuals who fall into this type odd personality I am about to expose. I was a city police officer during this time and was eventually the arresting officer of this suspect. She was very interesting and a strikingly beautiful young woman in her early twenties. She set one of the local elementary schools on fire in the middle of the night. She set several private residences on fire and she also tried her hand at lighting up a local fire station. The interesting part about this young lady was she called 911 so often to report she was sick or having breathing difficulties it got to the point that the dispatchers hung up. (The old days)

She learned that if someone other than herself called 911, someone would always respond - anyone in a uniform would do. She would pretend to faint in parking lots or public buildings and just lay in the middle of a traffic lane, on a busy road, or even a highway. She would lay there until a uniformed officer -fire, police, or paramedic - helped her up and gave her attention. She insisted on as much medical care as she could get at the scene, but always got well enough without a need and would refuse to be transported to a hospital.

One day one of our police officers was driving through the parking lot of a major grocery store and she saw him coming. When he looked at her, she dropped like a lead balloon to the ground. Several onlookers were nearby and the officer swerved his car around her. Without getting out he rolled down his window and said, "Oh come on Susie getup," (not her real name) and drove away. The Chief's phone rang for a week.

What the public did not know was that this young woman had more than 2,000 911 calls to her credit, all false except the fire calls that we had yet attached to her. Now you know why the dispatchers sometimes hung up, they knew her voice very well. It was suspected by those firefighters and officers who had given her assistance and the paramedics, who took her blood pressure, pulse and gave her oxygen that this was all a mental illness fulfilling a sexual need/desire. She had been booked into a mental institution once or twice, but they apparently could not help her. I do not know why. Maybe there is no help for these types of personalities.

One night the residence in which she was babysitting, went up in flames. Just prior to the fire she gathered the three kids, put them in her car and headed off to McDonalds down the street. She turned around and told the kids to stay put, as she had forgot her purse. The purse was lying on the floor board of the car, according to the oldest. She went in the house, doused it with lighter fluid and set the fire. She came out and went to McDonalds. From there she was able to observe the police and fire engines speed to the house.

According to the kids, she wanted to sit at a front window to watch the fire trucks come by. This was before the alarm went off and the call went out. After eating she drove the kids back to the house. There were numerous fire trucks and police, she was in heaven.

The officers recognized her and watched as she obviously had smiles of self-satisfaction on her face. They asked her what she was doing sitting in the car with the kids. With delight in her voice she answered, "This is their house and I am the babysitter."

After the investigation all the evidence pointed to her, I obtained an arrest warrant for arson charges. She gave a statement after I arrested her on the charges. She admitted to all the previous fires and this one. She made it very clear that it satisfied her sexually to watch the uniformed officers in action and loved it when she was able to get them, any of them, to just touch her. All they had to do was hold her hand and she was happy, but watching them work was the best.

You have to admire our firemen and women as they have their own kind of interesting characters with whom they must deal. In this case there was a standing inside joke about this young lady, she was hot in more ways than one, but as dangerous as any out of control fire could ever be.

Before I go on to the next topic let me tell you what the Hughes Aircraft plant had installed as part of the fire suppression system, when Mr. Howard Hughes was there. It was a "water wall" on most of the very large buildings. I have seen this elsewhere as well, but I do not believe they are in wide use today and I do not know why. Money is most likely the reason.

A water wall is a piped system that when a fire starts inside a building there is a wall of water that streams down every exterior wall from the roof of the building to assist in keeping the fire from spreading onto other buildings. I think every building should be built with a water wall if possible.

In the City of Susanville, California, years ago the wood mill caught fire. The heat coming from that area was so intense, the neighboring buildings caught on fire and the entire neighborhood burnt to the ground. I know this has happened elsewhere many times.

If all or some of those commercial and residential buildings had a water wall system, they may have been saved. You know water on the outside of the building won't do near the damage, because if you think of it they get rained on. Maybe even the insurance would provide a discount on home/fire insurance with a water wall system. Could there be another way to save money with this concept? If only we had politicians thinking of or listening to ideas on their own.

CHAPTER FIVE
The United States Military

This is a subject that is as close to my heart as Law Enforcement has ever been. The fact is; I owe my very life and I believe my outlook and respect for life itself to my experiences in Vietnam and subsequent dealings with our Government. At least the basic foundation of what brought me into a world, (a world of deep faith and the study of human behavior) that I used selfishly but did not appreciate or understand prior to enlisting and, more importantly, serving in Vietnam.

In my introduction, I spoke of having spent my active uniform time for the military in the jungles of Vietnam. Although there is a great deal more to my service during and after Vietnam, I will not be divulging it in this book as there is no need. Here is what most people around me, relatives included, know for sure.

I enlisted in the U.S Army, not because I was patriotic per se. However, I did believe in doing my part as I did not have any confidence in the media as a young man to tell me the truth about anything; I still don't. No, I enlisted to get the hell away from everything and everyone. I was an angry kid full of self-pity and I hated the world. I did not like myself very much either. After all "father" often yelled while beating me that I was "good for nothing and would never amount to anything".

I was running from the human race as I knew it. Anything was better than those who I knew did not know me; did not care whether I was there, gone or had been run over by a truck while hiding in the oleander bushes in the median of the San Bernardino Freeway (I-10 in Pomona, California) with some skanky girl.

I know that is not nice, but they were nothing more than a reflection of me in the opposite sex and I am telling you like it was. I had convinced many girls to hide with me on that freeway and play. This was a common occurrence and a great place to hide from everyone, whether it was for a few hours in the day (while cutting school) or an all night sleep over. Who would think to look in between eight lanes of freeway traffic for a couple of kids ditching school and "playing"? I was then an expert at finding the best hiding places; I made two adult careers side by side perfecting and utilizing these skills.

Why is all this important in this section of a book entitled *Simple Solutions for Complex Issues*? It is directly related to my experiences in and working for the U.S. Army and our Country. You see, it was in the heavy vegetation deep in the jungles of Vietnam where I learned what it meant to be human; I found a significant portion within me which only our Creator could possibly have endowed in each of us. Put simply, that is to be able to honestly analyze ourselves in the deepest confidence of our Creator; in doing so we find in ourselves a soul like no other life on earth. The ability to reason and determine that which is right and that which is wrong. The only question is what path we choose and how do we utilize this amazing gift of divine intervention.

It was also there in the far away land of jungles and creatures that I found what it means to take a life. Not only did we (many of us anyway, depending on the assignment) live literally on the substances provided by the jungles in bugs, animals and vegetation, we learned the meaning of being at the top of the food chain. The real vicious and difficult test, however, was the taking of life in the highest regard. The taking of a human life up close and personal will bring about a reaction you wouldn't believe, if you have not experienced it yourself. I hope that you have not or will never have to do so.

First and foremost is the physical reaction; then follows the psychological emotion unique to mankind that can, if you let it, demolish your very existence. On the other hand, if you didn't have any belief or self-worth before the occurrence, you can be changed into a deeply respectful person that you had no idea was within your very soul.   I am going to tell you something that many won't believe and many won't understand, but it helps make the point.

As I faced the North Vietnamese soldiers in a direct contact situation, it all became slow motion. I reacted to save my life and took theirs. Subsequently, I defecated myself and I could not stop heaving, this would not be the last time and there is no need to go into detail. I believe these trials of truth we go through, we must go through and both our actions and our reactions to these unbelievable human emotions are necessities that guide us towards a purpose of divine design and our Creator must intervene at just the right time to make it clear. I am not, as I said, a go-to-church type of person, but I most assuredly have a significant and deep relationship with our Creator and great faith.

It is perhaps important to point out my responsibilities/assignments in Vietnam, because the records may have been distorted just a bit. I was deployed with the 6th of the 29th Artillery. This was an air mobile 105 howitzer battery attached to the 3rd of the 12th Infantry, 4th Army Division. After two months, the Army sent out the word; they needed forward observers from the "guns" versus the infantry.

I raised my hand figuratively and asked, "Does this mean, I can stop shoveling dirt and filling these sand bags every time we move the guns?" (This was about every two or three weeks.) I was told, "Yes, but you will have a lot of walking ahead of you and you will be a lot closer to firefights." Not that the firefights didn't come to the guns often, they did.

Off I went to be a forward observer, after several months it was back to the guns with fire direction control. Subsequently, I was deployed with what was referred to as "a squad of 9" as the forward observer, to roam the jungle of the central highlands and on into Cambodia and Laos. The job: find the caches of enemy supplies - weapons, food and women. Report them and when possible destroy them as dictated by orders. Additionally, if we encountered any enemy advisers such as the Chinese, (sometimes the assignment) then we would interrogate to get as much information as possible before turning them over to command.

These units had first been referred to as the "Studies and Observation Groups" mostly made up of Marines, approved by President Johnson long before my time in the bush. To this day the word is these groups were disbanded. Or did they just go deeper into the bush by the time I arrived in country? We did. The media was scrutinizing everything in which the military was involved, as they do today, even if it meant placing our troops in harm's way, and the military simply went dark in numerous operations.

What a ride, what an education and what horrible experiences that would make anyone question their own very existence, while crawling very close to the ground and often times under the ground in rat holes that led deeper and deeper into the darkness. Your first greeters of that underworld were snakes; scary snakes that you were sure wanted a taste of that American flesh, but more often than not would just pass you by if you remained very still as though you were just another obstacle for them to get around. Then, some of the largest insects and spiders I have ever seen. Many of them would indeed take a little taste as you crawled over them or waited for them to go by. I guess they were more curious or angry than the snakes.

You would push on into a cavern sometimes as large as a common living room. These caverns were generally filled with enemy supplies: guns, ammo, even women, live chickens, and occasionally there would be a small pig or a goat. To this day, although I do not think I am claustrophobic per se, I do not like small confined areas, especially if they are dark. The dark part is interesting because often I found these underground rooms with very small holes cut through the ceiling lined with bamboo or wood and sometimes cardboard allowing sun light to enter. Many were very deep with ten or even fifteen feet of earth overhead and in these cases they simply had small sky light type tubes allowing the light through.

Here is a little story that occurred one night as I entered the perimeter of the field battery of 105 howitzers, Bravo Company 6/29th Artillery. This is the unit I entered country with and my good friend (who I still maintain contact with, though not nearly enough) was a sergeant on the gun crew and I snuck down into his crew's dug out. No one knew I had entered, but I needed some sleep so I lay down on the dirt floor.

During the night my leg slipped under one of their cots and my foot was caught. It was pitch black, and I do mean that you could not see your hand in front of your face, not even one inch from your nose. I awoke in a panic for some reason. Without a thought, I began to scream uncontrollably. Everyone, particularly my friend Billy Hart, jumped up. Most, if not everyone, hit their head on something, scared out of their minds.

Later Billy told me, he was sure that we were being overrun or someone had dropped a grenade in the dug out. He said he was pretty sure it was his time and that he would be going home in a body bag. Thankfully, he made it home just fine from Vietnam, but for a purple heart or two. If I did not say it before, he is a good friend of mine for whom I have significant respect.

No, I am not a crazy loon, as I am sure many are now saying. No, I am just a guy who like thousands of others has learned who I am and what it means to truly understand what is in my heart and soul. And without question I know what it means to be human and even though for years I questioned some of the acts in which I was involved, I know what it is to reach out and be touched by the Heavenly Spirit.

I have learned what it means to be respectful and professional and treat everyone with human dignity. This does not mean I am a bleeding heart or some might say a religious fanatic; far from either. I am not very sympathetic to a crying whimpering ideologue because someone did them wrong, or to someone who thinks they are owed everything in a free land where our soldiers gave their life for that freedom over the last two hundred plus years.

Get up and become self sufficient and take advantage of the opportunities this great country puts before you. I do not know why each of us have different trials and tribulations in life, on and off the battlefield - some horrific and some mild. I think it is perhaps a necessity for individuals to go through whatever it takes to see the light. I strongly believe in good and evil and one will win out over the other in each of us. It is that simple.

Our Creator has built in the will to choose a particular religion to help us recognize right from wrong when it is obvious. We learn to take the right road or we will return time and again to spend a bit more time in the hell of our consciences until we learn what it means to truly be human. So, with the Lord's help and the military backing the plan, thank you for helping me choose the right road, I needed the shock of my life in order to live it for the better.

Here is a simple solution for our Commander and Chief; allow your generals, who understand the trials and tribulations of a soldier's life in and out of battle, to make the line item policy and quit attempting to micromanage their vast experience.

Those difficult complexities in our military, like how many troops are necessary, what type of equipment will it take, what is the best battle plan and exit plan and other complexities such as "Don't ask don't tell", should be at the generals' discretion not the politicians'. Look, everyone is aware that homosexuality has existed in the military from the very beginning. However, don't you think that the generals and command staff can determine where these individuals can or cannot serve? Obviously, if there is a complaint that has been found warranted through investigation by a soldier that they are mistreated, they can and should be transferred to some other duty post. Further, if warranted, anyone regardless of rank should be appropriately punished for their actions. Let this be up to the military.

Keep those who worship the religion of hate, hell bent on killing our soldiers and American citizens, out of the military. I do not care if these people are touted in political nonsense as peaceful, they do not belong in our military. I realize we hold dear the right to practice any religion of your choice, but everything must have a line drawn in the sand, especially for the sake of our soldiers and our country. Why take the chance of putting our soldiers in harm's way from the inside? Don't they have enough to contend with in open battle and in bloody conflicts that turn their stomach and make them defecate themselves, and then having to deal with the aftermath of human conscience, perhaps at their own peril and destruction?

I know some are saying Islam should not be discriminated against and I did not say that. What I said, or rather what I meant, is to complete a diligent investigative recruitment before accepting a candidate. I have come a long way from the field of battle both physically and mentally accepting the reasons for my trials and tribulations, which have culminated into significant pride that I am an American and live in a free society.

No soldier should ever have to enter that battle by themselves, stop putting the enemy inside the barracks. Let our soldiers do their jobs with the confidence that they will not have to keep an eye of paranoia on their own foxhole buddy.

This business about bringing foreign immigrants to our ranks without first becoming legal citizens is ludicrous. If you need someone to speak a particular language, teach an American citizen and give them a raise for it. They will gladly step up. No need to go to an immigration pool just for the vote or to show the world that America is sorry for being America. What a bunch of liberal, ideological BS. Become a citizen first then subject every soldier to background checks and ensure they are not insiders for the enemy.

For those who do not know, the military years ago left the practice of issuing an individual service number to each soldier. They decided to simply use their social security number. That makes sense in one regard, but not so much when they began to put the full social security number in large print onto the duffel bags the soldier carries over their shoulder through public airports and everywhere else they travel or move.

A plan once again put into action without thinking of the most popular crime in history, identification theft. Now, I understand they have cut the number down to the last four of the soldier's social security number, but it is still in plain view. Come on, admit the mistake and go back to personal identification numbers and protect the soldiers from these types of international crimes, which have caught on expertly with the Taliban. Talk about leaving the door open!

It is not difficult to figure out our social security system and with the last four digits of a soldier's number being displayed in plain view these techno nerds can and have accomplished the task. Even if you're not worried about overseas, then just think about right here in and around our military bases.

I don't mean to expose a weakness that will bring harm to our military, but you must know. If you call a military installation and give your name they first ask, "What are your last four?" From there it's just a matter of requesting the rest of information in the soldier's record or at least enough to do harm in one fashion or another. What is it on the duffle bag? Oh I know, the soldiers' last four.

Let me discuss recruitment for the military. I know we want an all volunteer military, and we certainly want the best we can find from our citizens and those who can adapt to the strains, trial and tribulations of military burden and lessons. But I think we also need a readiness to react, God forbid, in a global or national emergency without delay should our troops be too far stretched in a world gone nuts. Since our politicians are often touting other country policies that are superior to the United States why not take on a bit of common sense from them?

We need to, and I might go so far as to say we must, get with it now. Implement a limited draft for those graduating high school. Send them to basic training and put them on notice, if they qualify to meet the standards. Who knows maybe they will at least learn respect and disciplined principles? They might even pull up their pants. At least we will have saved time in subsequent training should we need it, when we need it.

How many do you think might actually want to make a career out of the military when they get a taste of what it truly means to be a team player? I might also advise the military to get rid of this so called **stress induced** psycho babble and train the soldiers to buck up, grow up and be all they can be! Isn't that supposed to be the mantra/trademark? In my day if you felt bad - other than being physically sick - you stood, listened, learned and worked harder and ran a bit extra to build character and stamina that proved worthy on the battlefield where it counted.

Yes, I said stress, isn't that sweet. The way I understand it, if a soldier is being chastised by a superior and feels bad or gets their feelings hurt, all they have to do is report the hardship. Then go on sick call for therapy and medication with a complaint in hand for what? Revenge? Or is having to follow orders and be accountable like a real soldier, truly a mental challenge? What the heck is going on?

What is wrong with providing the opportunity to obtain a GED (Equivalent High School Diploma), if they don't have one when they are drafted or want to enlist? I was nearly illiterate when I enlisted in the U.S. Army. That is right. I could barely read, I certainly did not know the rules of writing and I was unable to spell. It was only by the grace of God that I was accepted; perhaps it was the Vietnam War that pushed me in as they needed warm bodies. For me it turned out to be my savior in disguise and in more than one way.

After I was indoctrinated, it wasn't long before I was forced to admit I really did not know everything there was and I was, in my opinion, stupid and embarrassed. I told myself; maybe the old man was right, I was good for nothing. I could not stand the thought of him winning, so I marched down to the USO on base. I sat and watched the ladies working there. I picked one out to manipulate into teaching me. I later learned she would have gladly taught me without my shenanigans. I needed someone who would not give up on me; I did not want to be put out on the street. I learned very young how to recognize and take advantage of people; especially an unhappy and distressed young woman and I knew we all have our secrets.

What I did not know then was there was never a need for me to manipulate anyone in the USO. They were happy to help and would keep everything confidential, something I was not use to or trusting. I picked her out and she, "Ann", was a pretty girl with striking features.

I on the other hand was not so striking. I was a kid who had not yet filled out and although I believed I was a man, I was not, at least not yet. This was one of my advantages and I knew it. I did not, however, use my childhood history, which was only my business and no one else's. I followed her and some might say stalked this girl for days. I was not infatuated and at the time I had no feelings in any way for her, not even distorted ones.

I was researching her; I needed to know her weakness and I found it. She did not, like many young women, think she was striking at all. She was shy and found it difficult to speak beyond her script from the USO, but she was friendly and dedicated. I moved in and made sure she took notice of a soldier with a problem, but afraid to open up. I gave all the right signs and even trembled/shook just a bit with an attempt to hide my hands, as she glanced to see my hands take cover.

I said I hoped she would teach me to read, but I was afraid of being discharged. I knew the colors she liked by what she wore when she was not working and made it a point to tell her she should wear blue as it was becoming on her. I then made a point to say, "Like my eye color." What a bunch of crap! I suspected she knew it, but by then she had committed to helping. I wrongly thought I did the right thing, as during those days I was very self centered and selfish.

Here is the point, she taught me to read and write. Although I still can't spell to save my soul, it was the military and the USO that gave me the chance I never really had as a kid. I became a good soldier and served for more years than any documented file in existence will confirm. I know there are those bone-heads in both the liberal and conservative camps wishing to believe that I was a part of some black helicopter conspiracy or want you to believe such nonsense, but that is far from the truth.

By the way, not every public or private agent is an assassin like what you may recall from the movies. Think what you will, it really does not matter now; there is no need for me to elaborate. For those of you who know me or think you know me, there is one thing you can say for sure, I have had an interesting life.

I hope you understand from the point of view of a troubled kid, I could not attend school. They would have learned and they often attempted to find out about the home life. I felt then that it would certainly have been disastrous. I hated everyone, especially authority. The military was my idea no one else's; therefore, I had to make it work. We can give a helping hand to kids that need it and the military can provide the vehicle that won't stop to pick them up anywhere else. If they can adapt, they will in short order. **If they are not adaptable, they will stand out and should be discharged.**

I would be remiss if I didn't pass on a true and meaningful story. I was on a United Airlines flight, having been discharged from the Army just hours before at Fort Lewis, Washington. I was traveling in my Class A Uniform. Unlike many soldiers, I was not concerned about all those stories of people spitting on them.

During those years I smoked cigarettes like most GIs, but I had none. Across from my seat were three ladies all from the same family and three generations. A grandma, a mother and a grandchild, the little girl kept looking at me and I noticed her mother had been smoking. I took the chance, introduced myself, and asked the mother if I might have one of her cigarettes. She gladly passed one over and then whispered into her daughter's ear. She then spoke quietly to grandma who gave her hat to the little girl. The youngster disappeared from view and I thought she was going to the restroom. When the girl returned, she presented me with a hat full of cigarettes. There were even a few dollars in the hat from the passengers. It was overflowing, both the hat and my heart; when I accepted, the plane burst into loud applause.

Go figure! The press never told any of the good stories and never gave credit to the humanitarian side of the war. I did not agree with the war from a political foundation, but I did agree with the war from a humanitarian foundation. Those people needed our help and they asked for it. We are beholding as human beings to reach out when asked and give our support to those who are in desperate need, to keep them from or stop them from being tortured and ruled by tyranny.

It really should not matter if we gain resources or anything more than helping our fellow man to have an opportunity to be free from pure government control and to pursue their God given rights as human beings. This is one of the main reasons in my opinion that our CIA and elite military forces must be a primary priority in this country's survival and our assistance to others throughout the world.

Here is a note to all those in the media and politicians who are under the false impression they make good points or think it is cool to speak so highly of "WOODSTOCK" and the drug induced idiots who participated. The majority of Americans and almost every soldier I served with were disgusted at this portrayal of our dirty laundry in the world news.

When I hear a politician of any stripe speak in good terms of Woodstock, they lose my vote every time. Proper protest is good for the Country; if you want to characterize Woodstock as some kind of protest, but it was not. It was, however, disgusting and shameful. The most powerful display of weak minds without any guidance or respect for anyone other than self portrayal and rebellion from what they just did not like, obeying the rules of society.

Let me include here something that I have been thinking of a great deal lately. That is the country without a government. Somalia has a pirate situation, the ruthless murders, the kidnapping and the demands of millions in ransom from unorganized thugs.

Why do we allow this to continue? What is wrong with not just the United States but every other country on the globe? I know this is a very expensive and very tall order and it seems to me an area we, as the United States and the most powerful force on Earth, should look upon as a humanitarian effort. We need to stop the piracy and bring order to the country of Somalia. The people who live in drastic poverty and disease with a corrupt system, I am not sure you can even refer to it as a government, need our help or anyone's help and they need it yesterday. We need to be on the ground and in the water over there and put a stop to this nonsense.

At the very least, if no one else will take care of business, then let the private shipping companies take care of it in the shipping lanes. If need be let them hire mercenaries as decoys; not to fire openly at anyone looking like they might be a group of pirates, but fire back on anyone who are pirates and engage them first, if they threaten a piracy act.

They need to simply blow them out of the sea and it won't take long for this ridiculous and tragic crime of piracy to stop. Don't try and give warning shots and try to advise them to go away just to pick on the next ship. Do not try and capture them. No, if the ships are fired on with weapons or threatened to be fired upon, then without any discussion and without any warning blow them out of the water; if there are no survivors, well too bad. Any survivors should be plucked from the sea and turned over to the international court and tried for piracy.

To be sure, the mercenaries should have absolute immunity from prosecution as long as an investigation fails to prove they mistreated the pirate. It should be pretty simple. Mandate in all cases that video film of good quality be exposed of each and every incident from the mercenaries' ships and authenticate the evidence via the FBI or the FBI equivalent in other countries.

The film should be required of every step from start to finish, from the time of first contact all the way to the point of turning over anyone plucked from the sea. That is right; everything in the water, on the ship, in the pirates quarters/cell, and every contact including feedings, etc. It is not impossible and it is very feasible and possible.

If a shipping company can come up with millions in ransom, then they can easily come up with the cost of filming equipment and redundant systems independently hard wired into the ship to ensure they have and will meet the requirements of video. If there is no film, then there was no authorization to intercede and there is no immunity. Might as well run like hell and hope the pirates don't get you with that handheld rocket. Or just keep paying the ransom and hope that works and no one dies.

Okay, back on land and inside our own military. Most of the "HUGGIE-BEAR-SMACKIE-POO" programs and wasteful, mandated entitlements do not work. Try a military program that worked for years, just improve them. Give the USO a more direct hand in helping our troops, under a set policy and military rules. I know we have psychologists who help with post traumatic stress disorders (PTSD) that help to some extent, but they have two deficiencies.

The first is the doctors are very expensive; the second is they inevitably give prescription drugs before any real debriefing has a chance to work. I say why not hire inactive or use active combat experienced soldiers who do not have PTSD as a kind of ombudsman whose conversations are protected by client privilege. When this does not work, then go to the doctors, if they must. I strongly believe that most of the patients I have come across with PTSD all snap after long treatments with medications; those who do not take the drugs go on to have problems to be sure, but they learn to cope and seldom snap into violent actions.

Can I approach the age thing again? Why does it take three years or more and/or special permission for a combat or qualified veteran over thirty-seven years of age to reactivate in the military? Just like in our police force, are we going to continue to overlook a strong and willing resource in time of need? Can't we serve up the appropriate test and get on with filling the ranks of qualified service men and women in a timely fashion? Just do it! If we did, maybe the draft would never be necessary again. Make no mistake; the time to address this question will surface again and perhaps sooner than anyone wants to admit. Tap the talent and use it for the betterment and the security of the Country, for our freedom.

You know how there are many, in fact thousands, of ex military personnel who retire from the military and get a second job then retire again with another pension. My uncle did; he retired as a Sergeant Major one day and the next was back doing the same job as a civilian for the next twenty or so years. You know the double dippers. As I said in the law enforcement section, just turn it around so to speak. After someone retires in their civilian career and they can pass the test for the military, let them in and leave their retirement check alone; this should not count against anyone. There should be no cap on earnings and no additional tax on their retirement as income.

It is not difficult to reintegrate anyone into a system where they once prevailed; even if there have been changes. If we were able to keep females out and now include them in any number of positions for whatever reason, then why can't we get past this physical age discrimination? I have no problem utilizing anyone in the positions for which they are qualified to participate and out of positions they can not participate. If you have older soldiers, then use that person in the appropriate position. Leave the logistics to them and the battlefield for the younger soldier.

While we are at it, can we please do something about those absolutely ugly utility uniforms? They might be practical and just fine for the battlefield; State-side how about we go back to khakis or anything but what we have now? At least implement a policy to insure they fit properly. Some of our soldiers resemble run-a-muck teenagers in the mall or, worse yet, some punk gangster.

Here is a bit of serious talk; not that I don't mean what I said previously, I definitely do. This is a subject that is of significantly higher priority and on the minds of the world not just the American citizen. Guantanamo, close it or leave it open and in operation? That is the question. I say, keep it open.

Before you slam the book shut, let's look at this from the necessity of national security, financial burdens and prosecutions. If we close the prison/detention center down, the enemy wins the psychological portion of the war on a global scale. This will dispatch a weakness of American political will and is set deeply into the ideology which runs rampant in the far left mindset. I did not say in the mindset of a liberal thought process, I said far left. Take note of who your politicians are at every level and with whom they surround themselves. Their mouth pieces are nothing less than a reflection of themselves and their ideologies.

This notion that diplomacy with our best interest of how we our perceived versus what must be accomplished will get your throat cut on the streets in police work and kill your international chances at negotiating from a foundation of strength. I have seen this play out on the streets, on the battlefield in direct combat, and in the back rooms of political gatherings and posturing. The only difference is the scale of gain and loss. This, of course, is where collateral damage is calculated into the equation, like it or not. Without that equation the formula is completely flawed.

We absolutely must consider all efforts of diplomacy, but we should not implement a strategy until we have taken count of the collateral damage possible. We should never jump to war or a display of arrogance. No one in their right mind wants war or any physical or political collateral damage, which is a fact. But it is always present and must be scrutinized. In Guantanamo we have total control through military tribunals and they simply need to be put into motion as soon as all the information is extracted from the defendant based on the interrogators final reports.

I am not in a position, neither is anyone on the outside, to say with any certainty that our Government and/or military is taking too long to bring these combatants to trial; however, it does appear this way. That said, it does not mean you jump to a civil courtroom just to posture with an arrogant attitude or to fulfill your own ideology, which is the way that decision appears to the masses of the American people. It means there must be some movement.

I suggest in every case possible start with the military tribunals immediately at Guantanamo. By the way, if a combatant pleads guilty, set the punishment; implement the punishment to be carried out; and move to the next trial. Show the world we have enough belief in our own system of justice, both military and civil, to stand by it and let it work. Quit posturing and trying to please the rest of the world with political correctness and HUGGIE-BEAR-SMACKIE-POO political ideological gain.

Financially, especially in these times of record deficits, it makes no sense at all to abandon the funds we have already spent on this facility, except in a world governed by arrogance and ideology which is the totality of the formula. In this case it seems that transparency is unquestionably evident without cameras or words.

Simply put, don't spend money where we have no need and do not allow the enemy an upper hand in the psychology of war and ultimate policy. As Bill O'Reilly of FOX news has stated jokingly, "For $39.95 we can complete these trials and move on." There is no additional money necessary for security, hundreds of millions; no need to overload the already weighted down criminal court docket; no need to give the enemy a platform; and we win the strength of psychology.

I think it is necessary to address these issues of aggressively going after our own for stepping up and doing their job. When this country sends out troops - this includes the CIA, DOD, NSA, etc. - to engage the enemy and they run into combat or obstacles of engagement to accomplish the mission, we must support them in everything they must do, except murder and or other criminal activity. Let us keep in mind that a military battlefield is not a street in San Francisco, like the far left mindset see it. In those streets we do have, in many cases but not all, a bit more discretion. The rules of engagement are very different and so is the collateral damage. It is, indeed, a necessity to understand what murder might mean given the circumstances.

This is a back-door, tell-tale sign that these people analyzing and preparing our foreign policy regarding engagement have no idea what it means to be on the battlefield. Well, I do. Let me tell everyone that when **necessary** during engagement I did and would every time beat the living devil out of the enemy. When that did not work I extinguished them, if that is what it took to save my life or another soldier or even a civilian in the place of combat and in the time set by the circumstances. Unfortunately, the killing often came first, because there was no other choice. I do not care if the enemy winds up with a bullet in them, a broken bone, or even a fat lip.

I understand there are and must be rules of engagement and the commanders in the field are held accountable to keep the human emotion and common traits of soldiers in check. Train them, trust them and let them do their job without the fear of being prosecuted for doing the right thing, instead of scrutinizing every move in order to find something to level the playing field on the battlefield. We are and should always be the strongest.

It must also be understood the word or definition of engagement is far wider in scope than a simple term. Engagement means every aspect of interacting with (inside or outside) the enemy camp to provide the required intelligence, and all inclusive battle plans for one distinct purpose, to win!

I am not saying the ends justify the means for those bone-heads who are trying to twist my words. I am telling you, engagement takes into account all measure of possibility cross-analyzed with collateral damage and the end result for the best probability to win strategically, psychologically, and politically. When we go after our own (especially in the global public eye) for nothing more than ideology, we expose a weakness to be taken advantage. You will be responsible for killing our own. Why? Our own will hesitate when they should not and the blood will be on the hands of those who made the policy that caused the hesitation.

I seldom observed a soldier commit a crime on the enemy. When I did, I stopped it and I reported it. The absolute necessity here is recognizing what is a crime versus what is a necessity. I do not condone, nor did I ever commit, any wartime or battlefield crime anymore than I ever violated a citizen's rights as a police officer. I completed the mission on the battlefield; I put the citizen first, then my partner and myself, regardless of which uniform I was wearing.

I am sure the far left mind reading this - if there is anyone still reading - must be horrified at what I just stated. If you cannot comprehend what I said above and you still insist that I said the end justifies the means, read what I wrote again and again until you get some sense that what I said is: as long as the soldier is acting within protocol and under the rules of real engagement, the means will never be an issue, because it was justified by the rules of engagement. So, get over it, and please never enlist in the military and never apply for a job with a police department. I do not want and, in fact, I fear the far left mindset in the fox hole with our soldiers or in the front seat of a patrol car. They will get themselves, their partners and the general public killed.

One day in Vietnam the squad was approaching what we were told was a friendly village high in the mountains. A young boy maybe ten or twelve came running towards us. He stopped approximately thirty feet and adjusted his baggy shirt. ("Black pajamas") Then walking again, he was stating "number one GI" in friendly terms with a smile. The boy moved to get closer, now approximately fifteen feet. He raised his hand up and pointed.

An old timer (a soldier that had been in country a while) shot the boy; as the bullet struck, the boy blew up. His body was rigged with high explosives. I did not know it, due to my lack of experience; I did not see the trip wire he pulled as he raised his hand. The old timer stated, "Sometimes you got to do the tough stuff, no matter what." His eyes were full of held back tears. He saved our lives. How close must we come before the far left mindset gets it? Will they ever? The Taliban have nothing on the Vietnamese, but they sure use the same type of tactics. The women and children are expendable; they use them up front, hide behind them and save their men's strength for the main battles. Nothing more than cowards!

Before I move on to any other issues, let me state what I believe is a tragedy. When our soldiers, police officers and firefighters get injured on the job, what is wrong with us? **We the people or the Government, whichever way you want to phrase it, (because if you don't get it, we are the Government) allow the injured veterans and their families to hang in the wind.** Although we seem to be doing better by taking care of veterans in part, we still do a lousy job in totality. We as citizens are indeed grateful and giving. I am amazed at how our brave heroes must depend on private charities to pay for their families to visit and stay in a hotel while they recuperate.

Why must a veteran's pay be cut, due to the fact that they are no longer in a combat zone after being injured, i.e., combat pay taken out of their salaries? For that matter our worker's compensation system for our police and firefighters being far less than their regular pay check? So much less, they must reassess what bills gets paid and who must wait for the payment, particularly during the process.   All the while, this screws up the soldiers', police officers' and the firemen's credit line and makes it even more difficult to provide for their families when they do recover.

Why do those who put themselves out there in front for our freedoms, our safety and our rights as citizens to live a peaceful and prosperous life go unattended with mounting debt and loss of life for them and their families? Why? I believe we, as a government, should ensure they do not falter in society after they have sacrificed.   After they become seriously injured by loss of limb or otherwise debilitated to the point they must take months or years to rehabilitate we should, we must, make absolutely sure they are not encumbered to the point of bankruptcy. For our soldiers we, as a federal government, should pay those additional expenses outright.

If they lose their life, we owe it to be sure their families have enough life insurance to cover their mortgage and other utility bills, etc., at the very least. Ensure their spouses and their children can get back on their feet and away from unbearable expenses.

I know we must debate what a serious injury is and what is common under, say, the fireman's rule. If you are hurt, it is part of the job so except that and go away; but that is in the negotiation process. I do not believe everything that happens to a soldier that is stressful is a serious injury. To those who do believe this, sorry.

Of course, there are always exceptions and I cannot speak out of turn against the experts per se, only as an ex-soldier who has been there on the battlefield and has lived with that unfortunate necessity. Look, Post Traumatic Stress is not only a fact of life; it is healthy and necessary to work through our trials and tribulations. I am sorry; but if their training is proper and their debriefing is proper, they will get over the problem or they will learn to deal with those problems in comfortable (at least acceptable) terms. Life will and does go on and we as active soldiers or veterans will adapt, contend and accept what we did, we did for all the necessary and right reasons.

This is perhaps the time for what I call pre-graduate counseling from veterans, who have been there done that and have gone through the trials and tribulations. It is, in my opinion, a good idea to have these pre-graduate counselors in good standing holding a Master's Degree, perhaps in Psychology. Believe me, even without a degree a true veteran can recognize when someone has or is about to transition from what is normal and necessary into a true disorder or dysfunction. It is when post traumatic stress turns into a disorder, or as I like to say a dysfunction, that we need the depth of medical counseling and/or medication; but not before there is a real dysfunction.

Now please keep in mind, I have not advocated endlessly paying bills or going deep into debt over these issues. I am only suggesting we keep our heroes above water and assist them fully in their recovery. The left side of this issue often tells me our soldiers receive plenty of counseling and drugs for their problems and they can go to the Veterans' Hospital for care. Indeed this is a great help, if you can get by the overwhelming amount of incompetent personnel who work in the Veterans' Hospitals.

Many of whom most likely couldn't get a job in the Department of Motor Vehicles; they screw up everything they touch, everyday. I can't tell you how many times I have had this conversation with veterans. One of their concerns is that if they do not get sick during the fiscal budget year calendar and had no need to go to their primary VA doctor, then they are removed from the doctor's patient list.

You say, so what is the big deal? They can't just call and be put back on the list; they must then go through an entire process of being evaluated again and then be put back on an active list. That, my friend, takes the Veterans' Administration months to complete. By then the veteran is very ill or dead, because their cancerous tumors were not caught in time.

Having said all this negative stuff about the VA; let me point out at least one exception with the name of an employee I hear often from veterans around Texas. Her name is Lisa McDonald; she apparently works in the main VA hospital located in Temple, Texas. This kind and considerate lady helps everyone straighten matters after the rest of her colleagues, regardless of their titles, screw it up. It is very interesting that the paper work seems to be in order and very plain in black and white.

The trouble is most of these VA employees are, simply put, too lazy to read the documents/report and follow through with their responsibility.

They just spout off a policy that no longer applies to the veteran with whom they happen to be speaking, because the veteran has already followed the policy. The VA employee mindset seems to be if there is a call and a question, we will list the policy and let it go without reading the reports. They might read one or two lines and they might even scan down a report briefly then spout off the policy. This action or inaction sets off a state of mind in the veteran of anger, distrust and abandonment.

Many have stated the military and local public safety personnel are like comparing apples and oranges. Like hell they are! Tell me, what is the difference between a soldier who volunteers or is drafted to serve on a battlefield overseas, or a police officer or a volunteer reserve police officer who serves in the battlefield of our streets and gets killed while serving? Dead is dead man! Losing a limb is losing a limb! Being placed in a wheel chair for the rest of your life is in a wheel chair! They put themselves in harm's way for all of us everyday, you and me!

What about the fireman, who climbs into a large truck, goes to a fire and enters a burning building to save you or your family's life and they lose their own life, often in a way that certainly compares to the open battlefield overseas? Can you think about napalm and how when it's dropped it burns everything in its path? Think about what it is like to burn to death. Ever receive a burn to yourself, perhaps a small very painful burn to some part of your body? I have observed people burning to death first hand on both battlefields in a foreign war and on our city streets. It is not pleasant, my fellow Americans. Their screams of agony will never leave my mind.

I have given you insights into real life experiences, because I think they make a point and carry recommendations everyone can extrapolate for themselves.

CHAPTER SIX
Proposal for State District Police

I must state that if you have not been bored up to this point, the following proposal may very well do it. However, I beg of you to suffer through it. The reason is simple; we can provide proactive policing as a priority vs. a wish list item. This proposal is a means of getting it done and it would affect all of us. It can be extrapolated from a management district to any State or City and any necessity, such as our borders.

In recent news the State of Arizona, is in fact, speaking in direct measures of this proposal. The problem is; they are developing the system into a militia vs. a police agency. My guess is because they are trying to avoid the unions. If the legislature will think a bit, they can get it done and the union membership will force the union to accept.

In Texas the most underused resource is the Constable Department. The following is written for Texas. However, all States can put together a division within large agencies as proactive, if done correctly.

The foundation for the plan:

Here is how I dealt with the situation in Houston, Texas. I could not have done anything without first having the support of the Board of Directors of the State Political Subdivision known as The Near Northwest Management District and the unwavering support of Constable Jack Abercia of Harris County, Precinct One. Constable Abercia commissioned me within his agency as Assistant Chief, and bestowed unto me in the form of a written job description, all the authority of this command position necessary to get the job done.

There was a significant twist to this appointment, some say a possible conflict of interest, but I still stand by the validity and the necessity of my appointment. I was the Executive Director for this State Management District which, like the twenty-two other districts in Houston at the time, was established by the State Legislature. The Districts' budgets come from taxing revenue, but only from the commercial businesses, not the residential property in the District. They are, for a lack of a better description, a supplement to all city, county and state services.

The Executive Director is in part a city mayor, city manager, and chief law enforcement officer within each district. The Executive Director answers accordingly to the individual board of directors, who are a reflection of any city council or county board of supervisors. Although this sounds like a bad idea and just another tax in a district, the assessments were set at eleven cents per one hundred dollar of value of the property taxed. It truly turned out to be a significant value with measurable and positive results, not only in public safety but in all areas of public service.

My district consisted of sixteen square miles and approximately eighty-five thousand in population in one of the worst crime ridden areas of Houston. The news media, both television and print, reported over several years that the center of this district, known as the "Antoine Corridor" and "De Soto Streets" (named after the main thoroughfare that traversed the length of the District), was the most dangerous area in Houston and maybe the State.

One day I would be developing a city park and trying to improve the traffic conditions. The next I was developing plans on how to attract new businesses to create jobs. Then, I would be developing an anti-gang initiative, followed by being in uniform weeks later to supervise and deploy eighty to one hundred law enforcement officers from numerous agencies, to carry out the mission of my program. The week would wind down with a visit to the local senior citizen centers, so we could improve their living environment. This included pushing, ever so gently, our State Representatives and city officials to help with such things as fixing the sidewalks, so the seniors would be able to easily travel to the grocery store one-half block away in their wheel chairs without falling over or getting mugged.

That takes care of a small portion of what my job duties were in the District and why I was appointed to the command position of Assistant Chief in the Constable's Office. Some say this was a conflict because the District contracted the services for the Constables to be the supplementing factor in public safety for the District. I looked at this from a different perspective.

First, I was already responsible for supplementing public safety in the District and I, unlike other executive directors of the other twenty-two districts, was already a commissioned peace officer in the State of Texas. I just needed to change the venue/agency where my commission was carried.

Second, the Constable did not receive anything more or less nor did I in the way of compensation. Third, at my insistence the written job description signed by both the Constable and I read very clearly that my commission and position would not in any way supersede the authority or responsibilities of my being the Executive Director; and I had this appointment approved by the Board of Directors for the District.

Further, it was my understanding that the Constable had the county commissioners and county legal department approve the appointment. If at any time I would have been advised formally by any authority in the loop that this was a conflict of interest, including the Management District's legal staff on retainer, I would not have accepted the appointment.

I readily admit I could not have accomplished the end result without all the other chiefs of police, especially Chief Harold Hurtt of Houston and at least one of his Captains, Randy Ellen of the Houston Police, North Command Station. There were many other chiefs and departments to whom I owe a debt of thanks, including the U.S. Attorney General's Office; the Federal Bureau of Investigation; the Drug Enforcement Administration; Metro Police; local school police; and although begrudgingly, the Harris County Sheriff's Office.

I do not think it was the Sheriff who had any difficulty. I believe it was his command staff, but I might be wrong. Either way, each of these agencies had some responsibility within the targeted areas as the District overlapped in the City of Houston and into the county area. Of course, the Feds play an important role in public safety everywhere, especially in the dynamics of today's law enforcement.

Due to the hard work of everyone on my staff and all the law enforcement officials working together, the District was awarded the covenant prize, proving the community policing initiatives were a resounding success.

This prize was one of only two Federal "Weed and Seed" grants in the State of Texas and one of only sixteen in the United States that year. For those of you who are not familiar with the tenacity it takes to write and provide on the spot changes in a continuous run of requirements for this one million dollar grant, believe me it is almost so frustrating you want to just bury your heads in the sand and pray to be run over by a steam roller or be fired.

On this note let me give deeply heart warming credit to my Executive Assistant at the time, Ms. Michelle Mitchell. To this day Michelle visits our home and is considered one of our extended family. Everyone in the community learned very quickly that this inspiring young woman had what it takes. In fact, the Drug Enforcement Administration did their level best to hire her away from the District.

What were the community policing initiatives that were implemented and why did they work? Herein lays a solid golden key. In my mind, the key was to introduce the bad guys to the idea that their best bet would be to run like hell and allow the community to grow economically in all areas of business and commerce.

The first thing we all must understand is that there is a duty by law that each primary agency within their jurisdiction is responsible: they must answer the emergency call (911) before they can even dream of proactive policing. Then, they must answer the secondary call for assistance, such as someone broke into my vehicle or my home or damaged my property or punched me in the nose and now the suspect is gone. It is after those calls that proactive policing is attempted.

You should not confuse proactive policing with undercover operations or drug task forces, they are not the same. For a lack of a better explanation, proactive policing is officers in uniform in the open and the others are in plain clothes and more or less out of sight.

There is some argument with others in law enforcement, but I standby what I know works really well, in uniform is the best type of proactive policing and undercover is one of the best ways of gathering intelligence that would otherwise not be learned. In my position I was responsible for supplementing public safety vs. being the primary agency and that is the heart of why we were so successful in conjunction, of course, with the cooperation of all the other chiefs in the greater Houston area.

In making the attempt to enact community policing as chief, you need to determine where within your jurisdiction the programs have the best, most cost effective and positive results for the community. Often this decision is made for you because the only reason you consider the program in the first place is based on demand from the general public and evil stares from the elected politicians.

I have been to hundreds of community meetings with many chiefs over the years, where the politicians would stand at the microphones and inevitably be confronted by the public (often the angry public) about not enough police services or timely services when they call the police or simply not enough police officers. Almost always the end response by the politicians would be to turn around give the evil eye/stare at the chief and loudly state with some reflection of disgust in their tone, "We need more officers, or Chief, we need to take care of this." Out of respect the chiefs would not often reply, but we would mumble to each other, "OK. Right, if you would only approve the budget I requested, I will take care of the problem."

Please note the dollars for these programs are the least in the budget and when the chief is forced to spend the money, it has to come about in the way of using overtime. In Houston, Chief Hurtt was desperately in need of taking care of business using overtime. One reason he had to use overtime was because the City of Houston's jurisdiction was 606 square miles and there were less than 5,000 officers on the force.

Spread those resources over a 24/7 time line in every category of policing and see how thin the budget becomes. He spent $53 million dollars in twelve weeks; and although he received great accolades for a job well done, the problems filtered back and the community rose up again with the politicians giving the evil stare. There are widely used analogies in police work. "We try everyday to work ourselves out of a job." "We can chase the bad guys around and cause them to go across the street. Like turning on the lights in a broken down apartment, the cockroaches will hide. But as soon as the lights go out, they come right back."

The program is State Political Management Districts currently in Houston, Texas and I understand several other concepts of the same type are in other states. These districts were created by the citizens and authorized by the State Legislature. In my District's case, it was developed and subsequently authorized and set into law by the 77th Legislature of Texas.

These districts are a taxing entity; Harris County collects the tax after assessing only the commercial properties each year in the boundaries. The County then distributes the appropriate tax amount to each district. The duties of the District Board of Directors are a reflection of a city council and the Executive Director, who answers to the Board. It is to supplement all state and city services. The district works both independently and collectively with the city, county, and the state. This means there are universal projects in the city limits and in the unincorporated areas of the district to benefit the district residents. There was significant interest in the public/private relationship concept.

What does all this have to do with my proposal in a new concept of proactive community policing? It has everything to do with it, as the proof is in the doing and not just talking about it.

We did it in Houston, Texas. We did it together, the chiefs and the officers as a team made up of every law enforcement agency in Houston and not with any special grants or State or U.S. Government help. This effort was a simple proactive dedication to the community and the initiatives worked, having historical and positive results. If you can't tell, I am very proud of the results and everyone who put in the effort to make it all come about.

The initiatives brought the overall crime rate down a whopping twenty-two percent in these most dangerous areas in Houston known for gang violence and drug trafficking. The crime rate drop studies were not done by the District; they were completed by third parties and the City of Houston. Although our effort in Houston was completed in the short term over a time frame of two years, it must be said that if these types of programs and initiatives are to have the long term impact so desperately needed, then someone must take the lead. There is a significant opportunity here for the State of Texas to do just that and utilize the Management Districts to their full potential in public safety. I would also recommend other states look closely at these types of districts and the way they can be effective for the community.

The Plan and Proposal:
The Texas State District Police

This proposal is introduced as a means to meet the spirit and the intent regarding public safety service to the community as set into law by the Texas State legislature which created State Political Management Districts.

It must be elaborated that this proposal is not intended to show disfavor to any current law enforcement agency. To the contrary, every law enforcement agency in the City of Houston and the County of Harris, Texas is doing an excellent job carrying out their primary and statutorily required responsibilities. Should there be anyone who perceives this proposal as a management or accountability issue with particularly the Houston Police Department or any other agency, then those individuals have missed the point of this proposal entirely.

It is imperative to understand that all common City and County law enforcement agencies are reactive vs. proactive by legal mandates. The meaning behind this is simple; they must respond to 911 emergency calls first and then common service calls followed by proactive desires. The word desire in these contexts is important because when an agency is under staffed and lacking resources and most are, then proactive initiatives are short lived with minimal if any positive impact.

This proposal provides for an interesting concept accomplished only within the Near Northwest Management District of Houston and will likely have a powerful and positive effect on the way policing can better serve the public if extended. In fact if this comes to fruition, it may be this proposal will have the same type of impact on uniform and community policing as the creation of the Federal Bureau of Investigation had on the Investigation side of law enforcement.

This proposal is for a 3 year pilot program and is not intended to replace or take over any responsibility of the Houston Police Department or any other agency currently in operation. Instead the "State District Police" would fill a void and supplement enforcement strategies, strictly from a proactive and reasonable enforcement practice. These officers will not be answering or handling 911 emergency calls as a primary or common policy. In the face of necessity there will be a mutual aid policy to ensure if requested by HPD or any other agency the State District Police will assist appropriately.

Furthermore, the Texas State District Police Department does not "privatize" policing. The agency would be fully accredited with State Peace Officer powers as described within the Texas Code of Criminal Procedure section 2.12 (4) and should be commissioned by the Public Safety Commission and/or the Director of Public Safety. They will operate in the manner required by law as peace officers.

There are limited resources and more importantly limited answers on how to approach the ever increasing problem of criminal activity particularly as the community grows and the agencies fill the ranks at the slowest pace in history.

The simple facts are that the City of Houston currently employs 4800 sworn officers at the time of this writing for a geographical area encompassing 606 square miles. There may be 240 officers on duty at one time, sometimes however, and more often, far less. Every thirty seconds there is a 911 call coming into the HPD. This generates almost an impossible task. There are numerous officers retiring on a regular bases and the population continues to grow daily. The recruitment is lower or slower then in previous years as a result of significant competition in the law enforcement community.

There will be an increase of 2.1 million people in the City of Houston alone and over 8 million in the immediate surrounding counties by the year 2035. It becomes obvious that even with a full complement of officers and or doubling the rank and file, the HPD will find it difficult to meet the requirements of our immediate future for 911 and common service calls. This proposal will provide current examples of other Cities for comparison to Houston as to strength and geographical area to be serviced.

I am well aware of the questions that are brought into focus with this proposal.

1. Policing the City of Houston is the responsibility of the City and the HPD so why create a new agency?

    Answer: Yes, it is the responsibility of the City and the HPD. However, the fact remains that this City and others, are in desperate need of supplementing all government service as evidenced by request and the demands of the people; culminating into the creation of the Management Districts by way of the State legislature in the first place.

    In fact, it is public safety that was placed as the number 1 priority based on the difficulty of resources and not ill management or accountability of current options. The legislature set the foundation into place addressing public safety but left the metrics on how to address public safety up to the Management Districts.

It is important to understand the legislature is very careful on its terminology on the passing of law. In this case they used the term "May Employ" vs. contract peace officers. Noted in both the State Political Subdivisions Law; Section 3811 and Local Government Code Chapter 375 section 375.096 is the structure of allowing Management Districts to supplement and govern their public safety issues.

This is imperative because a specific word is used to provide the appropriate interpretation. This is evidenced in other portions of the justice codes where the law states "the judge or magistrate "Shall" vs. "May" provide a specific penalty for a crime committed. That is very clear the magistrate has no choice when the word "Shall" is used.

Therefore, the legislature opened the door to allow Management Districts to request the specific authority to "Employ" peace officers. Thus having the "Texas Commission on Law Enforcement Officers Standards and Education" sanction those districts that choose to employ their own peace officers. By implementing this proposal each Management District would have the choice to use the State District Police via contract; allowing the spirit and intent of the law to take hold for the betterment of the community. This proposal is a far better solution than having each Management District request an independent police department which is implied by the current law. Additionally, as evidenced by a two year track record of the community policing initiatives to be used; this proposal is significantly more efficient and productive than the Status Que.

2. Where will the funding come from for this agency?

> **Answer:** Every management District is a taxing entity and has a budget arising from assessment funds on the commercial properties within the district. Every district allocates significant portions of their budget to public safety. Each district sets their allocation of assessments between $0.09 and $0.15 per hundred dollar value of a commercial property. Each District has a Board of Directors which is a mirror image of a City Council.
>
> Therefore the assessment amount is subject to change with the guidelines of State law at the direction and vote of each independent Board of Directors.
>
> In this proposal each Management District will have the right to choose whether or not they would like to participate in the utilization of the State District Police to fulfill their obligation of supplementing public safety. If they choose to do so; then they would allocate that portion of their budget to the district police by contract, in the same manner they currently do for county constable services, HPD officers or private security.
>
> It will be up to the commander or senior District Police official to manage that district's public safety initiatives appropriately in the same manner as it is currently accomplished, by the management district's Director of Public Safety. This of course will then free up the officers and or deputies currently used in this capacity to be reassigned within their perspective department to fulfill their department's statutory obligations. This will equate to the current departments having desperately needed manpower to answer the 911 and common service calls within a more acceptable time frame.

Additionally, by being an independent law enforcement agency, the State District Police will have efficient control over the initiatives implemented and be qualified to apply for both State and Federal grants from the Department of Justice. The Management Districts independently, can not apply for several grants without having a law enforcement agency. This is an alternative for productive and efficient long lasting proactive initiatives vs. the common based band aid effect from local and county agencies, which spends millions of dollars in overtime and "burns out the Officers".

3. If grant funding is an option doesn't this take away from the grant options for HPD who is in desperate need of that funding as evidenced by this proposal?

    Answer: No, not necessarily. Because there may be some competition for a particular grant; those with the best strategy, making a best case for efficient productivity and long term solutions vs. short term band aid effects, generally will be awarded the grant. Is that not the idea in the first place for the grant funding, to be spent in the most efficient manner possible for the betterment of the community?

    Outside of this reasoning there is the fact that the State District Police will be statutorily required to be proactive vs. reactive and therefore have the gateway to many grants for each independent District that the common law enforcement agencies would not have.

4. Why not give additional funding including the funding for this proposal to the HPD, no matter where the funds originate as long as they are legal and ethical?

Answer: Because this funding will be for proactive, long range initiatives vs. reactive responsibilities. The funding is far better put to use with an agency required to be proactive. Agencies that are required to be reactive can only use this type of funding in a short term initiative and this is greatly enhanced by those funds generated by a Management District; which by law can only be used within the boundaries for that particular District.

By providing these funds to the common agency it will be spent rapidly in overtime vs. regular salary. This is because proactive initiatives are almost always accomplished with overtime pay. Regular salaries are required to be paid for reactive staff on duty. Once again the common agency is a band aid effect, where the State District concept is a long range solution.

5. If the HPD has difficulty recruiting, then where will the State District Police recruit?

    Answer: This is a tough question for any agency. However, with the initial establishment of the State District Police Department, there is a phenomenon among law enforcement officers particularly seasoned officers to be a part of a new department.

    This is true specifically, in a new police department with the potential to have a significant impact on the culture of the community and thereby equate to true personal satisfaction. This is evidenced here, as there are already hundreds of officers who have requested a position within this agency.

Recruitment will be looked upon favorably with those seasoned officers having at least five years experience and recently retired officers that continue to meet both the psychological and physical requirements of the "Texas Commission on Law Enforcement Officers Standards and Education". New officers will be sought from individuals who put themselves through the state accredited police academies across Texas. Furthermore, there are numerous out of state highly trained officers searching for positions in Texas as lateral transfers, who meet and exceed Texas State training requirements.

6.   If this is a real solution? Why pilot programs? Why not establish the agency immediately and permanently?

Answer: Not every good idea turns out to be a positive solution and it is just good business sense to prove the viability and value of a new concept. Although new agencies are not a new idea by any stretch of the imagination; it is the matrix of how the State District Police Department will operate within the context of being proactive vs. reactive, that makes it vulnerable. Therefore, the department needs to be measured with quantifiable and independent observation. A significant part of this independent measure must include the cost effectiveness of expenditures vs. the productivity and effect; whether it is positive or negative of initiatives undertaken.

7. What will the pilot program cost?

Answer: The budget is extrapolated out from current expenditures of the Management District's public safety allocations. One or two districts should be considered to be served within the pilot program. It must be understood that these are projected cost.

There is a combination of what Management Districts currently spend and what equipment cost in the open market. The market cost is often off set through negotiation; particularly in purchasing safety equipment and vehicles. Therefore, it is suggested that the start up cost for the State District Police for equipment will be far lower than that which is projected prior to any negotiations. The salaries are within the current budget of Management Districts.

It is imperative to note that the HPD spends over 50 million dollars in overtime alone per year. The projected cost for the State District Police is far below these costs, which have become the standard and will operate on millions of dollars less for three to five years at a time vs. only weeks for just one or two initiatives with the same amount of money.

8. Where would the pilot program be operational and why that portion of the city vs. others, where the criminal activity is perhaps more prevalent?

Answer: The proposal for one District would be implemented in the Near Northwest Management District of Houston, Texas for specific reasons. Because for two years those initiatives that will be implemented - or more appropriately continued, as they have already been introduced and extremely successful -provide a current track record for what this proposal will accomplish.

These initiatives have successfully caused the overall crime rate to drop by twenty-two percent and years later continue at seventeen point four percent; overall calls for service dropped by twenty-nine percent within a focused target area.

These statistics are reported by the City of Houston and not the Management District. Even with these fabulous results, this target area still represents thirty percent of the District's criminal activity.

This same area two years prior to the initiatives - as reported by every media venue in the City of Houston - had the "Most Dangerous Street in Houston" (De Soto) and noted to be a "War Zone amongst Gangs" (Antoine and De Soto) along the Antoine corridor. As a result of the proactive initiatives just twenty months after implementation, the same area is in the process of creating a "Super Block Neighborhood".

This is a measure to bring all the property owners together and unilaterally implement private initiatives to yet again supplement the community policing efforts. This "Super block" effort would not have been possible without the community policing initiatives implemented by the district. The only way it will succeed is to continue the community policing initiatives that will not survive without the implementation of the State District Police.

A few of these initiatives did include the HPD and seven other law enforcement agencies in order to have an immediate and positive impact. These other agencies would not have been needed if the State District Police would have already been established. Other more constant initiatives were implemented. The time line is temporary because the Near Northwest Management District contracted only six Constable Deputies through the 20 month period.

Currently, the Near Northwest Management District has seven constable deputies effective January 1, 2008. However, the strain for these deputies is becoming overwhelming. Why because they must also meet the statuary requirements of the Constables office.

The positive ground gained in these initiatives is at risk of becoming just another band aid effect. Albeit, outlasting most others without a significant change in resources; which this proposal would provide.

It is very telling that six deputies assigned to specific and managed initiatives; can be as productive with significant and positive results, as the entire Houston PD North Command Station of more than 230 plus city officers. Again and it must be emphasized, that is because the HPD is reactive to 911 emergency calls first and then regular service calls second. Proactive initiatives are last and require significant overtime, which HPD must curtail wherever possible and attend to other parts of the city in need. The State District Police will operate four shifts 100% of the time (24/7) proactively. That will have an astronomical efficient and productive impact for all Houstonians.

If the proposal is implemented for two Districts, the State District Police would be assigned proactively in the Near Northwest Management District and the Spring Branch Management District. These two Districts share a common border and would easily be able to improve the effectiveness of initiatives as they would address shared gang members and territorial boundaries of the commercial industry, as business flows from one district into the other.

Additionally, the adjacent residential neighborhoods will improve in widely disbursed areas as they have in the Near Northwest Management District. Property values will increase due to the reduction in crime and make these areas a far safer community. In addition, because of an increase in property value, the residential and commercial real estate markets should increase as well. With the commercial market increase there will be a job influx and opportunity into the community.

9. Is there a realistic and positive impact to the city of Houston or any geographical area by implementing this proposal? Or is it just another redundant police force to muck up the communication and get in the way of criminal prosecutions and serving the public?

> **Answer:** This is a realistic proposal evidenced by the current track record of two years, implemented with the Harris County Constable's Office Precinct 1 via a contract with the Near Northwest Management District. Under the direct supervision of the management district's Executive Director, who also served as an Assistant Constable Chief, it works. However, the State District Police would place this responsibility with the commanders (liaison with district management) of each district participating in the pilot program.
>
> By moving this responsibility to the commanders, the district would be free to utilize the talents of their executive director in other important areas of service to the community. There is always a concern of complicating the public justice system and mucking up the communication; particularly with redundant agencies whose pride and practice get in the way of productive and efficient service to the public.

Pride should be self evident and always present in its proper form without arrogance or indignation and is the responsibility of leadership to foster the appropriate behavior, in addition to management (practice and policy) and both should always be held accountable.

This proposal is not necessarily redundant; because it will not be reactive but proactive and there is no law enforcement agency required to be first proactive and secondly reactive. Arrest and criminal prosecutions will increase and overall crime will drop even further then it did during the two plus years in practice.

Most generally, the State District Police will only be reactive by specific request of another law enforcement agency in need of mutual aid such as the case in severe emergencies; like that experienced from natural catastrophes where there will be the need to assist in evacuations from hurricanes, etc.

10. If the Harris County Constables Office Precinct 1 is currently doing the job, then why not just increase their manpower and funding?

Answer: As in the case of HPD, the Constable Office in every county has statutory requirements that do not include contracting with state political management districts. This is a financial benefit arranged and contracted through the County Commissioners Court and requested for approval by the Constable. Given this arrangement, those duties are only required to be filled by the Constable request vs. a requirement in law. Therefore, required services are losing manpower to a requested responsibility; adding yet another burden to the public safety services vs. providing a proper solution.

Again as in the case of HPD, the Constable Offices need their deputies to fulfill their required responsibilities. This proposal provides a real solution to that end.

11. Where will the liability rest in the case of inappropriate action and/or omissions?

Answer: There is no foundation in the law to subrogate liability under the premise of simple desire. Any agency or organization, whether public or private, has a duty to ensure there is appropriate liability coverage for their actions, errors and omissions regardless of the structure of liability; be it direct, indirect or vicarious.Generally, every incident in question on a case by case basis, will be taken into account on its own merits and pitfalls, and then litigated if necessary.

The following public safety measures were implemented and proved to be a significantly more effective way to police the concerns of the city; at least within the boundaries of the Near Northwest Management District. Having shown this to be a better way of proactive policing, which is evidenced in addition to the above by every short term program in every city across the nation; it is time to implement an agency such as the Texas State District Police as a pilot program now, with proactive policing as their primary action to service.

Public Safety Strategies in Action

Multi-Agency Neighborhood Deployment Anti-Gang Initiative

The Neighborhood Deployment Anti-Gang Initiative resulted in an immediate decrease in crime by eleven point nine percent, from July 24 - August 22, 2007. Calls for service decreased by sixteen point one percent. Moreover, a total of 142 arrests were made as a result of the four day long effort. Since then, crime has decreased overall by twenty-two percent and is holding at seventeen point four percent. This is a direct result of continuous proactive community policing initiatives. As a result of phase two over a two year period, the City of Houston, along with the Office of the Mayor, filed suit against the 300 (multiple) owners of Candlelight Trails Condominiums at 5600 De Soto, Houston. TX 77091. Candlelight Trails contains 240 units and has been known as a high crime area with high rate of calls for service, narcotic activity, and firearm disturbances.

The Condominiums were closed down, everyone evicted, and residents received alternative housing from the Office of the Mayor. Throughout these initiatives, officers were actively patrolling surrounding businesses in the event of displaced criminal activity. The following agencies were involved using a total of 71 officers:
- Houston Police Department
- Harris County Constable Precinct 1
- METRO Police Department
- Aldine I.S.D. Police Department
- Houston I.S.D. Police Department
- U.S. Drug Enforcement Administration
- U.S. Attorney's Office
- City of Houston Neighborhood Protection

Results:

Following the legal process; the entire complex of Candlelight Trails has been torn down. The crime rate within the management district at the time of this writing; still remains at seventeen point four percent drop or better.

Certainly for such an extraordinary affect, the Federal Government and/or the State of Texas, can pony up the start up cost for equipment and allow the management districts to take it from that point forward. Run the program for three years. If it works, it works and will stand fast. If not, then it will shut down as all programs that do not work should. At the very least this, should be worth a comprehensive study to determine the total cost and effect. Is this worth the dollars, or do we stay with the ineffective policy of today and doing business as usual?

There is another way we can implement a proactive policing effort across this nation, if our politicians in Washington D.C. and, frankly, the American people are truly serious about addressing all the issues of strong national security. I do believe the citizens of this great Country are willing, but I am not sure about most of our politicians.

Perhaps we need to adjust the above concept into a Federal Auxiliary Force, which should have been completed long ago and was discussed by every law enforcement official I know. Getting the inevitable argument out of the way; - This looks like a police state or the Federal Government should leave local policing to the business of local law enforcement.

I disagree with the first premise; it will not be a police state by the very nature of design. If that design is set into law, the policy will not be able to change. If there is a change attempted, then the law should hold accountable anyone who ventures out of policy.

However, I do agree with the second premise; leaving policing to the locals, and that is what I meant by adjusting and adapting the concept. Currently, we are paying for our police at all levels in our taxes. Unfortunately, we are not getting our money's worth. I believe those in charge and the great men and women in the ranks are most definitely giving their all, but they simply have too much to do.

Is there anyone who believes the Feds are checking up on all those individuals with visas that have expired? Or that the information given to support the visa is true and current, allowing these now illegal visitors to remain in our country unchecked?

If you think so, keep dreaming. The Department of Homeland Security states they are following up on all this but they do not have the appropriate manpower to get the job even half done, never mind with any efficiency. After all they spend a great deal of time and resources on chasing the "Chatter" and they should. But what about the rest of those in hiding and plotting outside the chatter?

Furthermore, the local agencies cannot do the job, because they do not have the funding in their local budgets. In the past and today the local law enforcement agencies apply for grants like the "Cop's Grant". If they were lucky enough to be the recipient, the money would be used to fill positions to simply handle the overflow of daily and current problems.

Often they would advertise these positions as a one year or two year term; not the best job security for a new officer. The funds were rarely used to support a proactive program of any kind. When they were, the regulations for the grant were limited in scope.

The agency would say better than nothing; and the public would become angry, when the department would not help in matters of other duties. There have been past grants allowing the purchase of motorcycles and the compensation for the officers to write citations, but not work any other detail at all. The best they could do was to receive money to cover overtime cost for a very limited program or current high profile case. The Lake and Ng murders of Calaveras County, California for example.

This is a famous case, where Mr. Lake and Mr. Ng kidnapped women and tortured them in a dungeon type setting of a house they purchased in Calaveras County, located out in the country. By the end of the case, few victims were identified, but several pounds of unidentified human bone were gathered in addition to the known victims.

In these cases, the Feds give the local agencies a loan; the local agencies then pay the overtime to their investigators and deputies/officers. The federal loans, although allowing the case to move forward, put the local agencies deeper into red ink and the people lose the appropriate policing efforts outside the case in hand. The deputies/officers spend a great deal of time working the case, instead of focusing on the department's regular duties. It is difficult at best to have it both ways and, more often than not, it is one or the other. Although it is often camouflaged by politicians, the chief law enforcement officer is forced to comply.

Further, when officers are addressing their regular duties they have not had enough rest between assignments and can be subject to poor judgment and negative reactions. When grants are given to special programs they have time lines; they come few and far between and are completed without anything more than a temporary fix.

Remember I said early on, without constant efforts in play, programs are almost doomed at the onset. Without a constant effort, it is equivalent to turning on the lights in a bad apartment complex and watching the cockroaches run for cover. As soon as the lights go out, the roaches come back. This is why we want transparency in Washington D.C.; we need to keep the lights on in political affairs. We must keep the lights on within the law enforcement community for the betterment of the community. Do not get crazy; I am not calling our law enforcement officers cockroaches. On the other hand, I am not so sure about the politicians.

This is the tough part to swallow, as we already pay far too many taxes; remember we must pay for everything. I have stated many times, I come from a very conservative government point of view. I would strongly suggest that Washington D.C. look at all the waste they spend on "HUGGIE-BEAR-SMACKIE-POO" programs and cancel them immediately. You will read more about these programs in the HUGGIE-BEAR-SMACKIE-POO chapter later.

A specific program of the kind I refer to is the type in the State of Nebraska, and I might add Texas; that allows illegal alien residents to be eligible for in-state tuition, but out-of-state U.S. citizens are not. You know this is somehow supplemented, if not completely paid for, by federal funds and certainly by state taxes.

Stop playing around with the programs that are truly unfair, ridiculous, and downright stupid. Here is a stupid program; Illegal aliens who pay no taxes at all can file a return. The Feds send them a check for $1000 dollars. We can all look around and find numerous programs to stop. Use those funds for something that works for every one of our citizens, and allow the positive consequences to be enjoyed by everyone in the Country.

If we must continue the unproductive programs (a waste of money), then we need to enact a federal law enforcement tax of one-quarter cent or one-half cent per one thousand dollar value on every property in the Country to pay for a Federal Auxiliary Force. (If not for this agency, then to pay off our debt and I will stop here.)

Oh wait, get rid of the... Department of Education and/or the Environmental Protection Agency or just the Internal Revenue Service and pay for this program. Ok keep the IRS but only the enforcement half, as the auditor half is not necessary with a flat tax. Did I say that, yes, I did.

This agency would be set up to assist all the other agencies at every level working under the supervision of whom ever they are assigned. Obviously, the President would have to appoint a Director to be vetted and approved by the Senate, unless the agency was simply an arm of one of the current federal law enforcement agencies.

In essence they would be Federal Reserve Officers, working full time with pay, at the ready; to be used and abused by any agency that needs help. Similar to the National Guard when activated, which in this case would be constant I suppose. The National Guard will not cut it in responsibilities of what we are discussing here. These will be law enforcement officers, properly trained, for all responsibilities as required.

I can hear it all now, "No way would this work; I can see the Feds inserting this force as a police state now." Oh, hogwash; we have federal police now. Just go down to the local federal court house or other federal buildings in any city and you will see the marked vehicles and the uniformed federal officers. I have not observed those dedicated men and woman marching into a legal civil crowd and dragging anyone away. If the idea of a new federal agency frightens you, then make this concept an extension with the U.S. Marshals or a uniformed division of the FBI.

In any case, we need officers to fill in the very severe gaps, if we are going to properly protect our citizens, our Country and our visitors.

Here is a message to individuals I admire; Mr. Glenn Beck, Mr. Bill O'reilly and a few politicians who I also admire like Governors Palin, Huckabee, Romney and Speaker Newt Gingrich. The message is: I promise I am not a progressive. I know that sounds a bit like so many politicians, or President Nixon when he said "I am not a crook" or when President Clinton said "I did not have sex with that woman" but it fits the message. I am not a progressive in the way our liberal friends have high jacked the term.

Any agency has a need for help, such as in the case of Calaveras County, California with the "Lake and Ng" murders. They received thousands of dollars - I believe it was somewhere in the neighborhood of $500,000 - and it put them deeply into the red, because they had to pay it back. Additionally, the deputies working the case were tired and the citizens lost out on patrol services, no matter what the officials tell you. I know because I was there in one capacity or another. In this case, I was a local citizen/resident. In later years, I would become an investigator with the District Attorneys' Office for the county, with an inside track on information.

How about instead of asking for money, they sent a request to the Auxiliary Force Offices housed in the Federal (FBI Office) buildings around the country for help, who then prioritized the request based on the requestors' needs and seriousness of the request? This is how it would work; an agency makes the request by contacting the Feds. There is a determination based on conversation and limited, but justifying, paper work from the requesting agency of the issues to be addressed.

How many officers it will take and for how long those officers will be needed, etc? The Federal Officers will arrive in their own police vehicles and in uniform reporting to the Chief/Sheriff of the agency who made the request. There would be a supervisor among them as a liaison to insure the Feds worked under the supervision of the requesting agency in the capacity desired/needed.

The requesting agency would pay for the gas, oil and any repairs to which the federal vehicles might succumb while working the agency's assignments. The Feds would pick up the tab on accommodations and meals when necessary. This means the local agency may be able to make arrangements in local hotels or motels with little or no expense to the agency and at a significant discount to the Feds.

I believe the budget made up from the one-quarter cent or one-half cent tax per thousand dollar value on every property across the land should be sufficient; if it was by law, strictly allotted for the Auxiliary Force. (Let me emphasize again! Any other use would not work, unless we forget the agency and simply pay off the national debt with those funds.) If, however, the agencies are required to pay back any of the cost and I think they should for the federal assistance, they could do so in a loan type arrangement.

This would be established by way of fifty percent of the cost with a five percent rate of interest amortized over the necessary time frame to keep the payments within the budget of the receiving city or county agency. This would allow the amount of time needed to pay back the cost of doing business, without any profit or loss to the Feds. In this fashion the cost would balance out and the general public would be served with efficient and effective use of their tax dollars.

The officers sent to the requesting agency will be law enforcement officers with no less than five years experience. Each Federal Officer sent to the state of request would have been a licensed (commissioned) peace officer in that state prior to becoming a Federal Officer. And they would regularly be sent to local academies in order to update and maintain that state's training and continued education requirements.

Of course, these officers would also maintain their federal training in line with the FBI or federal uniformed police standards. It only makes good sense to have these federal officers dual commissioned in the states where they are assigned, if need be to accommodate the laws, then the sheriff or chief of police can swear them in upon arrival. Cross training in many subject matters will suffice for both State and Federal requirements.

Assisting the federal agencies would be no different than any other federal agency, wherein these officers would simply take up the slack. When the FBI or whoever cannot run down the visa validations or if there is a need to run down pedophiles and other very dangerous criminals to verify appropriate information, then the Auxiliary Force can. There are so many tasks these officers could take over; it's almost a crime that we do not already have them in place.

In numerous jurisdictions, their resources are far less than the feds, and yet they have been asked for assistance to run down the visas and pedophiles and the locals say "Are you kidding?" Additionally, how many times have we seen in the headlines and asked why a pedophile is on the loose and no one knows where they are or what they are up to? These pedophiles, serial killers, spree killers and mass murderers do kill and rape and kidnap and torture, then get away and stay on the run far too long. They are just plain evil. We catch them, and incarcerate them. Then we let them out to repeat their evil deeds all over again.

We should at least know where they are and where they work. In this day and age how easy is it to commit identity theft? That could not be any easier. So the bad guy steals someone's ID and goes off to work. In what trade? Pedophiles like working around kiddies for example.

How easy is it to become a minister? All one has to do is fill out the paper work/application on line and bingo you are a legal minister. You can even obtain honorary degrees at the same time in religious foundation, Bachelor, Master's and Doctorate. I do not necessarily disagree with the churches right to provide these credentials but the point is that bad guys take advantage. In other words the bad guy scams their way into the perfect job to continue the evil and we do not know about it. If for no other reason, I say this is the justification to do far more than we currently do, not to mention the terrorist threats, etcetera.

I stated the Federal Auxiliary Officers will have been a law enforcement officer in the states they are assigned before they joined the agency and the department would be broken down into the time zones across the country. Each time zone would be a division and the division would consist of however many officers might be needed to serve the state(s) in that zone and the populations, serving as the criteria for number of officers in the agency.

Further, because these officers are federal, they would be available to transfer into special assignments anywhere in the Country to assist the other federal agencies, particularly in emergency situations. To help defer costs; I would suggest that we look toward military surplus for supplies and equipment that is still usable and generally sold in the open market.

This brings me to the Federal Government discriminating against age. As I wrote in the proposal of the Texas State Police, there is no reason at all to prevent well trained law enforcement officers who have retired, to fill these positions. If a candidate can pass the physical and psychological mandates of service as set out in every hiring process in the country for law enforcement officers, what is the problem?

Are we going to continue to ignore one of the best resources in the law enforcement community, because an officer retired? What? Today they are trustworthy and tomorrow they're not? How foolish! If anyone can give a solid reason why not, then let them speak.

The Feds claim the candidates must not have passed their thirty-seventh birthday in order to collect a federal retirement. Hog Wash! There are numerous law enforcement agencies all over the country that will hire at any age, as long as the candidate passes the tests. There are many where one can become fully vested in the retirement system in five or ten years. Which is why I state each Auxiliary Officer should have been a peace officer for five years prior to joining the force. So just put a sock in it!

Who cares if you don't catch a second retirement, for goodness sake change the policy. An experienced officer may be willing to do the job without any additional compensation beyond the direct pay (like benefits), because the past employer provided them with retirement health coverage.

What about those who will accept the cost of doing business, so there are no out of pocket expenses? They don't need any further pay or they just want to step up for their Country. How about half pay? Those who are crying about not trusting someone who wants the job for less than full pay, malarkey. I said each officer must pass both the physical and psychological test. Did I not?

There are many that will join out of patriotism and boredom of retirement. You might be surprised just how many will step up to the plate for nothing or very little, if the Federal Government can get their head out from where the sun doesn't shine. Just leave these retired officer's retirement checks alone; no restrictions on them as to how many hours they can or cannot work; and do not cap their earning potential over their retirements.

Of course, we can and should tax the new income but leave the retirement alone. They already earned and paid for that money. The Feds and the states must agree; no penalties for becoming a Federal Auxiliary Officer.

Some say there just won't be enough of the retired force that will want to participate. Well, that is a lot of baloney all in by itself. How do I know? I submitted a similar program first in 1993 and again in 1997, stating we need this program. Without it we are going to be in real trouble, just look at history. I was focusing on the trials and tribulations of Iran in those days. In 1997, I handed my proposal to Congressman John Doolittle in Northern California at a town hall meeting and followed up with his office several times. My answer from every politician was, "This is a great idea, but we don't need it."

Then at the end of September 2001, immediately after 9/11, I received several phone calls. (Not from the Congress) "Hey, remember the Federal Auxiliary Force proposal? Can you re-write that on a state level?" I did so, as the California Ranger proposal. I said that the way to pay for this agency was to take ten percent of the known fifteen percent waste in the California Highway Patrol budget, which the State Auditor's Office has proven every year. This proposal was written up and published in the October 2001 edition of the Peace Officers Research Association of California (PORAC) and I received nearly ten thousand positive responses and two thousand retired officers willing to sign up. Not to mention the active officers in agencies across the State who were willing to transfer into the Ranger program from their current agencies.

The only law enforcement agencies that said anything negative were the California Highway Patrol (Go figure?) and the State Rangers already in place for the parks – who complained about the name, but not the program.

I advised the Park Rangers, the answer would be to change the proposal's title from California Rangers to California Marshal's Office. The title – Marshal - was and is dying out in the State of California, as there are a limited number of local and county Marshals, most all of them have been absorbed by the Sheriff's Offices.

As for the California Highway Patrol, there was no appeasing the brass there. They were apparently unhappy about the exposure of their inadequacies in the operating budget. Hey, I have nothing against the California Highway Patrol; I just have a problem with any administration of any public agency that waste the people's money and knows all too well that is exactly what they are doing.

In this case as I said, the States Auditor's Office showed the waste every year for years past at fifteen percent. I only wanted ten percent of what was apparently inevitable. They could continue to waste the other five percent or maybe give their officers a raise, which in my opinion would be far better than throwing it out the window.

CHAPTER SEVEN
Huggie-Bear-Smackie-Poo

I have mentioned this phrase often and this statement is directed toward politicians, perhaps more appropriately what they say versus what they do. What they say is to get elected or reelected; what they do is far different from what they said and most of it boils down to political correctness. I believe if you truly listen to what they say, there are hidden meanings within their own thoughts.

No, I do not mean hidden from our conscious mind so our unconscious mind will pick the true meaning up, like some fool-faces have stated. You need to look close and listen closely to understand a politician. Many make their statements and intentions vague, so they can say, "I did or did not say that." They will use whichever fits into their explanation later with the caveat that we just did not understand what they meant at the time. If you doubt this, then think very carefully about what President Clinton said in response to the questioning over the word "if". He claimed it all depended on what you mean by the word "if" when you said it; there were millions who bought his argument. I consider these and many other issues as bunk or otherwise caricaturized as "Huggie-Bear-Smackie-Poo, BS".

As to hidden meanings, there is an area of study mostly in hypnosis and past advertisements that delves into subliminal suggestions. This was done with hidden messages in advertising, mostly in the movies but in numerous other advertisements, to get the observer to buy particular products, popcorn and the like. This type of business was brought to light and, supposedly, has been outlawed.

However, there are other more open ways to have you purchase stuff you hadn't thought about up front, like putting the candy at eye level for your child to focus on during your weekly shopping and it will be in the right color packaging that the company paid millions of dollars to study knowing it will attract millions of kids.

Depending on what kind of a parent you are, it can be hard to just say no to your child when they use those big loving eyes or a yelling tantrum to get their way. I was making an unofficial study for this book when I asked several large grocery store chain managers why they displayed baskets of candy and products like day old cinnamon rolls and soap at the cash register where you pay the final bill.

They all said the same thing. Management picks the items for display at the registers, because those last minute items produce between five thousand dollars and ten thousand dollars per day in sales. Now that is great marketing and what I call in-your-face suggestion at its best. They certainly got their dollar's worth of research.

So what do I mean when I use the term Huggie-Bear-Smackie-Poo? First, I use it because it brings about a smile or outright laughter from those with whom I am speaking, sometimes because they think it is cute and others because they think I am silly or nuts. My reason being, I will get their attention and they will then listen. It is a term that I coined for these purposes.

What I am telling them is the topic of conversation in other words is "the kiss of death" Like in your face suggestions that cause you to spend money you did not intend to. Or take the face value of what a politician is saying when he or she makes a statement like "I feel your pain" or maybe it will be more like "I did not have sex with that woman". They say what they think you want to hear, not what they feel.

Let's look to the recent news to illustrate true insight on how this applies particularly to our politicians. One of President Obama's White House advisers and Chief Campaign Strategist, David Plouffe, stated on NBC's Meet The Press (October 30, 2011) that Republican Presidential candidate, "Mitt Romney has no core." He elaborated, "If Romney thought it would get him elected by saying the sky was green and the grass was blue, he would do so."

What a bunch of Huggie-Bear-Smackie-Poo baloney that is. Why? Listen carefully now, to what is documented when he assisted then Senator Obama in his campaign for President. Mr. Plouffe, the candidate, and all the other high powered staff said the following in political ads, "Government run medical health plans are extreme."

1. After the President was elected, he fought and passed "Obamacare".

2. During the campaign they attacked the high debt under President George W. Bush as being far too big; then they came into office and raised the Nation's debt ten times that of George W. Bush.

3. During the campaign they were all about closing "Gitmo" and now they are for keeping it open. (Maybe?)

4. During the campaign they were all against military tribunals, especially for those housed in "Gitmo" and now they are all for the military tribunals. (Maybe?)

5. During the campaign they sated very clearly many times that raising taxes during a recession should never be done; now they will not move the Country forward. In fact, they are refusing unless - you guessed it - we raise taxes. Furthermore, the last any of us looked, this country is still in a recession.

6. During the campaign they stated if the time came to raise taxes, then certainly they would not raise the tax burden on anyone that makes less than two hundred and fifty thousand dollars per year. That number has

jumped around so much that my own head spins. But let us take them at what they said the first time, two hundred and fifty thousand dollars per year. But can we look just a little closer at "OBAMACARE" please, so we can determine just who will pay higher taxes?

A. Everyone who buys an insurance policy.

B. Everyone who goes to a hospital.

C. Everyone who buys drugs.

D. Everyone who buys or uses a medical device (and that comes with a list of what is considered a medical device by the administrators in Washington; meaning our politicians as opposed to you, me, or even our doctors. You know, this includes things like tampons and other daily necessities we all use.)

E. Every college student who obtains a guaranteed student loan.

We have looked just a bit closer at "OBAMACARE". Who in the list above makes more than two hundred and fifty thousand dollars, anyone? Every one of those individuals that fall into those categories will pay much higher taxes and that in by itself will raise all of our medical costs. Oh, I am sorry, weren't our medical costs and taxes supposed to go down? Didn't President Obama say all of that and didn't he say what he needed just to get elected? Doesn't he have any core?

Look a bit closer at our now President's voting record before he was President. He voted one hundred and twenty nine times as "present" to avoid a yes or no vote on such issues as partial birth abortions, concealed hand guns, and whether strip clubs should be allowed to be built next to schools.

As a United States Senator, he failed to vote three hundred and fifteen times on a variety of issues that without question were and are important to the American people.

I suspect his lack of voting here was also to avoid a controversial yes or no, all in the name of getting elected. Can he say he has a core or not?

Almost everything within the progressive mindset (having very few exceptions) can be found in all government departments - the Environmental Protection Agency, the Department of Education and the Department of Energy - as justification for their ideological agendas. Don't get me wrong; I do believe in the necessity of these issues. I do not believe, however, they need to know every little aspect of our lives or be allowed to control our lives as they see fit. The people should be making up their own minds.

It is not the responsibility of the Federal Government to do much more than be sure there is ample representation of persons (political office) to represent the numbers of population and control and protect our US borders. It should not be concerned with what type of toothpaste, type of vehicle or type of phone we, as a free people, have a right to choose on our own. Certainly, not what type of food crop we choose to grow on our own land. The free market dictates these types of decisions not government.

Speaking about free land, who does the Federal Government, or for that matter the local politicians, think they are by taking or allowing the Federal Government to take over State land, such as the National Parks? Frankly, we should have but very, very few National Parks. The rest should be under state control and the local populations where they stand. Maybe, just maybe, the locals might actually see the profits in upkeep (jobs) and visitors (money), instead of the bone-heads in Washington D.C reaping the rewards.

It is not the Federal Government's place to control local environments and local business endeavors. I don't care what title they place it under for all necessary needs or social justice mumbo jumbo; they believe the locals aren't smart enough to take care of business. Bull is what I say.

This socialist attitude being sold to us, particularly under the camouflage of commerce laws, is sickening and goes against everything this country has been built on for and by a supposed free people, not a regulated nanny state. If you hear a politician calling for social justices, get rid of them as fast as the vote or lack thereof will permit.

The rest of everything attached to social justice is nothing more than Huggie-Bear-Smackie-Poo. All of it is the kiss of death to our rights as a free people to choose and test on our own, which will determine our destiny in our free form of government.

Most of what these Federal Departments profess as a necessity for good stewardship is a poison to the American way. I believe these departments are a cancerous blot on the Country. We must demand the Government stop being so intrusive and stop taking over the enterprise and opportunity of prosperity of free men. We must demand our leaders understand that being an American is not an attitude of arrogance, but it is a symbol of great pride.

Have you noticed that whenever the politician wants to pass a controversial issue, especially a new tax, they attach children or seniors to insure the passage? If that doesn't work, then they use the Endangered Species Act or the Environmental Protection Agency to note or highlight unsubstantiated facts such as "global warming", i.e., climate change. When a candidate for political office stands up and speaks to the American people as a separatist representing only one group of the people from the outside, like a member paying only half dues, they should not be considered for office. If they can champion a cause to be considered in order to assist a particular group and mean it without just offering up what that group wants to hear, then we should listen to what they have to offer; otherwise, turn them away. You can usually tell by the way they speak. Do they have the same speech every time or do they address themselves differently in front of that particular audience?

As previously said, using segregating titles for race is simply keeping many Americans, especially those in the lower income brackets, in a state of anger and depression. Using a race issue should not come into play politically at any level, anymore than it should be used for profiling in law enforcement. To me it is reason to believe you might very well be a racist, or most importantly you are full of Huggie-Bear-Smackie-Poo. You know every race of people on Earth has fallen onto bad times, some for hundreds of years at a time, and kept in bondage at one time or another by a different race or regime and even been completely enslaved at some point in history. Used and abused, murdered, kidnapped, raped and beaten. America did not invent racism and it did not invent slavery.

We should never forget that and more importantly we should never allow this type of human abuse to take place again anywhere on Earth, if we have the power. We certainly should have the will, all of us. America has risen up above such things, which is why so many people from around the globe come here. We need to move on so we can create a more prosperous and productive environment in order to pursue life, liberty and prosperity. Our progress is great; we now must stop to analyze the deep divide keeping so many people down today. It certainly is not slavery. I believe, it is the insistence on separation, segregationist titles, and never ending entitlements just because you are in the minority or perhaps a bit different than most.

There are exceptions, such as special needs children and mental illness that we are just now coming to understand and more importantly accept, which need extra help. But if a person is healthy and mentally stable enough to earn their own way in a societal setting, regardless of their differences or disability, then they should be allowed to take advantage of hard work and prosper. There is no need to give them an upper hand apart from their neighbor.

Furthermore, if a business has shown itself to be poorly managed and poorly financed from its start and lacks any positive record or has bad history as to its products or technology, then it should be allowed to fail as anything within a free market should. It generally means our society is not ready or simply does not want the product being produced, no matter what the politicians say. Does green energy come to mind? Do green (electric) vehicles come to mind? Can anyone tell me how much it cost to electrically charge the new and unwanted "Chevy Volt"?

Tell you what, give me a Hummer H-2 that gets twenty-two or, better yet, thirty-two miles to the gallon and will still move fast when I need it and quit building these over grown tennis shoes that you call vehicles. I don't care what the fuel is as long as it works in my very large Hummer H-2, is cost effective, and gets me to the speeds I need to save me time and possibly my life.

A helping hand is fine in the way of grants for someone who can present a business plan with a good idea and the potential to thrive in a free market; but not, if the plan is attempting to justify the need because their ancestry or childhood has given them a bad break and especially not if the technology has proven itself to be ineffective and too costly.

The free market will continue to dabble with it, if the technology appears to work and if the bugs can be found and corrected. The Government should not do so. Chances can and will be taken with individual private money of our free market. But few, very few, chances should be taken with everyone's money in the form of taxes sent to our Government. A positive chance would be in the interest of national defense, like the development of the atomic bomb and other such weaponry for military use. If the Government truly wants to assist, then we need to offer free workshops to those who have the good idea but not the knowledge to create the business plan.

A business plan is complete from creation to banking a profit, not just what equipment or tools might be needed to make the attempt. Failure is okay (in fact often times a necessity) and should be allowed to be experienced if the idea or the projections did not work out; but nevertheless, there must be a plan. Progress, prosperity and opportunity arise out of failure and become even stronger the second time around. Stop giving out funds on a simple food stamp mentality; teach those in need how to fish!

If you hear a politician stand up and say that they feel your pain, he/she is only trying to lure you into a false sense of comfort and trust. Dog catchers work in the same fashion, where they coax the animal over with a kind word, a soft tone maybe an "entitlement" of food; when they are close enough, they toss the net over the top of them. They, then, haul them off to the death chamber. Our politicians might not be literally killing people; but they are certainly leading them away from prosperity and liberty with all these federal entitlements.

I stated in a previous chapter how to get those in our prisons clean from drugs and alcohol abuse. These ideas will provide a significant boost in helping our lower income areas up out of poverty, and into the free market with sobered skills. If we look at the extraordinary statistics of how many minorities in those prisons are drug users and drug traffickers not to mention the eighty percent recidivism rate, we may actually have a chance in a positive progression towards help. For the first time we might actually be able to state that there is a rehabilitation program that works, getting rid of the Huggie-Bear-Smackie-Poo syndrome of today. We might even encourage some of those who become incarcerated to go home clean and sober with the skills to be a parent, instead of absent for the sake of getting high on drugs and supporting their habit through criminal activity.

Just about everything involved with the Environmental Protection Agency is wacky. Nearly everyday is a news report about saving some endangered beetle, rat, maybe a little tiny fish or even a really big fish. The problem is every species is put in front of mankind's own needs and this leads to some sort of peril to humans. I very strongly believe in protecting against stupid and savage destruction without cause and without thought of what the collateral damage will be. I also believe in thinking out all of the different ramifications of progress or denigration from any program. I do not think that mankind should be the last element in the equation to be considered. I believe that mankind must be the first element in the equation, allowing progress in concert with the rest of our shared space and time.

Furthermore, as I speak to shared space as it relates to the Earth, let me state that our space program should not be allowed to die off and leave America behind, while the governments of our enemies jet propel themselves into advancement; wherein, we lose and they win. Has anyone else noticed how our current and, yes, past administrations are leading us into a path of socialism? Well of course, you have! Can we stand up and say it like it is? I continuously hear all the news media state that there is no need to be disrespectful or denigrate this or other administrations by saying they are socialists. It is not necessary to call them names and be mean. If I have ever heard HUGGIE-BEAR-SMACKIE-POO, then that is it! Let's say it like it is, take note of what this President has stated:

- "We are only five days from fundamentally changing America." Then he began to do exactly that by pushing, bribing, and browbeating the U.S. Senate and the Congress into passing a law against the people. The Health Care Bill and all of its devilish, socialist taxation and new big government mandates took us right into violations of the U.S. Constitution and violations of our freedom, prosperity and productivity.

- He has passed financial ruin onto this country by way of bailouts and, yes, the previous administration made their share of these blunders. Nearly all our representatives continue to do so. If I give much thought to the destructive matters of how this administration does business, I begin to believe that this President is trying to destroy our Country. It is very hard not to be cynical and I certainly do not want our Country to become so divided that it turns ugly and potentially violent as it did long ago and far away. I do not want to believe these things, but it is becoming more and more evident that this President is setting the United States up to fail.

- He has surrounded himself with self-confessed communists and socialists. He continues to back each and every one of them, trying to ignore or deny their very communist or socialist actions, writings, and statements. How many times must we read and hear from every expert throughout time; if you want to know the character, principles and values of a man, just look with whom they surround themselves? It is not a coincidence that these advisors have been placed into positions of power where they are not subject to vetting. If they were, they very likely would not have been confirmed, at least I hope not. If they would have been, then the Country is already lost.

- Not to mention the good and grand Reverend Wright. Give me a break; is there really anyone out there that believes the President didn't listen to his mentor and friend? "Like an uncle to me," is what he said.

- He removed strategic missile defense systems. Don't try and tell me they are not needed to protect our nation, Poland, or the rest of our allies for that matter.

- During the tragedy of the Polish President's death, our President went golfing instead of attending the funeral.

- He stopped funding our space program after we paid for building the International Space Station. Then will pay over fifty million dollars per U.S. astronaut to hitch a ride with Russia to go to the Space Station, which we paid for. Again supporting a country that has set out to support every country (our enemies) hell bent on destroying the United States.
- He created a tax base that will ruin most common citizen's businesses and he arranged to support the job markets in the countries of our enemies. Enemies who will one day take this land over, if we do not stop this insanity of going further into debt now.

Let me tell you a very brief story that directly relates to the new way out of debt this President and his administration are moving to implement now, before the November 2012 elections. You have heard of the "VAT Tax" (the value added tax) which will be put onto the purchase of everything you buy. LISTEN UP ALL YOU OBAMA SUPPORTERS WHO LOVED THE IDEA OF "FUNDAMENTLY CHANGING THE WAY AMERICA DOES BUSINESS". If you like pizza, especially while attending the university, you better buy a lot of frozen dough right now. While visiting Rome whose government is pleased to offer the VAT tax, my wife and I entered a local pizza shop and ordered three pieces of pizza, the size you get in a local pizza hut and two twelve ounce cans of soda. The cost was forty-two American dollars. Thank you VAT! Get ready America; here it comes.

It looks to me like this President is at best a socialist, if not just so ideological far left that he is simply weak and perhaps naive and inexperienced. Many people I talk with at all levels of the private and public sector are beginning to believe the same. Let me give an analogy. I listen to my new police officer, fresh out of the academy, as we drive towards the call for service.

He is well educated with a Bachelor's Degree from a good university in sociology. He lived with his parents until age twenty-six and entered into police work so he could help the people, particularly the lower class who have just not had a chance (taught by his professors). He has no idea what the people he wants to help have to put up with everyday, because he has no exposure or life experience himself. He only has experience with what his professor's thought and chances are they had no idea either.

We roll into a neighborhood on a family disturbance and he begins to try and help the young lady; she just received a severe beating from her husband who is a junkie heroin addict. He pulls the husband away to arrest him for the assault and "asks" the man to put his hands behind his back so he can be handcuffed. The officer turns from the wife. The man starts to comply, then turns to grab for a gun and shoots the officer, while the wife - the poor "helpless" young lady - jumps on the officer and stabs him in the neck for violating her man. She begins to yell, "Leave him alone, you bastard!" She tells her husband, "Shoot the lousy pigs; they have no business in our lives!"

The problem is the officer allowed his education in the classroom, which was distorted by assumptions, to get in his way and his enemy saw right through his weakness. He exposed the fact that he did not have any experience, first by asking for compliance and then by turning his back on the most deadly person in the room. Someone he mistakenly thought was his friend; because he was, after all, there to help her and with all good intention was doing just that. He not only jeopardized himself and his partner but all other persons around him, including the suspects.

I do not have a problem with a formal education. To the contrary, I have one and believe an education is a must have, especially for our public servants.

What is also needed is the experience to learn the appropriate application of that education and the only way to get that is to have real life exposure first. I realize that not everyone is going to move into the poor neighborhood to get that exposure. At least move out of your parents' house and do something on your own like pay your own college tuition, utility bills, rent, etc. In the case of our politicians, vote for those who have had some real life exposure to the world of politics and/or strong business dealings.

I believe this President is the young officer who means well but should not be on a call by himself. In the case of the example, thank God he was not or he would be dead. This President should not yet have been given the keys to the patrol car. Take those keys away in 2012!!!!!!!!!!!!!!! Remove the rest of those in power who are allowing him to drive this country into bankruptcy and very possibly the arms of our enemies! VOTE!!!!

As this chapter points out, this is all nothing less than Huggie-Bear-Smackie-Poo, the kiss of death to liberty and prosperity and the end of this great country and our values centered on the United States Constitution. VOTE in 2012 and vote with common sense, practicality and good judgment. Think about the far future not just our own life expectancy. I beg you all to VOTE!!!! Balance the power now peacefully or in fifty years, maybe less, this country will have fallen or been pushed into a bloody civil war, God forbid. Please vote.

I am not telling you to vote every Democrat or Republican out of office; balance the power and keep our government in check. The power not vested in the Government by our Constitution remains in full force resting with the people, of the people, from the people and for the people.

Do not allow our unalienable rights endowed by our Creator to be pushed into the thought process of being a granted privilege by the Government.

We the people have far more rights than the Government. Believe in the rule of law and follow it; do not let the Government distort the law right out of its constitutional boundaries.

Immigration

I can assure you this topic is repeated in this chapter for a specific reason. This issue is a political topic and there is no personal choice on the matter, if you are a United States Citizen. As a law abiding citizen there is only one choice; secure the border.

In matters such as drug addiction, drug trafficking, bank robbery, rape, fraud and a whole litany of other crimes, each of us have a choice to participate or not. Those are the issues where we must make the choice as to whether or not we get involved. Do we participate in the illegal activity, stand back and do nothing, or find severe punishment for those who participate?

For my money, to do nothing about those taking advantage of the desperate souls coming across and victimizing them is, in by itself, criminal. Sanctuary cities come to mind, where the criminals hide and they do so behind the very people they victimize. The politicians in those cities know it; therein, lays the Huggie-Bear-Smackie-Poo of immigration. Those who commit these crimes must be punished and deported. The cost of that process should be taken out of the aid to Mexico or other country from whence the criminal came.

Yes, there are the other crimes that attach to the initial problems of immigration, but the main and most important issue is securing the border. This involves keeping out all illegal persons. Not just Mexicans, but anyone who fails to process into our country by way of the U.S. rule of law.

For years every politician has had to deal with this issue and no one has ever accomplished any real solutions. Unfortunately, even President Ronald Reagan screwed this one up, by giving amnesty to those who were already here.

The issue is complicated, but not as much as the politicians want us to believe. The issue has now reached a national security level that is dividing the Country into a hard line hatred and violence never before seen in strength, not to mention the disguised complexities of what the politicians put out. They pass a law to prevent an action - good or bad - and then they pass several laws to "people proof" the original law. My friends, that is impossible. We cannot "people proof" anything under any circumstance. Don't fall for it any longer, just enforce the original law; or get rid of it altogether and replace it with a law that makes better sense, is more inclusive as necessary, and holds up our original principle of securing the border by priority over and above any distraction.

The majority of politicians are only interested in votes and more acquisition of money to control. I hope there are some exceptions, but I can no longer be sure. What then can I recommend that would fit into the title of this book, *Simple Solutions for Complex Issues*? I cannot nor can anyone fix everything, but this book is intended to provide simple solutions which constitute a foundation from which to build and move the Country forward.

I have spoken extensively about creating a Federal Auxiliary Force for law enforcement. These officers would be able to assist the border patrol agents in ways that are essential to controlling the security. They would be available; they would be cheaper; and they would be federal and have worked in the border state assigned as local police officers, prior to their positions as Federal Auxiliary personnel, which would take care of the jurisdiction issue regarding immigration. Oh, no, do I mean working together on a significant problem that is basically being ignored by the current federal administration?

I repeat that our borders with Mexico and Canada are extremely diverse in topography, presenting every conceivable type of training ground for our military. Why not allow our military personnel to train in this terrain? Special Forces of each branch and both fixed wing and helicopter pilots would benefit, while at the same time providing intelligence to our border patrol and the Federal Auxiliary Rangers. After all, a great deal of the land is federal and the Federal Auxiliary Force would be federal officers.

Politicians apparently do not want to send troops to the border for security purposes; this might offend the Mexican people. But there is nothing wrong with training our troops on our land, is there? Ever had a military jet fly over the top of you at very low altitudes; or looked up to see a hovering Apache attack helicopter or Blackhawk helicopter; and then observed several armed troops repelling down?

Do you think the drug cartel will be willing to take on our Marines and other Special Forces groups, even if they are only involved in training exercises? I do not. If they did - if they actually had the guts - do you think that would finally be reason enough to turn the exercise into a mission of security? I do and I do not think the Mexican President or the Canadian President would stand in our way.

I do not think it's a good idea to build a military base or post on the border; but certainly, we can build some outpost off but close to the border for the purpose of this extensive and continuous training exercise. I know there will be yelling about the environment that might be damaged from our military troops tromping around.

That is bunk! I have not said to train the tanks and the artillery in these areas, although I do think that should be done. I said train the Special Forces, helicopter and fixed wing pilots. They will not create anymore havoc on the environment than the hundreds of thousands of illegal aliens coming across.

Once again if you hear a politician who talks about how complex these issues are and how we must give every break to those illegally coming across, vote for someone else. This includes the President.

Before I leave this subject, I would like to address the issue that gives illegal parents an edge, because their child was born here. I know this is a tough issue in by itself, because our Constitution - as stated by liberals - mandates any child born on U.S. soil is a citizen. Personally I think there is a Constitutional argument that proves otherwise. I believe they need to read the Constitution again and discuss what the document actually says, not what they want it to state. For the liberals and the ideological far left, this means amnesty for all.

I say we should absolutely not give amnesty to all illegal aliens who are currently here. This will instigate a run on our border, so their children will be born here. However, and this pains me greatly, if we set a specific date of birth (in the past not the future, perhaps January 1, 2005), those born here can stay. Their parents must then process thru the lawful and appropriate procedure to become citizens. Those born after that date must be deported with their parents, but will be given priority passage into this country.

A priority will be given to the parents with an appropriate visa that must be monitored, encouraging and assisting them to become citizens legally. If the parents do not become citizens within two or three year's time, the parents will remain out of the Country and the child will remain out of the Country until the child's eighteenth birthday. Anyone born in this country after the proposed date of birth must follow the above doctrine without exception.

I call this a partial amnesty and I do not like it personally; but there is, I guess, a compromise in all matters. At the very least we must do something. I believe the ideas put forward, perhaps dovetailed into Republican Presidential candidate Newt Gingrich, will work.

Manipulate the formula and length of times, but get the process started and be done with it as soon as possible for strict immigration policy at all levels of government.

Side note: How many of us are aware that a person here illegally can apply for child assistance through the Federal Government? They do not have a Social Security number, they do not pay income tax; but they can receive a child credit. They can receive $1000 dollars per child. Can we say Huggie Bear Smackie Poo?

CHAPTER EIGHT
Relationships: Personal and Professional

I have addressed several areas of concern and these issues relate and transcend the boundaries of one another. Each of us starts with a clean slate and each of us has the power of choice, as soon as we leave the guidance and demands of our parents or circumstances from which we were born. As they say, we can't choose who our parents will be, at least not as far as we are aware. Where our parents happen to be at the time of our birth is where we begin.

Before I continue I must state the following; there is no doubt that my wife has carried the lion's share of parenting our two children. That is the cost of working very long hours. She gave her all, everything she is. Everything she has done has been with complete devotion to me and to both of our children. Her love, her common sense and her intellect have, literally, carried me through life. Further, her motherly instincts have supported our children and together we have given them the tools to grow and be productive citizens. I will be forever appreciative in this life and beyond.

This gives rise to that age old question of how much our environment plays in the forming of our choices. I want to point out something right off the bat; I keep saying choices. I do so, because it is obviously what I strongly believe. Even under the strain or good fortune of our parents, I believe we begin to formulate our own personal choices as intended by our Creator. Maybe we need the belief in our Creator before we can make this affirmation. Although I did not have a deep faith in my younger years, I think I was always hopeful and later at the moment I needed it most, my heart and soul were opened. I found it in myself while doing my duty in those far off jungles of Southeast Asia.

Having said this, I would not want to mislead anyone, it took me many years in order to work out some of the confusion or perhaps that which I considered conflict in my heart. I must say in all fairness; I made several, in fact a basket full, of poor decisions in my life, particularly in the years prior to my serving in the U. S. Army and my serving the Government and population in other public service endeavors.

From my personal experiences across the board, I do not believe there are but few exceptions on who turns out good and who turns out evil, when choice is the qualifier. There are those who truly are insane and without the ability to make a choice. Those are driven by an impulse they are unaware of or do not understand and go about their deeds, good or bad, without any real thought behind those deeds. That's correct; good or bad.

However, the many that grow up in an environment that is dysfunctional and even abusive still have a choice and are well aware of right and wrong, good and evil. Their choices are not a product of their environment but of their very own exclusive decisions. Oh, I agree that there were some pre-adult incidents, very likely a string of them, which may even fall into the category of evil by themselves, perhaps extensive abuse by one parent or the other. But in my point of view (I base this on thousands of interviews with just about every personality type there is and, of course, my own dysfunctional family), these people make the choice.

Let me ask anyone who differs in this opinion to explain how a person who suffers from torturous treatment in their adolescence or formative years can grow up and find some unsuspecting person and torture them just like they were? I suspect there are many psychiatrists and psychologists (which I am neither) that will disagree and I get it, they must defend their profession and the drugs they prescribe to make their patient "all better".

Yeah, right. How many are let out of prison and go right back to the same violent behavior as before, raping and killing? Do you know the majority of these "doctors" in the prison system don't even know or take into consideration the convicts' past deeds or circumstances surrounding the violent crime for which they were convicted? Yet, they stand there and offer up these violent offenders to the general public again and again to repeat the horrific evils onto a trusting and naive society.

I agree they are very likely insane or at the very least not normal because sane and normal people don't do these things? Do they? I say, they do. Regardless, they all know right from wrong and they certainly know the difference between yes or no in the case of rape. If we argue that they were tortured and/or coming from an evil environment, then they certainly know the difference between discomfort and pain, which includes torture.

Before I leave these types of people (meaning those who commit crime of all categories, especially those who are violent offenders), I believe there are very few exceptions to who makes a choice and who can't really help themselves. Although I believe it is a good idea to have more police (particularly specialists) and build more prisons, the real answer is in tough love.

I often hear we need more love; what we really need is more tough love. Love is paramount in the formative years and how a parent handles their child makes a difference, but this will not alter anyone's personal ability to choose. I am speaking more directly towards the time frame after the parents and before the violent behavior. Tough love is what must be incorporated into how relatives and society alike should handle those who make bad or evil choices.

There is also another class of individuals who grew up with what is referred to as having a "silver spoon in their mouth". I do not mean to separate these individuals from the rest of us; but it is important, because for some reason many take advantage of this statement in order to point a finger.

There is the majority who fall somewhere in between tin, silver and gold spoons in their mouths. Please do not get the "silver spoon" confused with the "silver tongue". There is a significant difference. Anyone who can master the "silver tongue" can use this talent for good or evil. This is a double edged sword like many things provided by our Creator, i.e., water, fire and technology. How we use these gifts is what choice is all about.

I know there are those who will say this guy is crazy, because our Creator did not give us technology. What the heck is he talking about? Once again I disagree, because I believe God gave us the gift of reason, which leads to ingenuity, which leads to invention. And that is technology; because without these elements, occurring only in the human mind, there is no technology.

I sort of skimmed over parenting which to me means establishing a relationship of trust and respect. Love is for the most part built into our psyche and is they say inherent to our relatives, especially our parents who are the two people who gave us life. Those who become our parents and siblings as a result of adoption can only build love from the first two elements in the equation, trust and respect. The inherent portion of love simply is not present, whether you know you're adopted or not, at least not in my opinion. This leads to the reason so many adoptees want to locate their "real parents".

Behavior problems are also inherent within human beings as is their reaction to new things, to include those behavioral difficulties. Why do I use the term inherent vs. an intellectual process? It is because I think we have been programmed to believe love is inherent, as are behaviors.

I believe the capability to love is inherent but none-the-less is a learned process; whereas, behavior is inherent. We learn and that is where our parent's reaction and understanding is developed towards how they treat each of us. This is where the love comes in and it starts from the very beginning of the child-parent relationship. Again, this may be at birth or when a child is adopted. Why is it that siblings can grow up within the same environments, as it is observed from the outside, and turn out very differently from one another? I believe it is all based on our individual personalities and our perception of the way our parents respond to our behavior good or bad; whether we absorb that reaction to be an understanding or a lack thereof.

Therefore, based on my own childhood perceptions from what I strongly believed to be at best a dysfunctional family, my wife and I made sure to understand the best we could as parents why our son or daughter did something which provoked an immediate reaction. We loved both our children with all our heart and soul, but it is a learned and lasting desire fulfilled. To put it another way, we are very proud of both our children and we like them.

Let me give one example regarding our son at the age of four. He had been taught not to handle or play with those items around the house that most of us would consider knick-knacks. Our concern was twofold. First, these items were sentimental and several were fragile. Second, we wanted them to have respect and manners, ensuring they would not go into other people's homes and handle their knick-knacks. He had plenty of his own toys, as did his sister.

One day my wife entered the living room only to find our son and his sister sitting on the floor playing with our wedding picture in an antique picture frame. The glass was out of the frame; he and his sister, coming to his aid, were trying to put it back together before mom found out.

Mom said to him, "Why are you playing with those, you never took them off the shelf before?" Our son looked up at her and stated very clearly, "Well mommy, I couldn't reach them before." Our daughter said, "I was helping him fix it mommy." It was common for this type of assistance between them and there was no reason not to believe them. Of course, he was given another verbal lesson on why he should not play with the knick-knacks and to play with his toys, but not the items on the shelves. If he wanted to see something that he was not allowed to play with, he must first ask. Mom did not see any reason to smack his little butt, this time.

Unfortunately, as a police officer I have seen this very type of scenario play out in numerous homes I was dispatched to regarding family disturbances. When I arrived at these homes the outcome was very different from the way my wife and I handled these matters. Often - way too often - the child would have received a severe punishment to include several strikes with belts, branches from trees or just plain old fashion beating by fists.

One parent or the other was catching hell for what they did to the child and many times the call came from a sibling or other family member or even the neighbor stating these events were continuous. These families, if you some how can give them this title, as we say were at best dysfunctional. Interesting enough, calls regarding many of these incidents were so frequent to police officers that the dispatch received nothing more than the address. We were familiar enough with all parties involved and the circumstances surrounding them, because it was routine.

My wife and I are not in anyway the type that believes you never spank your child. We do believe, however, if you make the effort to reason and understand why your child acted out, then the answer of what type of discipline will be evident.

As I recall, it was necessary to spank or paddle our daughter and our son on several occasions causing their behinds to sting a bit, but we took care not to injure anything but their pride. Other times where discipline was needed, we found other ways that hurt them far more than striking them, like staying in their rooms, grounding them from events, and taking away privileges they would have to earn back.

I have no intentions on addressing every issue under the sun herein because as stated there are simply too many and I do not have the answer for all of them. Some might say; I do not have the answer for any of them. Just because we differ here doesn't mean the discussion stops, because every opinion should be heard. Talk about this, especially with your partner.

So let's talk about one other area in parenting and that is the relationship between our children as it crosses the boundaries of our schools. There are many different subject matters we should discuss. Like those of teaching history the way it actually occurred without the teachers' version of what occurred. We could also address why it is so important to teach the fundamental basics like reading, writing and arithmetic (mathematics), as they said in my day.

Have you ever been in a retail store when there was a problem with a cash register and instead of counting out your change after providing a twenty dollar bill for a small purchase of thirteen dollars and twenty cents, everything came to a screeching halt? I know some will argue that in this day and age with computers nothing works without electrical power.

The fact is, numerous times I have been in this position and the kid behind the register, to put it simply, was unable to count out the change correctly and needed assistance. That, my friend, is a society completely dependent on technology and completely lost without it.

What happened to the parents in this matter? I believe parents need to teach their children the basics and stop depending on a third party to do it for them. Before our children reach the classroom they should already know how to read, write, do basic math and know all their colors, at the very least. Further, they should have a basic concept between right and wrong.

This is my point in several areas of where and why this country has turned so far off course; if we don't address our very basic elements of survival, we are in big trouble. I am not advocating we drop our advancements or progress in technology. I think we should enhance our efforts, but we cannot let go of how we got here either or we will lose ourselves in the circuit boards of electrical pulses as though we are in a game on a computer. This is a serious issue and it is not only in our schools; it is prevalent throughout our government and private sector. We depend far too much on technology and not nearly enough on ground rules of basic understanding and knowledge.

I want to address the one issue I think is perhaps debilitating the weakest of our young children and I fully believe there is a plethora of evidence to prove it everyday. It is the issue of bullies. Bullies in my day were dealt with generally on the spot or at least within a reasonable time frame. They were dealt with either between the kids themselves or between reasonable parents or as a concentrated effort with the school.

Today, they are dealt with in the courts and with the absent, lazy or forced parent. How sad we have become when we get a call from the school and we are told the kid did this or that and the first thing the parent says is who is to be blamed. Generally, it is the parent. If they are asking, they already know who is to blame; they are simply looking for a scapegoat.

I said debilitating our weakest young children, why? Here goes the controversy. Humans by nature compete and they have since the beginning. This is part of what we are as a species; those who bully teach us very good lessons. Not to say I like them, I do not. In fact, I despise them and dealt with them far too severely in my day.

I got a reputation for being very aggressive and I was, no doubt; but, I was in the war alone (from my perspective) with two selfish adults who gave up their parenting cards (as Dr. Laura Slessinger would say) long before I needed their guidance. I also realize that many cross over the line and the basic disciplines do not work at that point. What I am addressing is the up front and more minor problems, which we turn into extreme issues when they need to stay on a small scale.

During our son's fifth grade year, there was a kid who was by all definitions a bully. This kid, for whatever reason he had, picked on the more timid and at the time my son was timid. The kid would physically push others around and to the ground; knock their books out of their hands; laugh and often push some more. He would threaten to beat the others up and called them names. My son one day pushed back and the teacher admonished both for fighting. The teacher, who I liked, said they would both be suspended from school and a permanent record would reflect in their behavior and possibly their grades if it continued. As often happens, the bully did not listen and his bully tactics worsened.

My son came to me and told me he tried but nothing, like ignoring this kid, was working. The kid would just seek him out and he did not know what to do. The school had failed and the other boy's parents had failed. I could have gone to the school and the parents again for additional talks. But this did not work the first time, so I gave my son advice from the old way of taking care of a bully. I told him the next time the kid grabbed a hold of him to push him back.

Then, tell him directly without shying away at all, "Look at me! If you touch me again, I will punch your lights out." I told him to say nothing more and if the kid came after him, to do just that. He was concerned about getting in trouble. I told him I would stand up for him, but do not engage the kid unless he started the problem and only after he told the kid what I said, if he did not stop.

It did not take long, as I recall two or three days, and sure enough the kid struck out against our son. Our son followed the advice to a tee and he did not have to hit the kid at all. In fact, the kid stopped almost all of his bullying towards everyone. In a matter of weeks, they were playing together. I believe the kid found a mentor and our son was no longer one of the shy and timid, instead he became even more popular as did the other boy.

I know that not every situation can turn out this way. It was not luck; it was a learning experience for both those boys and other kids who watched this play out. When I said a human competition we need to understand that is what this was all about; competing for the lime light, if you will, in one way or another. We must occasionally let the human condition play out and stop interfering with kids who must take what God gives them and deal with it. By the way the other kid in this incident with my son was not a very attractive boy and I think he was trying to overcome his own inadequacies as he viewed them. His parents failed to provide the type of encouragement he needed and allowed him to be mean instead of accepting what he had to deal with.

It would be hard for me to believe that Chris Farley did not get bullied about his fat; that Barbra Streisand passed through her childhood without kids making fun of her very large nose. How about Jimmy Durante's nose, Babe Ruth's fat? This list can go on as long as any. I think these people and millions like them became better people and, very likely, it is one of the things that drove them to succeed. It brought them out of their hiding places and into the spot light of life.

If you are too young to remember these real people or you're tuned out of what is common and believe political correctness is right, then I guess you will agree with the idiots who are yelling about "Rudolph the Red Nosed Reindeer". They say because all of the other reindeers made fun of him, they should be expelled and punished. I say it again for those of you who live in these fantasy worlds, Rudolph made it to the very front of the pack because of his nose that is so red you would even say it glows.

From my perspective and experience, bullies are not only a way of competition but also a significant learning process; wherein, we come to terms with how to handle the hurt. Parents simply being content as an outside observer will always point the finger at someone else for the wrong doing of their child.

I know the bullies often hurt us and, especially these days, they go way too far; but, it is because we have failed them and others to deal with the problem correctly when the time is required. Stop allowing our children to run and hide. If we don't get them to deal with it early, they will forever be in the dark and they may get hurt physically and psychologically, often they will be very sad and very lonely. Bottom line here is that parents must stop passing the buck. Let me leave this particular subject by saying numerous parents would respond to me as a police officer, "My kid got in with the wrong crowd." My reply often was, "Your kid IS the wrong crowd." Although they were angry at the truth, they understood.

I don't mean to sound aggressive, rude or ruthless as some might say. We must recognize when the truth must be told and when to hold all the truth back. That is, when we know the truth hits the nerve that is necessary to change someone's behavior rather than simply using it to hurt them. We should tell them what they must hear, tough love.

When we know that others most likely will be hurt unnecessarily from all the truth or any of the truth, such as children who have no need to know or understand the matter, we hold back appropriately. Why cause psychological pain when there is no gain for anyone? This is the example we as adults must teach and it is a difficult one for sure, especially when we grow up without parental guidance.

There are many children who grow up without parental guidance at all; there are, as I see myself, those who had words to guide them in the eyes of their parents, but no action to back any of the words believability. My parent's actions were, in my view, completely opposite of their spoken word; void and empty of any truth, meaning or merit. What then do we do as outside observers in these cases? As a police officer I often find it necessary and I am required by law to call in social services and remove the children from these environments.

In the days when people included common sense and understanding to the problems and hopeful solutions in these cases, the system worked fairly well. However, in today's society with common sense all but gone and no understanding at all, the only thing that has any priority seems to be political correctness and potential law suits. The environments, the parents and, unfortunately, the child only come into play for the purpose of filing criminal charges and civil law suits. We are so intent on addressing everything but the necessary; we overlook the harm we cause by separating siblings.

Placing children into environments that are unhealthy and often times dangerous because we fail to follow up or complete the intense backgrounds to prevent anyone other than good decent people who truly want to help. I have observed hundreds of foster homes that are in it for the money and care less about the children.

I further realize, there are wonderful and selfless foster homes, like Congresswomen Michele Bachmann and her family with big hearts; but this does not negate the fact that there are I think more harmful foster homes than good ones.

My solution for this is old fashion, but I truly believe we would go a long way in putting a fix to a great deal of the problems in today's foster homes. First, allow only those homes that have been fully and extensively investigated. Secondly, never break up siblings unless there are egregious extenuating circumstances, such as incest rape. Third, re-establish the old time orphanages where regulations and unannounced inspections are policy without regularity. If anything is out of policy or if any complaint is outside that which is healthy or normal, remove all staff employees immediately with interim part time staff members from a stand by list of individuals who have previously been vetted.

Subsequent to a full and impartial investigation completed by law enforcement without delay, any staff not suspected of wrong doing would be allowed to return. Any criminal act will be prosecuted and any unethical acts will be fined with the circumstances dictating other punitive actions, if warranted.

I further believe if we want to have significant and positive impact with these children, the orphanages should be allowed to establish schools within their organization from K-12, readying those students for extended education based on their abilities, whether college or trade schools.

Within the learning process and communication aspect of these schools the facts of our country's birth as should be taught. This part of our history is apparently being distorted and perverted in today's public schools system.

I do not want some bonehead making the attempt to distort what I am saying here either, so let me be very clear. I have no objection to global events being taught as well, all inclusive to other religions as long as they are taught without the distorted opinion of the instructor.

In other words, just the facts should be taught, allowing the student to question the premise of what they are learning, analyzing the true results of history and the real documented effects of content. The instructor should be stimulating the students' thought processes by only inserting perspective not ideological opinion. This means to allow the student to process the information and come to a point with an independent mind.

All of our relationships between each other boil down to communication in both verbiage and actions. These two elements of relationships carry more meaning than any others, whether positive or negative. Outside this communication is the spiritual communication between each of us as individuals and our Creator, whether you refer to the Creator as God or otherwise. In any regard, forcing these interactions or communications either by extreme demands, rules or out of fear will always turn towards the negative.

Earlier I made mention, when we break free or grow up and out of our parent's immediate guidance and childhood environments that we all have individual choices. I realize even as children we have that God-given ability of choice. Those choices have an impact of immediate lessons to keep at bay the destruction of our entire lives.

I chose to move from childhood and parenting into adult relationships because that is the way life plays out. Our adult relationships are where we begin to utilize to their full potential those lessons of communication learned early on.

Hopefully, we learned that respect is one of the most enduring elements of human behavior. We should have respect for ourselves, other people, their belongings and all that concern others, everything that is socially acceptable and some that is not, as long as that which is acceptable to the individual brings no harm to others or that which is acceptable to society.

If that sounds like Huggie-Bear-Smackie-Poo, it is not. It is instead, as noted, one of the most important elements of human behavior and we are losing that battle in today's society.

Unfortunately, we have turned respect away from human dignity towards excuses for political correctness, sexual harassment, discrimination and frivolous law suits. For example in the work place, should someone give a compliment to another worker (usually the opposite sex, but not always) stating they look very nice today; that their clothing fits them and compliments their appearance, this can bring on all the above.

If respect is so important, how do we use it as good human behavior? Easy, show respect to everyone. Do not use foul language; do not use drugs; do not abuse alcoholic beverages; do not dress like you just got out of prison with your pants below your behind; do not dress like a street walker; do not destroy others property in any way, including putting your foot or any other part of your body on someone else's bumper or hood of their vehicle; do not assume the co-worker is a potential date or that the co-worker who gave you a compliment is trying to "hit on you".

Above all else, show respect to your partner, because love is simply not enough my friend! When you enter into a relationship, you should be open and be honest. Look, we all play the game of casually courting (generally with more than one person) before we begin a relationship that has real meaning and we might actually start a life long journey where courting turns into commitment, marriage and/or children. I personally prefer marriage as this is or at least should be a final commitment with value and principles.

There are several issues that I have observed by way of investigation through interviews that have destroyed relationships.

As I have mentioned perhaps more than once, I have interviewed thousands of individuals from all walks of life and these interviews always shed light on people's relationships.

1. Girl's night out and boy's night out are common place and common reasons and excuses that destroy relationships regularly. Why? Because people fail to consider their partner's feelings and put themselves into places and situations that display a complete disrespect for their partner. They give rise to issues that cause any human being to wonder and worry. Jealously is the green giant, but trust is not the violation here; it is respect. Just because your spouse or partner trusts you not to participate in any activity that is unfaithful, does not mean they are not deeply hurt by your ignorance.

   Furthermore, there is no way any person can trust others not to make the move (if you will) and cause embarrassment to both of you. This may sound shallow and unimportant, but let me assure you, it has been the cause of horrific casualty, both psychologically and physically. If you must have a night or time out without your spouse or your partner do so in ways like playing tennis with those of your own sex; having lunch; going to a movie; or playing ball with your friends and most of all stay out of any alcohol serving establishment where people go to "get lucky". If you are one of those unfortunate individuals who came to the relationship as your second or third time around and you met your new partner in one of these places, hanging out there only ignites the fumes for disaster.

2. If you are always having business meetings, try to keep them within working hours. If possible, invite your partner occasionally and simply advise those who you're meeting that your spouse will be joining. If those meetings are after hours, invite your partner. If they cannot be in the meeting, then go home with little delay or have them meet you. I have observed the constant business meetings to be over the top in fighting and detrimental to the children resulting in hundreds of breakups. Sometimes it is said that it can't be helped and I know that is true, but do not use this as an excuse. Communicate honestly and effectively; meaning positively not negatively with your partner. Yelling statements, like you don't trust me, is a camouflage to keep from communicating with invested interest.

3. Finances have absolutely destroyed relationships time and again. This was one of the constant troubles in so many families. One of the main reasons it was problematic was this business about my-money-your-money. I believe when you are committed to a relationship, it is all inclusive and money is a big part of getting by, prioritizing needs, desires, etc. If having your own account is so important, maybe you need to have your own totally private life that does not include someone else. If you are intent and stubborn enough to have your own account, have it openly; even if there is no access by your partner to the money, don't be so concerned that your partner knows about it. I guess there are reasons for separating accounts in matters such as taxes, careers and perhaps separate gift monies, but don't hide the fact. This too has been the cause of disastrous harm.

4. Selfishness is one area that inevitably will give rise to real trouble. This is because more often than not, our priorities go out the window when we want to fill our desires before our needs. We tend to lie in order to have what we want, somehow diminishing the needs as not so important and perhaps there are other ways to achieve the need. Where this plays out with great devastating impact is when our selfish desires are set in front of our children's needs.

When we take on the responsibility of children, whether we give birth to them or become their step-parent. At the very least this is an oral contract, if not a marriage or some other adoptive agreement. The child becomes the first and most important priority, no matter what our desires might be. If we put that child or children into second place during the time they are in our direct or indirect care, we are not in my opinion any better than an abusive parent.

Compromise is not out of the question in these matters, of course. Any compromise must include the needs and must include input on the part of both parents, before the desires. Let us not lose sight of this issue being extremely important without children being involved as well; because lying will come to only one conclusion, no relationship at all. One day someone like your neighborhood police officer will be stepping between you and what little, if anything, you have left to keep the peace.

I imagine that this subject might go on for thousands of pages. Instead of providing more of the common and devastating issues that seem to many as small until they find themselves overwhelmed in this tainted soup of human entrapment, I will move on to recommendations I have found work in my thirty-eight year marriage.

I have read the Kinsey Institute completed research which has shown that thirteen percent of married couples have sex a few times per year. Additionally, forty-five percent have sex a few times per month, thirty-four percent two or three times per week and seven percent four or more times per week. To the best of my recollection, this study included only those couples who are living together in the routine of daily life.

I don't believe the study include those on extended business trips, separations away from home as a result of extenuating circumstances, or soldiers deployed on assignment. Given these same circumstances, I can tell you that couples definitely do not have sex anywhere near as often as they should. I have heard directly from those I have encountered many times through a variety of investigations; people who tell me their spouse or partners are simply not there for them sexually.

I would say any time you can muster up the desire, enjoy your time together; as time in by itself is far too short. There is nothing like intimacy to bring about a quiet close connection and spirit filled relationship with your spouse. In my opinion the highest percent of interaction or intimacy possible should be in the weekly categories. Live these experiences together, not apart in fantasy. Fantasy outside your communication and relationship leads to trouble, my friends.

I believe there are but very few exceptions to replacing the human fulfillment of sexual desires. Perhaps individuals, who choose to be celibate for religious reasons, are one of those exceptions and I admire their conviction.

However, from my experiences if they are family orientated with spouse or partner outside the church and not having sex at home, they are being satisfied somewhere, somehow. Like I said fantasy outside the relationship, especially the kind we act on, brings real trouble. As I noted, there is no relationship at all, as it only becomes a facade, if there is no trusting respectful communication.

I know there are those stating about now that relationships are not built on sex or sex alone. I am well aware of this and don't mean to imply it does. I am saying to you that sexual frustration will close the door on honest communication and your relationship will begin to wither. Would you like to hear the number one excuse stated to me when I have caught individuals committing infidelity, often in the act, during my regular patrol duties as a police officer or while they were under surveillance?

They were all the same for the most part, "My wife or husband (whichever the case) does not satisfy me." An excuse perhaps, but it is one used regularly and I don't put a lot of stock in coincidences. I heard my sister say once, "Never allow your spouse to leave the house dissatisfied". I think if you heed this advice in more than just sex and apply it to confusion and anger as well, your relationship will grow vs. wither.

I have never worked on our wedding anniversary. I have made it very clear to my employers' that I would if need be, call in sick just to stay home. To my surprise and my luck, the employers I have had went along with me and gave me the time off. That might have something to do with my offering to work any other day, including holidays to make up for the time off, which I did occasionally. I believe my relationship at home is worth more than my work, as much as I have loved my career. Additionally, I took off every year on our children's birthdays (as long as they were living at home.) Lucky for me, we only had two children or I might have had difficulty with this one.

I have never given my wife an appliance for a gift, such as a vacuum cleaner or such. I did give her, on one occasion, a hand lotion warmer, and another time an electric popcorn maker, because she loves popcorn. I think you are far better off giving gifts of the heart and personal gifts are the best, not ones that you gain from her having.

Vacations are fine, as long as your spouse gets to vacation also, not stand around cooking and cleaning as usual. Now those types of getaways are fine, as long as they are discussed first and not a gift of surprise. I believe strongly in travel as this is one of the best educations and fun times anyone can have.

I think anyone committing to a relationship that will include children should have a minimum of three years together before having them. This will give you both time to get to know each other well enough to be sure children are right for both of you. Obviously, this is a conversation to have before you even become committed, but so many fail to do so.

My wife and I, after a brief courtship, had this conversation and began trying to have children three years after we married. God found it necessary for us to wait nine years, only He knows why. Maybe we will learn why in the hereafter. I know there are many thousands of couples that enter the commitment already with child/children. But even then, especially before final commitment, you really need to have that conversation. If one or the other is dead set against children, I recommend reconsidering marriage. It will surely be a strong wedge in the relationship for years to come.

Careers must be one of the topics of conversation before commitment. It should be well understood that each person has different wants and needs to fulfill their lives, as well as the very serious conversation about religion. On the topic of religion/holidays, can I give you something to think about?

If you celebrate Easter, let me tell you what I do. Every Easter I buy my wife a different Easter basket that she keeps as an ornament or knick-knack around the house. Things like a painted or crystal glass bowl, or a statue with some type of porcelain basket attached. A couple of times it was a planter for her flowers in her garden. I do this out of respect for my wife. My point is to give her something she can place sentimental value on along with the celebration of the holiday.

This next recommendation is one for everyone to keep in mind, as I have observed this inconsiderate desire to be vindicated, tear relationships apart. If you have a particular problem with your spouse or partner and you can't solve it or you are afraid to confront your partner with it, do not talk about it with your friends.

I recommend you speak to a counselor of sorts. I would first go to the church; they are free and can provide you with guidance from a spiritual point of view that may very well assist in resolving the issue. If they cannot help, often they will guide you to someone who can and that service might also be free. If for whatever your reasons, you do not go to the clergy, then hopefully a psychologist or your parents will be of some help or maybe a very close sibling.

I am directing you away from your friends. I have observed this go very bad, very quickly. It has been said that "A man (woman) if he is lucky will have made only one or two true friends in his lifetime". You tell this "very close friend" private concerns and troubles (that should never have been disclosed) with the caveat never to tell anyone. We all know how that turns out. However, the real problem is when there is nothing to gain on the part of those telling other than gossip! Gossip, unfortunately, comes easy to most people and often it is used as a tool to get nothing of value and only selfish recognition at other's expense.

When we talk about keeping other's personal issues in confidence, I am always amazed at why we continue to pry, particularly in areas that have no concern to us at all. You might have realized that I failed to mention anyone by name in my examples particularly when the issues are of a personal nature, even though each are true renditions of what has or is occurring. That is because none of us need the names and I don't feel the necessity to prove anything to anyone. I am giving you what I think in areas of real concern but there is no obligation on your part to believe me at all, it is only advice or recommendation and nothing more.

My point here is back to gossip. Why is it necessary to know someone's medical history or their personal trials and tribulations when it will not be of any help to you at all except maybe in the gossip arena? When people ask me for information, I respond with why do you want to know; or I tell them straight out, sorry there is no need for you to have that information. This in my opinion is a nice way of telling, them mind your own business and I think everyone would be better off doing the same.

In this way you don't have to say "please never tell anyone no matter what", unless you are testing them that is. The only test, however, with any substance is the one where you only give that information to one person and no one else, waiting for it to be exposed in gossip. I suggest however that the information you tell is not true and will not cause any harm.

Before I leave gossip, I would be disingenuous if I did not advise to consider the information and why you might need to tell. For example, if you hear that a person might be contemplating suicide, you need to tell. Why is this different from what we might call general gossip? Because you have nothing to gain and the person you are telling on has everything to lose, if you do not.

The work place relationship is an area of true value and employers must recognize their employees are the most important asset. I spoke of this somewhat in previous chapters but want to reiterate the point. This will stabilize your employment, promote your product, and grow your customer base, increasing your revenue. This means jobs and job security upon every decision.

There are many excellent businessmen that you hear talk about their customers being their best asset. I would disagree in the working environment itself; because if you don't treat the employee right, they won't treat your customer base right.

If anything there might be an argument for vertical importance. Either way, I advise listening to your employees and most importantly answering those voices.

Provide what you can in the way of compensation and benefits, but be sure your employees are aware of the circumstances leading your decisions. Reasonable people will always come to terms with management, if they know they are part of something positive and trustworthy. The exception to this is union executives which have proven their unwillingness time and again, destroying businesses.

Why? Because they won't have a job, if they don't have the union; and you do not need them! Representation with and between management and worker can and should be addressed and managed through a group of in house association members directly from the ranks, not outsiders.

In closing this chapter, let me tell you what I consider very likely the most important relationship for all of us. That is our spiritual, but most importantly our faith in and relationship with God and the church. I have exposed a small portion of my trials and tribulations with you, so you will know that I speak from the heart and real life experiences. I do not guess, per se, at what I have told you; I believe it all based on my life.

I am continuously learning with an open mind and moving into a realm of understanding vs. fighting what I previously thought was intrusion. You see anyone who I perceive to be prying, gets turned away very quickly. Also, when anyone starts to tell me that they know what I need to do without even listening to what I might say, they are also turned away.

I still have questions and now on my bucket list is to sit with Father Jonathan Morris who wrote the book "*God Wants You Happy*". I am not looking for someone to make confession; only someone I will trust and respect to hear me and answer me in earnest about my religious questions.

I have discussed these matters with my wife and she has been a significant model with her upbringing and twelve years of private Catholic schooling. She is my steadfast reassurance in all matters. Nevertheless, I/we would delight in an in depth conversation in these matters with Father Morris. As I told you, I am not a go to church type of religious person; but, I do consider myself as having a true depth of faith in our Creator and I do pray nightly for his "whispers", as Father Jonathon refers to God's communication with us. Therefore, I strongly recommend that everyone should read the Father's book "*God Wants You Happy* - from *self help to God's help*".

I have this theory about why it is there are so many different religions and divided religious orders. This also plays into why I believe each of us goes through so many different trials and tribulations as diverse as human psychology and our spirit itself. The theory is that everyone is designed to learn in only the way their particular personality will allow them to learn. For example, if I did not go through what I perceived to be nothing but a negative childhood and having been in a place with no choice but to take human life, perhaps I would never have come to terms with who I am as a human being and a man.

When I began to understand those situations in my life assigning, if you will, reasons and giving them perspective, I began to grow spiritually. I began my conversations with the God I recognize as our Creator and that also gives me perspective as to our purpose. It seems to me that every religion carries a message of similar faith at least to the point of what we hopefully accomplish as a "Junior Partner" with our Creator. "Junior Partner" is a term I have borrowed from Father Jonathan Morris, and I do not think he will mind me doing so, at least I hope not. You see, my point here is that we need the diversity of religion to match the diversity in our psychology in order to find our way.

I also believe when a religion of any standing is distorted by radicals this is where the devil hides. He confuses our psychology which instills irrational behavior, whether there is a perceived purpose or not. This is where the devil gains strength and holds those souls in debt. I pray for those souls to see their destruction before they act. I don't know how this theory relates to everything being a divine design; but I know this: we have been given free will to choose and in that we have the opportunity to grow in all relationships.

CHAPTER NINE
All in a Nutshell

I am going to begin this chapter with a disclosure, if you will, about what many have perceived to be insults towards many different types of people. I know I have been blunt and even sarcastic in the many subjects covered. Please understand that my intent here is not to belittle anyone or bring thoughts of anger, just recognition to the issues of the day.

Allow me please to illustrate what I mean and why I chose to address these issues in the way I have. I told you, as a guest speaker on the issues herein and many more; I have stood on the stage numerous times and offered up solutions in very kind terms and felt like I was offering a breath mint or a piece of gum to someone with really bad breath. Have you ever been there? You sit with someone in meetings, perhaps a co-worker, and friendly business conversations doing whatever it is you do and they have really bad breath everyday. You kindly offer up the gum or breath mint and they say thank you. Then, they return the next day with the same bad breath and you repeat your kind offer. Instead of them getting the hint, you become known as the nice person who always shares his gum. You have accomplished nothing accept political correctness and perhaps a gesture recognized as being a nice person.

In one other example; I had a subordinate who I believe due to allergies, did not use deodorant and everyday in short order they truly had pungent body odor! I was in a position which no CEO or supervisor wants to deal with. I had no choice here because there were regular complaints from both co-workers and customers.

I sat and thought of the lectures and admitted I did not want to go wrong here with a long and drawn out process. It was time to address the issue up front and be blunt enough to affect a change in their hygiene. Lucky for me, this person was gracious and understanding. I brought them into my office when others were not around, offered up the issue as a necessity and told them straight out what the problem was.

No beating around the bush and no offering of deodorant. I simply told the truth bluntly, but with respect. I was relieved to see they took the discussion with respectful understanding and changed their hygiene immediately. What was interesting to me was they did not use deodorant; instead, they went to the restroom every two hours or when needed and washed. Also, they did not wear heavy clothing which kept them from perspiring as much.

So within my disclosure let me state very matter of fact that if I have insulted anyone, I only apologize if you consider me to be disrespectful, that is not my intention. Regardless, you get it and I hope you will look within yourself to make the change you need to in your personal life style, your work and your relationships and with respect towards others.

Under the following captions I will sum it up in each category with priority.

HEALTH CARE
1. Pre-existing conditions should carry though with the insurance carrier with who you had a policy when you acquired the major illness. That insurance company will be responsible for everything that can be medically related to the illness. All other insurance coverage will be taken care of through your new insurance company coverage, minus the catastrophic cost you pay to the previous company. It should not matter where you live

or move. Your catastrophic coverage payment must have been segregated in all insurance coverage at the time you acquired the policy. In other words, your catastrophic payment/portion may be $210.00 per month paid to company A. All other coverage will be paid to company B minus the $210.00. Costs are examples only.

2. Health care should be allowed without federal restriction to be sold across state   lines by every company who meets the state requirements.

3. With a dilemma surging regarding families who cannot afford health insurance, especially if they get a catastrophic illness; there simply is no hope. The answer following the above recommendations is to overhaul the tax system and at least have a choice of a flat tax. However, without the flat tax perhaps those who have only the catastrophic policy as previously outlined and who are on the poverty line or below can use the entire premium and any cost associated to receiving the treatments be totally tax deductible.

4. Emergency rooms should only be used for emergencies, not the common cold. If you come into the emergency room with an amputation and you do not have insurance, then doctors stop the bleeding and do not reattach the arm. If you have insurance, even if it is only catastrophic, then they can reattach and you're covered.

5. If your doctor prescribes what they believe is a medical necessity, the insurance company must before denial, whether it is a medicine or test, sign a legal document

that holds them fully responsible, if your condition worsens at their refusal to allow the doctor to treat. That document must be provided immediately to the doctor and a copy to the patient. Alternatives may be substituted, if agreed by all parties, within a reasonable time with priority of the patient's condition.

6. Tort reform is absolute in medical malpractice. Caps with five years of potential earnings the patient could have earned in the state of the patient's residence. Unless the mal practice was of extreme gross negligence, then no cap.

7. All insurance fraud proven must carry no less then $15,000 dollar fines for each count and/or jail time without leniency.

8. All medical school students in good standing should at the time of graduation be allowed to deduct a minimum of twenty-five percent of their school expenses including tuition, if no grants were involved, ten percent if grants were involved. Providing that formula levels the paying field between grants and no grants. If not, there is a formula that will work we just need to figure it out. We need doctors, as there is a shortage.

POLITICS AND POLITICIANS

1. If your politician is set on displaying political correctness vs. political politeness VOTE FOR SOMEONE ELSE!

2. If your politician has served more than 16 years in their current office, send them home. If they are running for a different political office that is okay, as long as you study their voting record. However, in no case should any of us vote a politician back into a political office at all (except the Presidency or Vice Presidency) if they have already spent more than 20 to 24 years in office. No exceptions, find someone else; there is always someone who you will agree with on several if not most matters.

3. Social Security must be grandfathered out. I went into detail previously on how to accomplish this important entitlement. Now wait a minute buddy, are you saying you are for entitlements? In this case I believe Social Security, the way it was established, is an entitlement for those who have paid into the required by-law program. It was and is referred to as the "Safety Net" and it is for millions of Americans. I call it entitlement because those that paid should receive the payments of their money with the interest promised by the government for using their money.

   Isn't this what all other investments are required to do? This so called safety net was promised to never go broke and the only downside was you would not get as much interest as you might with an investment that has no guarantees. However, the government, like just about everything else, they mismanaged the program and took the money for their own. Getting them reelected through pandering by paying for programs that had nothing to do with the original Social Security promised and only used it for unrelated socialistic and ideological programs.

Programs like the one my friend's nephew (God rest his soul) was paid for directly out of Social Security. His problem was by his own choice he acquired full blown AIDS from his homosexual desires. Here is the rub, he never had a job and never paid a dime into the system. So how do we fix the program? I call the answer a PUBLIC/ PRIVATE partnership concept, well known to many and not so much to many more. We keep the same basic rules currently in play with Social Security.

The government will continue to mandate your employer take out whatever the percentage rate is at the time from your check, and then report that deduction to the IRS. The difference is your employer also reports what financial institution they sent the money to as a deposit into your "Personal Social Security Account". The institution must be FDIC insured and all the same rules apply; meaning you can not withdraw any of the money on deposit until retirement age, whatever that turns out to be at the time of your retirement.

Of course as I said, the same rules apply to you. So if you are disabled and meet the rules for early retirement such as a catastrophic illness, you receive your monthly allotment. By following this type of program, first you will receive your money as in a true safety net and a far larger return on your money. I would propose that one rule might change and that is you would be allowed to match donations as in a 401K and perhaps twice the match or more which will likely take you to the grave.

I would also purpose that any funds remaining would be willed to your dependents as noted in your will. Your dependents would either pay tax on the full sum or transfer the funds into their own retirement accounts equally among them, but only as your legal will dictates. In the case of no will, the sum will be inherited as usual through probate with the full burden of taxes. Furthermore, the bank must not be allowed to use the money as collateral in order to borrow funds for operational cost. If the bank is audited and is set to go bankrupt, then your funds must be reported immediately to the Government and transferred to a financial intuition of your choice within ninety days. The funds, if unavailable, will be covered via FDIC as outlined within those procedures. I know I cannot cover every detail herein, but at least you get the point and it can be done.

4. As far as the other two big entitlements "Medicaid" and Medicare", if we simply start improving our prosecution and conviction rate in these areas regarding fraud with very stiff mandated penalties; put reasonable time limits to the eligibility in receiving funds; and stop paying for additional children birthed while receiving benefits, we will go a long way. Regardless, if we do nothing else, we must get the Federal Government out of regulating these entitlements. Allow the States to run these programs with only a basic guideline, such as we should do in the healthcare rules. Set the base and the Feds get out of it altogether.

5. Repeal "ObamaCare" now!!!!!!!!!!!!!!!!!!!!!!!!!!!!!!!!!!!!!

6. If you care about our Country's debt, it is imperative that we push all our elected officials at all levels federal, state and local to spend wisely vs. just to spend on anything at all in order to please a particular group

over the majority for what is needed. For instance, if they vote or use money to build a bridge, then the need must be there at the time they need the bridge.

7. I believe this Country needs to revisit the voting age. I truly believe with all the service calls and investigations I have completed that eighteen years old is, simply put, too young to vote. Young adults, if you will, do not have the exposure to everyday life in order to make informed decisions on matters of such great importance. I know there are exceptions; I have stated this time and again. When the argument was made to change the age from twenty-one years to eighteen years the primary stand was, "If they are old enough to be drafted and/or join the military to fight for the Country, they should be allowed to vote".

I say; if they join the military, then let them vote at eighteen. While we are at the revisit issues, can we reestablish the draft, at least on a basis of boot camp; and be ready with a brief refresher course when we will need them for the next big one. It is surely inevitable and if we can't face that reality we have deep, deep problems. If the eighteen year old goes to boot camp only and they don't stay in for a full enlistment, then they do not get to vote. Of course no one wants war, but it will come and we have to be ready.

8. Can we talk about the significant issue of "EARMARKS" in the legislature? Here is how we might be able to fix it. No, I am not talking about line item veto like almost every President has wanted. It is as simple as; "IF IT DOES NOT PERTAIN, THEN IT DOES NOT REMAIN". It should never make it out of

committee by law. If you have a highway bill then we can allow for a bridge to be built in the bill.

However, if in that same bill there is an earmark for financing a new concept vehicle or a rebuilding of a historical building at the center of a township in Mississippi, then it is out and anything else that does not pertain to the title of the bill; no matter what the bill is. If every quarter the legislature would have an EARMARK bill with everything, in fact anything else that was not attached to other germane bills, they can argue those items all year and the Country will continue to function just fine. All the important stuff will be in bills such as national defense, finances, immigration, etc. The politicians will tell us; that is not how it is done! I say; it is about time to start, right now!

Economics, Business and Jobs

1. As previously stated, each of these fundamental aspects of our Country are intertwined, but I have put these solutions into the categories I feel best fit their impact. If we want to create jobs and improve our economy, we must release the businesses both small and large from ever tightening rules and regulations. The burden is so great today that everyone is, simply put; sitting on any funds they have, waiting for what relief, if any, is coming their way. If we do not mandate that relief, we will see a slight surge to fool the Government for tax and other burden reasons, while the businesses hide and or run with their money and get out of business.

   I recommend we take the worst offenders out of the Federal Government as quick as the economy allows;

so as not pushing us into a deep hole of resentment and even more power struggles between government and private business. My suggestion is to immediately incorporate two very large out of control agencies, the Department of Energy and the Environmental Protection Agency. I would rename them the "Department of Energy and Environment Protection" or "DEEP". Why do this when in reality the environmental agency really needs to go altogether? Because there needs to be a transition back to the States regulating their own environments, again with a base line only.

Many reply, why would you do that when these two agencies are stark enemies? My reply is simple; when you combine them they reassert themselves into a common goal under one management. Within these agencies there are experts who can write the base line with the subsequent approval of Congress and Senate, while at the same time incorporating a real strategy for energy independence. Take these two agencies; cut their budgets in half; make one agency and move to drop the environment side from the Feds to the States. States and private businesses will undoubtedly hire several of these employees who are removed from the Feds.

Our Country will move with priority to becoming energy independent, while at the same time do so with common sense controls that protect our environment and foster the needed reform. While we are at it, can we find someone like Governor Sarah Palin to be the new director, to ensure it gets done appropriately and efficiently with the correct priority? I can think of no one better to take this task on and get it done. Why her? She understands as well as anyone, the ins and outs of both industries and where the priority can be accomplished, taking account of the people and the Nation's necessary standards and security.

2. We need to come to terms with the facts about our Department of Education at the Federal level and abolish this agency with minimal delay in transition back to the States. Since it's creation in the late 1970's, every fact surrounding our children's education has a failing grade in comparison to just about any other country in the world; especially in those countries we should be most concerned about in competition for any standing, whether it is energy, trade, business development, economics, science, mathematics or arts or even space exploration. All of which equal jobs.

    You see, we must look ahead of our child's graduation and take a close observation of what they are in pursuit, career wise. It is in those children who have graduated and those who are unable to accomplish a meaningful beginning, which we measure and qualify what we have done and continue to do. Once again, I believe that those who lose their Federal position will be absorbed by the States and or local school districts and those who simply prove themselves unable to transition will filter into the private sector. Perhaps, they may even create a small business of some kind and actually provide a job or two for others.

3. Taxes are, of course, one of our major obstacles today. I have stated the real answer here that everyone knows; it is to completely reform our tax code. The problem is not the change itself; it is the metamorphosis we must go through to get that change. Plain and simple, it is a very scary proposition. In the end if we take the right path, it will work out and we will be far better off. I

use the analogy of the butterfly, when it crawls it simply cannot see over the horizon, but when it makes the change, it becomes more beautiful. Now it can fly high above the spiders that wish to eat them. Let us change this archaic system and get with the flat tax. Okay, without radical change in the process we need to do a few things of importance now.

First, repatriate the off shore money held by American corporations with no tax penalty, or a very small five to ten percent rate. Get those funds back into our economy, creating jobs. Second, drop the overall tax rate on business to be competitive with other countries in the global grab for business. Exempt full cost of equipment from tax and allow for growth. I would say, drop the corporate tax to zero and at the very least listen and adopt the "Laffer curve".

Arthur Laffer was President Ronald Reagan's foremost adviser on the economy and taxes. It is his plan that brought about one of the strongest, if not the strongest, economies in history. It worked, so why not use it? Third, allow all retirement plans to match twice or three times the employers' contribution into a 401K with total exemption. In response to the transition into a flat tax, if we consider the Public Private Social Security Retirement Account recommended earlier in totality, then that is no longer a problem is it?

Additionally, if we incorporate that system under the current tax policy with only the changes to implement such a social security program, which of course keeps the safety net in place with far better foundation of support and earnings, then we might not have to worry as individuals on what retirement programs our employers offer. That my friend creates thousands of jobs. In any regard, we must stop this nonsense of taxing our money that we already paid tax on at the time of earning.

I am addressing inheritance tax. This needs to be dropped altogether, talk about double dipping. If we cannot do it, then why should the government be allowed to? Look, the only way to truly eliminate any program that has been dependent upon, especially an entitlement program, is to grandfather them away. The best way to do that is, first, have a plan that replaces them and, secondly, grandfather them out in increments so as to even out the pain of metamorphosis and prove the alternative.

4. Let me now address the unions. I stated earlier that my recommendation is to create Associations vs. Unions. Given my first hand experience investigating the union's affect vs. the association's affect, those without unions are far better off in every aspect of the work place. Unions have significantly higher dues and employ executives that are way over paid. Put bluntly, they cause grief and significant expenditures for your employer. Employers become more resistant to increased benefits and wages remain stagnant for longer periods of time. Unions take the issue into court and dues eventually rise.

Often employers go out of business when there was no need and all the jobs are lost. In any event the morale factors in union shops destroy hope and customer base, decreasing production and product quality. I have been asked, what is the difference between associations and. unions? I just answered the question, because the opposite is true where associations are concerned. Associations do not run roughshod over entire industries; they only negotiate within one work place with equality. Without unions you reinstate competition between employers, even if they make the same products such as vehicles, which is stimulating to our economy.

Competition is every bit as important in attracting employees as it is for products and customer base. Wake up; if you do not have high union dues and ridicules union rules, the chances are always better through negotiations directly with management to acquire better wages and benefits. If your employer will not budge even when they can provide fair and equitable earnings, then look towards your competitors for a new job. Believe me; your employers do not want your skills, talents and the money they have invested in you walking down the street.

There seems to be a lost understanding of competition for the customer. This means, if the vehicle plants would compete against one another, then we might have vehicles that run longer without major repairs; maintain a higher rate of appreciation; and the upholstery might not fall apart in a few months just because the owner is a bit overweight. We the people would produce and purchase better products than any other manufacturer in the world, again.

I made an observation during the time I was investigating these issues as they related to union shops. Those products made overseas in years past made significant gains on quality when compared to American products. Why? Unions moved aggressively into American shops and they were not yet in the sweat shops overseas. Now, I don't like sweat shops anywhere, but is it not interesting, that when the unions moved into the overseas markets (even if it was simply by embarrassing the employer in the media to affect the market share), the products began to falter in quality? Bring the American production back without unions and you will see an across the board improvement in jobs, wages, productivity and quality. Look, the sweat shops are gone and people will not stand for substandard environments any longer. You do not need the unions.

Ask this one question; why is it that the State of Wisconsin went from having a 3.6 billion dollar deficit to being on the road with a 300 million dollar surplus? In effect, they provided job security for public employees, gave more money to the welfare state system, and lowered taxes. Oh, I know they curtailed the union powers and now the unions are mad as heck. It seems they are the only ones without job security; except, of course, those who don't do their job and say "give me some money". I wonder are they talking about "Obama money".

5. I want to point out an area or perhaps an era of times past in the minds of most entrepreneurs I have had conversations with over the past five years. A lot of what they say is based on the dreary outlook of success. They want, more than ever, a sure thing and that is very difficult to find these days. This attitude tends to stifle their attempts. Mostly, this is a direct result of regulations placed upon their intended investment.

After compliance with all the regulations, they are out of money or so far in debt they can't see a way out without further borrowing; it becomes a vicious circle working for the government and not their families. Although I have found this mostly in the large cities

(Los Angeles, Sacramento, Houston, Dallas and others), it also plays out in small cities. It all boils down to the Federal and city regulations. Often the real problem is city officials are unwilling or cannot work with any real meaning with the entrepreneurs. They offer up some small concessions, like an unconventional permit to build a different type of entrance into the new property and the like, but it is little help overall.

The only help they seemingly get is through the different States, but even then, local government is hard pressed to budge and a lot of that is due to their own out of control debt. Here is my recommendation to those entrepreneurs. Take a closer look at the old mines of yesteryear. Yep, the diamond in the rough.

Let me give you a prime example in Texas right off Interstate 45 located at exit 211 and 213, with some 4.5 to 6.5 million vehicles passing by continuously. This incorporated city, Streetman, currently has a population of 247 people. It has been there and incorporated since 1906, one hundred and six years. They have a mayor and city council and, of course, city services, such as water mains, electrical power, etc. There are no businesses, except a U.S. Post Office and a liquor store. Interestingly enough, the U.S. Post Office serves approximately 1500 hundred homes and a few outlying businesses, such as the service stations on exit 213.

This community sits truly in the hub of four other cities and on the county line of Freestone and Navarro Counties. There is within its U.S. Postal route the third largest lake in the State of Texas. Richland Chambers which is twenty-six miles long and three and a half miles wide. The fishing in this lake is superb, with a variety of species of catfish, black bass, and so on. The homes built around the lake, both at waters edge and just off the water, are mostly new and middle-to upper-middle-class. There are large cattle farms and equine ranches, in addition to power plants. The grocery store is anywhere from fifteen miles to forty miles one way for anyone in Streetman or around the Lake, which statistically accounts for approximately 5000 persons.

In addition to the residences, the lake is popular, but not too popular, with fisherman and second home owners that arrive on the weekends and holidays. This means all these people must pack the cooler for the thirty to eighty mile round trip, just to get their groceries home without defrosting or spoiling. All business, including the grocery, is conducted within the two primary cities of Fairfield (fifteen to thirty miles one way in Freestone County) and Corsicana (fifteen to forty miles one way in Navarro County).

My recommendation go there and other places similar; talk to the city officials; and make some deals to build grocery stores, hotels, barber shops, shoe stores, fishing equipment, saddle shops, you name it! Are you listening BUC-EES are you listening Kroger's or HEB? Here is a shout out to IN & OUT Burgers or someone of their mindset; go to these places and do an onsite analysis by conversing with the city officials and community.

I know there are not enough retail customers available for large stores, but has anyone ever heard of good old fashion "Mom and Pop" shops or half to three quarter size stores (I am talking to both Kroger's and HEB). What about the opportunity to tap those millions of customers passing by continuously on Interstate 45?

These places are set to grow, as they were in the early beginnings of yesteryear. With the troubles for businesses in the previously secure, well established cities, it is time to take advantage. What these places need are the old school entrepreneurs of yesteryear. Just like their communities, they don't need to get rich; just take care of their families and maybe help their children into the universities.

Hey, they may even create a job or perhaps together maybe a few million across the nation. How often do we hear about the good old days? There is a way to get back there and make a decent living. Quit crying about Wal-Mart and other large chains, take these smaller communities back or they will blow away with the dust storms. Take a small chance, work hard and prosper in a pool of opportunity. I hear all the time about, "how can we compete with Wal-Mart and other large chains"? Think about what I said regarding how far these people must drive to go grocery shopping, hardware, and everything else used day in and day out.

Now think about the cost of gas and the offset not having to make the drive. If they pay less and I might add a lot less in gas (the national average at this writing is $3.39 plus a gallon and moving to $4.50), the money saved is substantial. They can walk or drive just a very few miles vs. thirty to eighty miles. If they are paying a few cents or even a dollar more for milk, they still save hundreds and maybe thousands as a result of convenience. Don't they? Look, we are not going to see $1.50 or $2.75 a gallon gas again, my friends, and this is about how low it needs to go before this equation reverts. So look to the small communities like Streetman and Ranger, Texas or their duplicates across the nation.

6. Let me point my finger in the direction of another opportunity that lingers in what some would call the land of minority. This land is that of the "Native Americans". This title actually rides off my tongue better than any other because, if we are honest, these indigenous people to the Americas really are "Native". Although, I still don't quite understand why there is so much uproar at the mention of the word "Indian". Maybe it is hard for me to relate because I played cowboy and Indian often as a kid and, yes, I played both roles.

Oh well, maybe I am just insensitive. I absolutely mean no disrespect. In any case, there are lands of abundance in/on the different nation properties. Their tribal leaders have nailed down the casinos action and the tribes prosper in many ways. However, I am told **(without any confirmation)** there is also a great deal of shenanigans, deception, crony politics and possibly fraud among the leaders. What I think the tribes should do is get their hands around textiles and manufactured products wanted and needed.

However, can I respectfully provide some advice? Produce only a small amount maybe twenty-five to thirty-five percent of your native heritage products with the turquoise and beads. These items are nice, especially when it has high quality, but not as desired in the broader markets. Instead, produce clothing lines without the beads in high quality leather goods. A little bit of native attachment, but not everything. If you go after the soft deer hide products, you're onto a popular and expensive line of desired clothing. Try making shoes and boots for normal casual and business attire.

You get the idea; I am sure, by now. Run wild with your intuitiveness and skill set. But before I leave this can I ask why the Native Americans have allowed the Mexicans to highjack the total market on tortillas? I know the tortilla very likely originated in Mexico and the Native Americans may have adopted this food, but often those who inherit improve the product. Not only have I had mucho better tortillas out of the Native American kitchen, but their native dishes can stand up to almost any Mexican dish. Their "Indian Fry Bread" (a common term not mine) is to die for. Take advantage of your heritage in the best most prosperous way you can, by promoting it with hard work and respectful recognition. The rewards will be astonishing. Look out Mission Tortillas, here comes the competition.

7. There is a great deal of discussion on building the oil pipe lines and I agree whole heartedly, along with building several refineries. We will need them for the hopeful drilling we will be doing under subsequent administrations. Also, we should not forget that this country exports more oil than we import. We need to look at why this is so important, so we do not use it as an excuse to not drill for ourselves. Here are a few notes to consider. Federal policy can not regulate the cost but federal regulations can sure have an effect on the cost. Greed, mostly by speculators; plays a large part, perhaps the largest.

8. There is another commodity we all need desperately. Water, water, water and we need it every time there is a significant drought. Additionally, in some cases, there is simply put, too much water and that happens every time we have floods. My recommendation, which

I have been talking about for years, is a National Aqueduct. I know the arguments, that cost far too much and there is no way to pay for it. Where would we build it and who would build it? It would take 100 years or more, wouldn't it? Well, let me answer these questions.

Can I start at the bottom and work my way up the questions? So what, if it takes 100 years or more; maybe if we go about implementing the project correctly, it won't take that long. The water will be needed here or there forever and it needs someplace to run off when we don't want it in our living rooms. Remember when I addressed the real and true meaning with a plan for rehabilitation for our prison population. Does that not answer most of the cost in labor and who?   That leaves where; how about along the interstate highway system? Is it really all that hard?

You know when they repair the highways, (it seems they are always ripping some portion of the highway apart) they could actually put in the water pipeline. What about the environment? Come on, for goodness sake, its water that falls out of the sky and we need it off the roads, out of our living rooms, and in the reservoirs and farm crops. While we are at it, can we think of how many jobs this might actually create? I bet the steel industry will prosper along with every other position on the job sites. I know I said use prison labor, but you can't do it all on their backs. Nevertheless in the Department of Corrections jobs lost if any (because we revamped that system), could return as watchmen over the Aqueduct job sites.

Immigration

1. Immigration is perhaps a lower priority in many people's minds than economics per se and, of course, there is the connection made by millions. Mostly the connection is when they say the jobs that "undocumented" (illegal immigrants) take are those that Americans just don't want or won't do. They may be correct in this lazy day attitude of our younger generations (meaning sixteen to thirty-five year olds), at least to a degree.

   But whose fault is that? I say it is mostly the parents of lazy kids who think they should have everything given to them just because they are alive. Fact is, if we quit giving everything to the kid as parents and government entitlements and make them work for their money, they will do whatever job they can get. Ok, maybe that is just a pipe dream, but can we put aside for a moment that those who are taking the jobs are ILLEGAL! That leads us to one of the primary duties of responsibility of our Federal Government.

   Our Constitution states: secure the borders of the United States of America. We must demand that Washington and every politician in the Capitol of our Country and, for that matter, our States do their job. Enforce the current laws and deport as soon as possible, after we catch the illegal. If your local or state representative fails to cooperate with taking a stand, vote them out of office. That is the hard way and like millions say, it is lacking compassion. I do not think it lacks compassion, if we are deporting immediately; only if we wait twenty years to start the process. I know this hard measure seems to be the only thing we, as a supposed free people, have left shy of rebellion and I do not want that; nor do I believe anyone does.

So maybe, we need to get this right once and for all. Appropriate work visas would be a beginning and those who were born here to illegal parents can stay, of course, but their parents must go through the process of becoming legally documented and in the shortest possible time frame. Becoming legally documented with a visa will give them a break on learning English, but anyone from anywhere who wants to be a United States Citizen must learn English within two years or goodbye.

Without question, the way to citizenship in this country by enlisting in our military, must stop now! I could go on and on, but I did that in the narrative of previous pages on ideas about doing something about immigration. I will leave you with one thought that upsets many; if a child (not eighteen years of age) is born in this country (a U.S. Citizen) to undocumented or illegal immigrants and the parents do not begin and process through the new policy for visa or citizenship themselves, then they all are deported. When the child turns eighteen, they may return as a citizen. That will put an end to the free ride.

2. I think technology, like flyovers with unmanned drones, is great; but they are far more expensive than officers on horse back and officers on ATV's with K-9's. I say, use less drones and more horses and ATV's as we will save money (millions), create more jobs, and catch more offenders. Want to place a bet on it?

3. There are many who have suggested we use the military on our borders and I do not disagree. After all, this is the duty of the Federal Government says our politicians. However, the administration is opposed to this suggestion. Their problem, it seems, is that they don't want to show a military action on the borders in fear of upsetting the Mexican Government?

My recommendation is to use our borders with its vast and diverse terrain for continuous training of all our special forces from each branch of the military. Furthermore, we could also put the regular troops out there for any training exercise we need. That is not necessarily a military action, per se. Do you think the drug cartels will attempt to engage those Special Forces? How difficult do you think it will be to sneak around a battalion or two on night and day maneuvers? It isn't easy to run by a fifty mile-an-hour tank. (Ok, it is just a thought about the tanks. I get the environment thing.)

I know it will take some negotiations with private property owners, but somehow I think many of them are ready for even temporary solutions. In between our troops, maybe the law enforcement officers will be able to contain the rest. I recommend they think about the Calvary Oh, I am sorry, "mounted officers", ATV's and K-9's also. Personally, I might even volunteer for one of the mounted slots myself, what a cool job.

Law Enforcement

Before I go into my recommendations here, let me make it very clear that law enforcement officers are not judge and jury. They are, instead, the Arch Angels (if you will) of our government to protect each of us individually with priority given to our well being and those God given rights; the rule of law stated in our Nation's founding documents, which I believe were defined with Divine Intervention.

Law enforcement officers are responsible for arresting the wrongful acts of persons against other persons and all God's creatures. There should never be prejudices of any type inserted as a factor of an officer's duty. Any prejudices should instead be replaced with compassion, understanding and dignity; but, in all cases any arrest must be made in accordance with the law of the land and undertaken with precision and only the force necessary to accomplish the duty.

We as a society, do not judge. Instead, we hold those transgressors accountable, including the death penalty. In the end God will judge everyone. Perhaps I am splitting hairs between terms? Maybe, but I use them as independent of one another. I realize there are those that will disagree with me in my statement above and may even be angry or simply ignore it.

However, I have followed this mindset my entire career and read it in context in the Bible years ago, specifically "The Living Bible" Romans 13: 1-7. This rendition actually used the description of "policeman". I was thrilled to read it.

1. I said a great deal about law enforcement previously, but there are priorities that I believe need to stand out. I know there is a great deal of opposition when I say our police officers have gone to fat in a hand basket. As

a career law enforcement officer and a citizen, I am frankly disgusted with how out of shape we have become. Most agencies have a physical agility test to get hired and a few academies have a physical fitness program. However, all that work and money spent to give the test and go through the program is thrown out the window after they are on the job. Why? The managers and leaders of the department are also out of shape and stopped leading by example long ago.

Those of us who want to return to the days an officer could actually do the complete job are shot down by lazy officers, unions and budget constraints. If my 5' 4" wife calls for assistance, due to a prowler in the yard and a cop shows up at the door that is so fat they can hardly get out of their cruiser, she tells them to go away noting they are not a help, but a hindrance. She'd just as soon go outside and take care of the prowler herself, as an instructor in martial arts she would have no problem. Why call the cops? Because she does not want to get sued or arrested for beating the crap out of the criminal.

Herein lay several problems. First, the cop is too fat and in my book unfit for duty. Second, criminals should never be allowed to sue the victim under any circumstances. If you enter someone's property in or out of the house **with intent to commit a crime,** you should be forbidden to become a victim yourself in any regard (criminal or civil) as a result of attempting or committing the crime. Third, why do we continue to spend the money for the test and or the programs, if we are not going to hold the officers and their superiors to staying physically fit? We need to put that to a stop because the officer by being overweight, and in many cases extremely overweight; is putting the officer and the public in harm's way.

If we look at this from all equitable sides, we are putting the offenders in a position that leaves the officer no choice but to use far more force than necessary. Like shooting them, because the officer can't fight them in order to control the situation and he may be killed. Texas and other right-to-work-states can make this right, if we as leaders - the department head and the city mayors, managers and council members - will put the physical fitness program into the department policy and procedure manuals.

Every sworn officer, regardless of rank, should be able to take and pass a physical agility test at least every two years. The test should be graduated by age, and of course, illness and diseases must be taken into account. Remember, if we start them young and keep them fit, the issue of illness and disease will be far less of a concern and far less loss in medical expenses, i.e. workers' compensation cost.

2. Uniforms should be clean, neat, fit properly and be practical. But all departments should have a dress uniform.

3. Those of us in the law enforcement community have been working desperately for years, particularly since the attack on the Twin Towers in New York on September 11, 2001, to become more interoperable with each other. The word itself restated as "interoperability" became the standard use and even the key that opened the vault in grant writing for our agencies. Unfortunately, there seems to be a back slide

in many agencies and I believe this is due to the lack of available funds in and through the grants.

We must not let go of this extremely important fact of necessity in law enforcement. As the leaders of our agency, we must keep up the inroads and never allow a road block to keep us out of the board meetings amongst ourselves. We must find the time, and the general public need be aware of how important the neighboring community is, especially those with which we share a border. I have heard too many times community leaders, such as the city managers and city council; complain about their chief or sheriff visiting away from the department.

It is also important for us as the department heads to convey to our hiring authority the necessity to work with our counterparts. Everyone in this day of vigilance and short falls in the budget and the great threats to our communities must depend on each other for support, suggestions and assistance. That equates to interoperability. Without this element we will have, at the very least, an extremely difficult time protecting our communities with a positive and professional measure.

4. Proactive policing is the dream of just about every chief, sheriff, manager and sworn officer in law enforcement. We all do our very best to make it happen, but the strict budgets and the necessity of priority 911 emergencies and service calls make it nearly impossible. When it is possible, it is short lived. This plays out in drastic measure within our large cities and heavily populated rural areas. Within the previous pages I spelled out a way to accomplish proactive policing and, in fact, proved it can and did work in the

City of Houston. It is a tough task and seemingly impossible in many jurisdictions; but, if we study the concept, maybe we can find a way to accomplish the idea in those cities willing to try. Texas has a special opportunity to put into place pilot programs, as the constable departments are the most wasted resource available and would easily be the most useful in proactive policing.

5. This is, as I have stated many times, the era of possibly the smallest budgets in history. There has been in the past and continues on a small scale, utilization of retired officers who still possess the physical skills and the psychological ability to do the job. Unfortunately, there is opposition to use these officers to the maximum they are willing to work.

First, State and Federal laws and regulations surrounding their retirement earnings prevent them from volunteering more; either for little compensation or even in some cases for free. Second, the unions keep them out because they would be "taking paid jobs away". There are no paid jobs and no one can afford to hire anyone, at least not at full wages you idiots! When and if the budget increases, then we might talk about not having as many retired personnel on board. My suggestion is similar to some States that allow the retired person to work at full wage less the benefits.

That is great, but I think this does foster using too many for too long. I would instead advise that we use the retired at half the wage, no additional benefits, and do not tax the earnings. If you must tax the earnings, then only the additional earnings should be taxed. The retirement should not be part of the calculation; if someone is going to do a job with all the risk and make less money then they would not doing the job, why then would they apply in the first place? It is similar to accepting a promotion at the first line of pay, say becoming a sergeant who earned less than the top pay for your senior position as patrol officer. It makes no sense and it is why we had to change the pay scales long ago. This then gives the unions (if we must have them) an argument when the budget does increase.

Why do they have an argument in this case? Because if the employee remains in the part time category without benefits, the contracts do not mandate their being retained. Part time is less than thirty-two hours in most situations and no additional benefits save approximately forty percent for the employer. When we can equal the budget to services, the full time positions return.

6. I have found, what I believe, is a real problem within our judicial system. As the prime example: in Navarro County Texas, the courts are regularly issuing summons as jurors to active peace officers. This gives rise to issues of true concern, both judicial and potential physical harm.

   a. First, it is a violation of the defendants' U. S. Constitutional Sixth Amendment Rights to a fair and impartial jury. Certainly, active and or retired career peace officers have no business serving on a jury anymore than a career criminal does. By placing either of these individuals into the jury, sets a foundation to argue in favor of the sixth amendment violation. The jury has been tainted or poisoned.

b. In the event a peace officer sits on a jury, especially in a criminal case and a conviction is the result, subsequent query of the jurors would only take one to state they reached a guilty verdict based on what the peace officer said vs. the evidence. This would give rise to a mistrial or foundation for appeal. The same would be true if the career criminal sits on the jury and a not guilty verdict occurred. Regardless of the evidence, there stands a common human trait of factual perception; wherein the juror is bias and feeds the allegation of violating the defendants' right to a fair and impartial trial.

c. Outside the violation of the Sixth Amendment, I believe this corresponds to Texas D.P.S. v. Cox Texas Newspapers L.P. et. at., 343 S.W.3d 112 (Tex. 2011) decided July 1, 2011. Texas Supreme Court recognizes a "Physical Harm" exception to the Public Information Act. Therein, the "Physical Harm" provides exemption to issues concerning the release of information regarding D.P.S. security detail for Governor Perry. The ruling does not segregate only D.P.S. noting that employees of government agencies information falls under the exception such as the officers, names, addresses, etcetera.

The Attorney General of Texas and the Texas Supreme Court ruled that there is a "Special Circumstances" aspect of common law privacy that requires this type of information be withheld. Without doubt, this does correspond to a peace officer who sits on a jury. It is common place, especially for the defendant, to acquire this type of information regarding jurors from public records. Although all jurors are subject to this inquiry, the peace officer and their families stand out as a primary target for revenge in the minds of the convicted.

d. The current practice is to summon an active or retired career peace officer for one purpose, although camouflaged by political correctness stating "everyone must serve and peace officers are not exempt". The truth is even officers on duty and in uniform report and are never called to serve. They are only used as a strike for one side or the other. This waste of time and money puts our system into a controversy that should not take place. Even if an officer does serve, they should not, based on the above.

Currently as an active peace officer and a forty year law enforcement veteran, I learned this practice is not only common, it is abused. I have personally observed several officers in uniform and there have been officers on duty at the time of summons, which interfered with their responsibilities and, frankly, cheated the community of their services. Officers are held in the jury pool for up to seven hours, which was my experience. I was advised second hand from another officer, with fifteen years or more, that there have been officers ordered to ignore a subpoena in separate active cases in order to report for jury duty. I have not confirmed this portion of practice, so I question it for now.

Officers who are required to serve on a jury where their co-workers, subordinates, and superiors, are the arresting officers, is ludicrous; an injustice to the community; and violates the defendants' Sixth Amendment. So, why are they summoned at all? Please put a stop to this practice in our Great State of Texas and any other State where it occurs. Write new legislation preventing this activity, by providing a clear exception to peace officers from jury duty.

Firefighters

1. Small communities that depend on paid firemen and do not have volunteer fire departments should consider cross training their police and fire personnel for budget and safety concerns. This will also increase the pool of candidates significantly in these communities.

2. Water walls should be considered in every structure, where they are feasible. This is a system that runs down the sides of a building when there is a fire inside it or a fire in the building next door. I believe it might be a real plus for residential properties as well as commercial and I am sure the fire liability insurance will decrease. This will allow for management of the fire spreading.

Military

I spoke about the decay of our police officers physical fitness, poorly fitting uniforms and public language. All of these issues apply every bit as much to our military personnel. I see hundreds of out of shape soldiers, both male and female, where their uniforms do not even come close to fitting.   And come on , can we at least "Stateside" go back to something that looks more like professional uniforms, like khaki's or anything other than camouflaged pajamas. I know they are practical for the battlefield, but not for roaming around our shopping malls.

While we are on the uniforms, can our generals and other command staff wear their dress uniform to all funerals and other supposedly formal gatherings? Think back to the Fort Hood, Texas funeral services and review the film coverage. What an insult to those killed or injured! Uniform of the day?

There should have been Dress Blues! As for their language, well that needs some leadership. I recall my Drill Sergeant demanding that the troops hold their tongue when we went off base and/ or in earshot of civilians. I also recall my uncle, a Sergeant Major, telling a story of dressing down his soldiers for their bad language in earshot of civilians, and he was retired at the time.

1. I have discussed this next topic time and again over the years and to follow I will spell out what I think should occur as soon as possible. The Purple Heart Medal; should be awarded to military Veterans who were affected with the chemical Agent Orange in Vietnam while fighting in a war zone for their Country. This chemical is highly toxic and laced with dioxin a significant carcinogenic. First, let me state what the administrations and military policy indicate is the

reason for not awarding this honored medal. The United States Military rules state the "Purple Heart Award" is not issued to those affected or injured because: Under U.S. Army regulations 600-8-22 (11 December 2006) Personnel General Military Awards 2-8 (page 19-20 (H- 4) notes; "Chemicals, Biological, or nuclear agents not released by the enemy".

From my perspective all other requirements under the same rules on page 19 and 20 of those general policies that state the Purple Heart will be awarded, settles the matter in favor of the Purple Heart for Veterans affected by Agent Orange. Why? Look, it has become recognizable that the preclusions is nothing short of an excuse designed to deter law suits and other such reaction to those affected.

For whatever reason, this is a ridiculous argument on the part of our military and whatever administration is sitting in the White House.

Read the section in its entirety (you can find it on the internet) and I am sure you will come away with the same view point I have. Let me say this: the reason for not awarding the Purple Heart under this contradictory excuse is nothing less than a post dated flaw and I might add blind understanding of who and under what circumstances Agent Orange was utilized.

You see, the Purple Heart is awarded, if the soldier is wounded by what we refer to as "friendly fire". The military states "we do not want to blur the lines" and noted that friendly fire is only that from our own forces which include everything else and chemicals used via the enemy force, which would cover the award. But our own chemicals by "friendly fire", precludes the award. Well, that confuses me. How about you?

Let me make it very clear for those who don't get it and try to indicate that Agent Orange was not a weapon to be used against the enemy and classify it only as a defoliant - (as the military does). The primary argument seems to be that it was "Just a defoliant" and not used as a weapon. Well, that is plainly put, BS.

Our troops in the field, field officers, forward observers and combat squads, provided the intelligence to command on where to drop Agent Orange explicitly and purposely for destroying the enemy's food supply and camouflage (vegetation or jungle) they utilized for traversing the terrain. Where they hid weapons and themselves to injure and kill our soldiers.

The destruction caused by Agent Orange was one of the primary reasons we were able to locate the enemy's fortified stationary positions, weaponry and food supply; not to mention the "Ho Chi Men Trail", resulting in fire fights, injury and death.

If Agent Orange was not a weapon and the troops were not struck by this friendly fire, then the helicopter gun ships that struck our troops often could not possibly be friendly fire, as they laid their barrage of fire down to find the enemy and bring them to the open as much as they caused injury and death to our troops.

Furthermore, the troops in the field who were dependent on food provided by nothing more than the jungle, consumed this deadly dioxin in the things they ate and the smoke they breathed; not to mention, actually being sprayed with the stuff and crawling in it while it was still moist. Tell me please, was "napalm" a weapon and did it or did it not create massive smoke plums (with Agent Orange in it) that our troops sucked down their lungs while engaged in battle?

Look, I know that the military provides health care for those affected, but they also provide health care for those who took the bullet or pun gee stick. This might not mean much to those making the decision; but, it means a great deal to our veterans, especially those lying in the hospitals waiting for the cancer to take their life, already recognized and agreed to as a result of Agent Orange. It might also mean a great deal to those family members they leave behind! Here is a proposal I have resurrected from a State of Utah resolution and wrote as a resolution from the State of Texas, will our Governor, you and your representatives join me and right this wrong now? Will the President of the United States?

RESOLUTION URGING THE PRESIDENT OF THE UNITED STATES TO AWARD THE PURPLE HEART
2012 GENERAL SESSION
STATE OF TEXAS

A concurrent resolution of the legislature and the Governor urging the President of United States to award the purple heart to members of the United States military forces serving in Vietnam who were exposed to agent orange.

Be it resolved by the Legislature of the State of Texas, the Governor concurring therein:

WHEREAS in 1961, the U.S. Government signed orders allowing Agent Orange, which contains trace amounts of dioxin, to be used in Vietnam to defoliate areas of jungle growth and to destroy crops;

WHEREAS 18 million gallons of Agent Orange were reported to have been used in South Vietnam;

WHEREAS Agent Orange caused Vietnam farmers to lose about 70 percent of their crops;

WHEREAS regretfully, the effects of Agent Orange spread to American military forces serving in Vietnam who were exposed to the chemical;

WHEREAS regretfully, exposure occurred from three primary and accepted sources by the
U. S. Government and the Military armed forces to be that of skin contact, smoke from fire containing the chemical of burning vegetation having been sprayed and eating insects and other dietary supplements from the jungle and sprayed vegetation recommended by the U. S. armed forces for survival;

WHEREAS currently, thousands of Americans who served in Vietnam suffer from the effects of exposure to Agent Orange, which range from cancer to memory loss;

WHEREAS the Purple Heart for merit, commonly called the Purple Heart, is awarded to members of the armed forces of the United States wounded or killed in battle;

WHEREAS the criteria for receiving the purple heart includes injury caused by chemical, biological, or nuclear agents released by the enemy, and the medal can be awarded if injury is the result of friendly fire designed to inflict damage or destroy enemy troops or equipment;

WHEREAS Agent Orange's use as a jungle defoliant and crop destroyer was intended to inflict damage on enemy troops by depriving them of hiding places and food;

WHEREAS American soldiers exposed to Agent Orange in Vietnam have received no medal or recognition for the injuries sustained by exposure to the chemical;

WHEREAS the fact that the United States Government provides medical treatment to American soldiers exposed to Agent Orange and their descendants clearly demonstrates that it is an injury deserving of recognition;

WHEREAS American soldiers suffering from the effects of exposure to Agent Orange in Vietnam should receive the Purple Heart in recognition of injuries sustained while standing in harm's way for their country;

WHEREAS Members of Disabled Americans, American Veterans, and Veterans of Foreign wars support the granting of Purple Hearts to these Veteran soldiers; and

WHEREAS the President of the United States should act to ensure that the sacrifice of these soldiers does not go unrecognized:

NOW, THEREFORE, BE IT RESOLVED that the legislature of the State of Texas, the Governor concurring therein, urge the President of the United States to grant the order of the Purple Heart to American soldiers who were injured from their exposure to Agent Orange during the Vietnam War.

BE IT FURTHER RESOLVED that a copy of this resolution be sent to the President of the United States, U. S. Senators of the State of Texas and representatives of the State of Texas Disabled American Veterans, American Veterans Association, and the Veterans of Foreign War

I have presented this proposed resolution to several State of Texas Representatives and the Governor's Office. Will they respond and will it be in the affirmative or not? Hopefully, by the time this book has been printed we will have accomplished the task and the President (who ever that might be) will finally award those who are long over due their recognition.

3. I have discussed the age requirements for law enforcement and it is, in my opinion, just as applicable for the military and for that matter all industries. When times are tough and qualified personnel are lacking because the budget has short falls, then why not tap those who have the training and skill set to get the job done. Help the system get back on track and prosperous, so we can start hiring the youngsters and train them. In the military especially, it seems to me

that Stateside positions, which are absolutely necessary for smooth operations here and overseas, can be filled by retired personnel who have the skills for the needed positions. This is another area that I am sure many retirees would be glad to step into. Take their expertise in law enforcement or the military and commission them to a rank of equal standing comparable to their civilian position. Pay them half pay: leave their benefits and retirement alone, regardless where that retirement is earned; and they will do the job. Let the young soldiers concentrate on training for the battlefield and send them anywhere we need them. We might not ever need the draft again, if we did this. We will need the draft on our current course if we don't do something now. Bet on it! If not, we will fall.

4. PTSD, "Post Traumatic Stress Syndrome", has been high jacked in the same fashion that progressive has been. Look, post traumatic stress is normal. It is okay to grieve, feel guilt, and cry your eyes out, if you have uncomfortable memories and even nightmares now and again. Just because you scraped your knee as a child is no reason to be so afraid at the sight of blood that it turns into a transfusion, when you have only cut your finger. I don't dismiss the fact that our soldiers and other professionals go through some extreme situations and absolute horror. They do and, in fact, I have. But not every incident is reason to medicate and cause a perfectly normal and prudent person to walk around in a lethargic stupor staring into space or, worse yet, at you when you're speaking to them. There are those individuals who truly need medical help and likely medication on a case by case basis. If you are having normal reactions to the horrors of war on the battlefield or other similar situations and you think you need help, by all means go see a professional. However,

don't let them talk you into medication without seeking a second opinion. Get that opinion as soon as possible. (Note to the professional, you don't need to write a prescription for everyone who comes to seek your help. Try the old school way and have them talk it out.) If you need further guidance on this, ask a veteran who has been there and done that. Try looking to those officers who spent many hours reconciling with themselves on the trials and tribulations of the battlefield and giving orders that sent soldiers to their injury and death.

5. Criminals vs. Combatants: if you go after the United States of America; if you are a terrorist and you are captured on the battlefield anywhere in the world, including in the United States, you have committed an act of war and should be considered a combatant. If you are a United States Citizen, that's all folks you have committed treason.

6. If you commit a criminal offense not noted above, you are a criminal in either the criminal court or the civil courts of America. You will be afforded the rights of the Constitution and the laws of the land. If you are an illegal person in this country, you should be held accountable for your crimes; upon completion of your sentence, be deported without delay and without any further notice to anyone accept your victims.

7. If you are incarcerated or have been incarcerated in this country for a crime as an illegal person, you will not be afforded the right to become a citizen, ever. Furthermore, you will never be allowed into our military.

Relationships; Personal and Professional
Personal

1. Do not put yourself into a position where your partner will be disrespected or have reason to worry about your loyalty. In other words, stay out of the cocktail lounges with the boys/girls and away from the strip joints.

2. When I say disrespect, there is no reason for anyone to tell their friends intimate and private issues concerning their partners. For that matter, there is no reason to tell your family (such as your mother, sisters or brothers) either, unless you really need their help to prevent a tragedy or injury. If you have a problem or difficulty with your partner, talk it out and resolve it between the two of you.

3. Do not use foul language; it sets the standard in and around your household for your partner and your children. Do not use foul language in public; it makes you look and sound stupid.

4. Do not do your children's homework for them; give them guidance and assist at the very most.

5. We taught our children to read and write the alphabet, count, and know their colors, before they ever entered school. However, we did this in the form of games and story telling, not as a work load or mandate. This allowed for close bonding and fun together. Let your children be, and have lots of time to be, children. They

will start the games of learning with you after they are introduced to the joys of pointing and making the statements, "I know what that says and what color that is mommy or daddy". Have fun raising your kids into young respectful, productive and perceptive adults. Childhood should be fun and adults need to learn that going back to fun is a great way to maintain interest in the world at large.

6. It seems to have been forgotten that kids are really resilient to falling down and putting it back together. I cannot recall all the times I fell off my bicycle, out of trees, off the "jungle gym bars", etc. I even fell off a two story house twice, and numerous sheds; not to mention, the cars I fell out of at speeds of up to thirty miles per hour. No broken bones, no hospitals, and no doctor appointments; guess I was just lucky and I don't need therapy. Okay, that one might be a matter of opinion.

7. If you drink alcoholic beverages excessively, stop. If you use drugs, stop. If you peer into or use the porn sites, stop. If you smoke, stop. If you can't help yourself in any of these "addictions", that's a cop out; but get help and stop it. Make the choice and pay the consequences; or live the happiness staying sober and drug free will bring. After all, we are really big eaters and your food will taste better.

8. I highly recommend you get off facebook and twitter and quit sharing your personal information with everyone in the world. I know you think you're only sharing with people with whom you are "friends". Not true; you're sharing with anyone who wants to know about you; and millions that don't care who you are,

but just want to see you more personally, if you get the drift. Don't be so naive. Don't be an idiot, thinking you control the information, words, pictures, etc. You don't!

9. If you're going to cheat, get a divorce or work it out. If you have cheated and can now control yourself, stop it. Keep it in the bag, unless you're out to cause more hurt and ride one of the saddest ever-rolling, never-ending nightmare roller coasters for life.

10. Get your head right with your faith and ask questions of your choice, if you have those questions. Be satisfied with your understanding of whatever faith you choose. Keep in mind that if there is a radical or perversion of good and evil, you might want to have a better understanding of what that means. In other words, if the faith is calling for the death of others just because they don't believe or follow every tenet of the faith, that is a diversion from God and a path to the devil, no matter what name you use to refer to them.

Professional

1. If you are an employer, listen and communicate with your employees respectfully.

2. If you are an employee, listen and communicate with your employer respectfully.

3. Whether employer or employee, do not use foul language in the work place or in front of your customers. Even if your customers have the foulest mouths you have ever heard, do not follow a stupid sounding person's lead.

4. Instead of employing the unions, try to utilize an association. The difference is amazing, as the association is for your shop only and management will be far more lenient with wages, training, and benefits. The non-union shops always have less stress and better work environments; and are far more open to suggestions. I know there is a lot of argument to use unions; but take it from me, I have seen the very worst of unions and associations and I will take the association every time.

5. Never stop looking for a job, even if you're happy with the one you have. However, never jump into a new job without completing due diligence regarding the employer and workers, if possible.

6. If you work in a shop that alters the safety equipment, don't use it. Even if they fire you, refuse and report the problem unanimously to the authorities if necessary.

7. Be a productive employer and a productive employee. Do so by setting the example. Earn your wages, don't demand them. The same goes for respect.

HUGGIE-BEAR-SMAKEE-POO

I spoke a lot on this subject within the previous pages and suggest you read them. But I want to close out the entire book with this one last mention.

In the sixties this Country was inundated with "arteeest" in the music and show business. I agree many of these, especially the musicians, had gobs of talent. (Like the Beatles, those rock and roll sensations that have endured over time.) But in the end and this is where I really get into trouble, these guys (meaning especially the Beatles) glorified everything wrong and very little right. They sung about grand drug trips of the mind, as though removing yourself from reality was the best and only way out, ignoring everything. They degraded women by using them for nothing but sex objects, whether they camouflaged it or not. They rallied against the laws, established religion, and stay-at-home moms. They promoted open sex with everything that moved.. Their songs went on and on, mostly I think, about the glorious use of death dealing drugs.

I can think of one song that was made famous by the legendary John Lennon which says it all, "Imagine". In his book John Lennon wrote (about the song), "it is anti-religious, anti-nationalistic, anti-conventional, anti-capitalistic, but because it's sugar-coated, it's accepted."

His lyrics promoted the following;

Imagine there's no heaven, imagine there are no countries, and imagine no possessions, or no religion..........
And a bunch of diatribe to pull the drug infested numbskull and, unfortunately, the naive numbskulls into working to that end. If that is where our Country is to wind up and I believe it may be, if we don't put down the junk and get back to our real values and principles this Country was founded upon, the Judeo Christian beliefs...

Well, I would rather witness the apocalypse.

NOTES

Alinsky, Saul. *Rules for Radicals.* New York: Vintage, 1989

Beck, Glenn. *Common Sense.* New York: Mercury Radio Arts, 2009

Charlesbois, Derek. *Lifestyle Cut Diet.* www.lifestylecutdiet.com

Coulter, Ann. *Demonic.* New York: Random House, Inc, 2011

Douglas, John. *Anatomy of Motive.* New York: Mindhunters, Inc, 2000

Giuliano, Geoffrey. *Lennon in America.* Cooper Square Press: 2000

Hasselbeck, Elisabeth. *The G Free Diet.* New York: Center Street, 2011

Huckabee, Mike. *Do the Right Thing.* New York: Penguin Group, 2008

Lennon, John. *Imagine.* (Lyrics) 1971

Morris, Dick. *FLEECED.* New York: Harper Collins, 2008

Morris, Father Jonathon. *God Wants You Happy.* New York: Harper Collins, 2011

Palin, Sarah. *Going Rouge.* New York: Harper Collins, 2009

Schlessinger, Laura. *How could you do that?* New York: Harper Collins, 1997

Skousen, Cleon W. *5000 YEAR LEAP.* National Center for Constitutional Studies, 2006

The Declaration of Independence and the Constitution of the United States.
    Washington, D.C: Cato Institute, 2002

Webster's New World Dictionary, fourth edition. New York: Wiley Publishing, Inc, 2003

.

www.ingramcontent.com/pod-product-compliance
Lightning Source LLC
Chambersburg PA
CBHW060235290526
45789CB00001B/55